Participatory Democracy and Political Participation

Democracies have developed a sense of crisis regarding levels of civic engagement and their own legitimacy, prompting government initiatives to reform the institutions and procedures of liberal democracy to provide more opportunities for political participation and bring citizens back in.

Participatory Democracy and Political Participation provides the first systematic evaluation of most visible and explicit efforts to engineer political participation via institutional reforms. Policies of democratic reform aim to increase the level of political participation by implementing institutions of participatory democracy. Such policies are debated in established democracies as means to counter downward trends in political participation. However, there is little empirical evidence whether this approach is actually able to increase or sustain political engagement without compromising other values of modern government.

This new volume investigates this topical issue by integrating three different research approaches:

- Theoretical analyses that aim to bridge the gap between the normative and the empirical level of participatory democracy.
- Comparative large N analyses that focus on the empirical link between participatory institutions and political behavior.
- Case studies on the structure, the politics and the behavioral effects of concrete reform initiatives within various established European democracies.

The leading contributors analyze participatory institutions on the basis of empirical models of democracy such as direct democracy, civil society and responsive government and analyze the impact of these models on political behavior in general.

Providing a detailed assessment of democratic reform, this book will be of strong interest to students and researchers of political theory, democracy and comparative politics.

Thomas Zittel is Researcher at the Mannheim Center for European Social Science Research (MZES), Germany. **Dieter Fuchs** is Professor of Political Science at the University of Stuttgart, Germany.

Routledge/ECPR studies in European political science

Edited by Thomas Poguntke

University of Birmingham, UK, on behalf of the European Consortium for Political Research

The Routledge/ECPR Studies in European Political Science series is published in association with the European Consortium for Political Research – the leading organization concerned with the growth and development of political science in Europe. The series presents high-quality edited volumes on topics at the leading edge of current interest in political science and related fields, with contributions from European scholars and others who have presented work at ECPR workshops or research groups.

1 **Regionalist Parties in Western Europe**
Edited by Lieven de Winter and Huri Türsan

2 **Comparing Party System Change**
Edited by Jan-Erik Lane and Paul Pennings

3 **Political Theory and European Union**
Edited by Albert Weale and Michael Nentwich

4 **Politics of Sexuality**
Edited by Terrell Carver and Véronique Mottier

5 **Autonomous Policy Making by International Organizations**
Edited by Bob Reinalda and Bertjan Verbeek

6 **Social Capital and European Democracy**
Edited by Jan van Deth, Marco Maraffi, Ken Newton and Paul Whiteley

7 **Party Elites in Divided Societies**
Edited by Kurt Richard Luther and Kris Deschouwer

8 **Citizenship and Welfare State Reform in Europe**
Edited by Jet Bussemaker

9 **Democratic Governance and New Technology**
Technologically mediated innovations in political practice in Western Europe
Edited by Ivan Horrocks, Jens Hoff and Pieter Tops

10 **Democracy without Borders**
Transnationalisation and conditionality in new democracies
Edited by Jean Grugel

11 **Cultural Theory as Political Science**
Edited by Michael Thompson, Gunnar Grendstad and Per Selle

12 **The Transformation of Governance in the European Union**
Edited by Beate Kohler-Koch and Rainer Eising

13 **Parliamentary Party Groups in European Democracies**
Political parties behind closed doors
Edited by Knut Heidar and Ruud Koole

14 **Survival of the European Welfare State**
Edited by Stein Kuhnle

15 **Private Organisations in Global Politics**
Edited by Karsten Ronit and Volker Schneider

16 **Federalism and Political Performance**
Edited by Ute Wachendorfer-Schmidt

17 **Democratic Innovation**
Deliberation, representation and association
Edited by Michael Saward

18 **Public Opinion and the International Use of Force**
Edited by Philip Everts and Pierangelo Isernia

19 **Religion and Mass Electoral Behaviour in Europe**
Edited by David Broughton and Hans-Martien ten Napel

20 **Estimating the Policy Position of Political Actors**
Edited by Michael Laver

21 **Democracy and Political Change in the 'Third World'**
Edited by Jeff Haynes

22 **Politicians, Bureaucrats and Administrative Reform**
Edited by B. Guy Peters and Jon Pierre

23 **Social Capital and Participation in Everyday Life**
Edited by Paul Dekker and Eric M. Uslaner

24 **Development and Democracy**
What do we know and how?
Edited by Ole Elgström and Goran Hyden

25 **Do Political Campaigns Matter?**
Campaign effects in elections and referendums
Edited by David M. Farrell and Rüdiger Schmitt-Beck

26 **Political Journalism**
New challenges, new practices
Edited by Raymond Kuhn and Erik Neveu

27 **Economic Voting**
Edited by Han Dorussen and Michael Taylor

28 **Organized Crime and the Challenge to Democracy**
Edited by Felia Allum and Renate Siebert

29 **Understanding the European Union's External Relations**
Edited by Michèle Knodt and Sebastiaan Princen

30 **Social Democratic Party Policies in Contemporary Europe**
Edited by Giuliano Bonoli and Martin Powell

31 **Decision Making within International Organisations**
Edited by Bob Reinalda and Bertjan Verbeek

32 **Comparative Biomedical Policy**
Governing assisted reproductive technologies
Edited by Ivar Bleiklie, Malcolm L. Goggin and Christine Rothmayr

33 **Electronic Democracy**
Mobilisation, organisation and participation via new ICTs
Edited by Rachel K. Gibson, Andrea Römmele and Stephen J. Ward

34 **Liberal Democracy and Environmentalism**
The end of environmentalism?
Edited by Marcel Wissenburg and Yoram Levy

35 **Political Theory and the European Constitution**
Edited by Lynn Dobson and Andreas Follesdal

36 **Politics and the European Commission**
Actors, interdependence, legitimacy
Edited by Andy Smith

37 **Metropolitan Governance**
Capacity, democracy and the dynamics of place
Edited by Hubert Heinelt and Daniel Kübler

38 **Democracy and the Role of Associations**
Political, organizational and social contexts
Edited by Sigrid Roßteutscher

39 **The Territorial Politics of Welfare**
Edited by Nicola McEwen and Luis Moreno

40 **Health Governance in Europe**
Issues, challenges and theories
Edited by Monika Steffen

41 **Republicanism in Theory and Practice**
Edited by Iseult Honohan and Jeremy Jennings

42 **Mass Media and Political Communication in New Democracies**
Edited by Katrin Voltmer

43 **Delegation in Contemporary Democracies**
Edited by Dietmar Braun and Fabrizio Gilardi

44 **Governance and Democracy**
Comparing national, European and international experiences
Edited by Yannis Papadopoulos and Arthur Benz

45 **The European Union's Roles in International Politics**
Concepts and analysis
Edited by Ole Elgström and Michael Smith

46 **Policy-making Processes and the European Constitution**
A comparative study of member states and accession countries
Edited by Thomas König and Simon Hug

47 **Democratic Politics and Party Competition**
Edited by Judith Bara and Albert Weale

48 **Participatory Democracy and Political Participation**
Can participatory engineering bring citizens back in?
Edited by Thomas Zittel and Dieter Fuchs

Also available from Routledge in association with the ECPR:
Sex Equality Policy in Western Europe, *Edited by Frances Gardiner*; **Democracy and Green Political Thought**, *Edited by Brian Doherty and Marius de Geus*; **The New Politics of Unemployment**, *Edited by Hugh Compston*; **Citizenship, Democracy and Justice in the New Europe**, *Edited by Percy B. Lehning and Albert Weale*; **Private Groups and Public Life**, *Edited by Jan W. van Deth*; **The Political Context of Collective Action**, *Edited by Ricca Edmondson*; **Theories of Secession**, *Edited by Percy Lehning*; **Regionalism across the North/South Divide**, *Edited by Jean Grugel and Wil Hout.*

Participatory Democracy and Political Participation

Can participatory engineering bring citizens back in?

Edited by Thomas Zittel and Dieter Fuchs

Routledge
Taylor & Francis Group
LONDON AND NEW YORK

ecpr

First published 2007
by Routledge
2 Park Square, Milton Park, Abingdon, Oxon OX14 4RN

Simultaneously published in the USA and Canada
by Routledge
270 Madison Ave, New York, NY 10016

Routledge is an imprint of the Taylor & Francis Group, an informa business

Typeset in Times by Wearset Ltd, Boldon, Tyne and Wear
Printed and bound in Great Britain by TJI Digital, Padstow, Cornwall

British Library Cataloguing in Publication Data
A catalogue record for this book is available from the British Library

Library of Congress Cataloging in Publication Data
A catalog record for this book has been requested

ISBN10: 0-415-37186-4 (hbk)
ISBN10: 0-203-96931-1 (ebk)

ISBN13: 978-0-415-37186-5 (hbk)
ISBN13: 978-0-203-96931-1 (ebk)

Contents

Contributors

Jacob Aars is research director at the Rokkan Centre at the University of Bergen in Norway. His research interests cover local government, democratic theory, political representation and recruitment. Recent publications include co-authored articles in *Scandinavian Political Studies* (with Hans Erik Ringkjøb and with Anne Lise Fimreite).

Simone Baglioni is a research fellow at the Bocconi University in Milan, Italy. Previously, he has taught social capital and civil society at the University of Geneva and carried out research at the Swiss Forum for Migration and Population Studies, Neuchâtel. He is the author of *Société civile et capital social en Suisse* (2004) and has authored and co-authored publications on civil society and migration.

Neil Carter is a senior lecturer in the Department of Politics at the University of York in the UK. His major research interests are in the areas of environmental politics, political parties and participation. Recent publications include *The Politics of the Environment: Ideas, Activism, Policy*, Cambridge University Press (2001) and (co-edited with Arthur Mol) *Environmental Governance in China*, Taylor & Francis (forthcoming).

Dieter Fuchs is professor for political science at the Institute for Social Sciences at the University of Stuttgart in Germany. His research foci are in political theory and empirical analyses of democracies.

Reuven Y. Hazan is a senior lecturer in the Department of Political Science at The Hebrew University of Jerusalem in Israel. His research interests cover political parties and party systems, elections and electoral systems, and legislative studies. His most recent publications include *Cohesion and Discipline in Legislatures: Political Parties, Party Leadership, Parliamentary Committees and Governance*, Routledge (2006) and *Reforming Parliamentary Committees: Israel in Comparative Perspective*, Ohio State University Press (2001).

Grant Jordan is professor at the Department of Politics at the University of Aberdeen in the UK. His major research interests cover public policy making, interest group membership issues and influence. His most recent book is *Shell, Greenpeace, and the Brent Spar*, Palgrave (2001). Most recent articles appeared in (with D. Halpin) *British Journal of Politics and International Relation* and *Political Studies*.

Peter McLaverty is reader in public policy at The Robert Gordon University in the UK. His main research interests are in the theory and practice of democracy and public participation. He is the editor of *Public Participation and Innovations in Community Governance*, Ashgate (2002).

William Maloney is professor of politics in the School of Geography, Politics and Sociology at the University of Newcastle in the UK. His main research interests are in the areas of interest group politics, social capital, political involvement and non-participation. He has published extensively in these areas and is currently completing a volume with Grant Jordan entitled *Interest Groups and the Democratic Process: Enhancing Participation?*, Palgrave (forthcoming).

Silvano Moeckli is associate professor at the University of St. Gallen in Switzerland and president of the Parliament of the Canton of St. Gallen. His major research interests cover direct democracy, demography and politics, and democracy assistance. His major recent publications include *Die demographische Herausforderung. Chancen und Gefahren einer Gesellschaft lang lebender Menschen*, Paul Haupt (1999) and an article in *Zeitschrift für Politikwissenschaft*.

Stig Montin is associate professor in political science at Örebro University in Sweden and a research fellow at the Centre of Urban and Regional Studies (CUReS). His main subjects of research are local and regional governance and democracy. His most recent publications include *Moderna kommuner* (Modern Municipalities), Liber Förlag (2004).

Sue Morris is director of MorrisRichards, an independent social research company based in Aberdeen, UK. She was senior lecturer in public policy at The Robert Gordon University from 2001 to 2004, and before joining RGU was principal researcher in the Scottish Parliament Information Centre, responsible for political and legal research services for Scottish Parliament committees and MPs.

Gideon Rahat is a lecturer in the Department of Political Science at The Hebrew University of Jerusalem in Israel. His research interests include political parties, electoral reform and candidate selection methods. He has written or collaborated on articles that appeared in *Comparative Political Studies*, *Comparative Politics*, *Electoral Studies*, *Party Politics* and *Political Studies*.

Eric M. Uslaner is professor of Government and Politics at the University of Maryland–College Park (USA). He has written seven books, including *The Moral Foundations of Trust*, Cambridge University Press (2002), *The*

Decline of Comity in Congress, University of Michigan Press (1993) and *The Movers and the Shirkers: Representatives and Ideologues in the Senate*, University of Michigan Press (2002). His current research includes a book in progress, *The Bulging Pocket and the Rule of Law*, which examines the linkages among corruption, inequality and trust.

Thomas Zittel is researcher at the Mannheim Center for Social Science Research (MZES) of the University of Mannheim in Germany. His research interests cover normative and empirical theories of democracy, electronic democracy and political representation. Recent publications include (co-edited with André Kaiser) *Demokratietheorie und Demokratieentwicklung*, VS Verlag für Sozialwissenschaften (2004) and articles in *The Journal of Legislative Studies*, *Zeitschrift für Parlamentsfragen*, and (with Eric Uslaner) in *The Oxford Handbook of Political Institutions* edited by Rod Rhodes, Sarah Binder and Bert Rockman.

Series editor's preface

Democracy is inconceivable without citizens' participation. Hence, despite the growing number of countries that have adopted democratic procedures, there is little reason for complacency – after all, it is not only in some of the newly established democracies that public engagement in politics leaves a lot to be desired. Many established democracies suffer from similar problems: turnout seems to be declining, parties find it increasingly difficult to recruit candidates and members, and local democracy is in danger of drying up due to a lack of interest by those living in the communities.

Even though, as the editors rightly point out, the jury is still out as regards the empirical evidence on some of these aspects, it is the perception of political elites that matters from their perspective. Here, they are on fairly safe ground: politicians across modern democracies tend to bemoan the decline in citizens' involvement. Furthermore, as most of them are *party* politicians, they have a sound empirical reason for their generalization. After all, party membership has been declining across the board. As a matter of fact, there are few trends in comparative politics which are so solid and unequivocal.

As a result, different shades of participatory engineering have gained prominence in democratic countries, and this timely volume combines an interesting theoretical discussion of what is normatively desirable and theoretically meaningful or plausible with a broad range of empirical studies on different examples of participatory engineering. The common point of departure is the assumption that, at least in principle, institutions matter in that they can promote or obstruct popular involvement in politics. However, how much involvement is theoretically possible is less consensual.

There is an interesting tension between the two theoretical chapters by the editors which set the stage for the subsequent case studies. Thomas Zittel takes a rather dramatic view in his introductory piece and calls for democratic reform in order to increase the quantity and the quality of political participation. In his view, it is the latter where improvement is particularly important: citizens need to take part in decisions instead of merely selecting delegates who will then decide for them. Dieter Fuchs takes a far more sceptical view and argues that much of our modern democratic thinking is still guided, or rather misguided, by the ideal of Athenian democracy which represents the epitome of self-government. In highly complex modern societies such self-government is, according to Fuchs, unthinkable, and this renders true self-government an unrealistic ideal. Furthermore, personal life plans in the modern age are far more removed from the political sphere. As a result, it is only rational for the modern citizen to invest comparatively little energy in political involvement. A logical consequence is the emergence of a class of professional politicians whose full-time job is political involvement. Furthermore, as Rahat and Hazan argue, there may be a tension between increasing the range of participatory opportunities and the quality of the involvement that this may evoke. After all, costs attached to certain participatory acts may be a good idea as they may prevent meaningless random choices like the popular Internet votes or Big Brother contests. To be sure, the often cited phenomenon that more people voted in the UK's Big Brother contest than in the general election does not necessarily mean that British citizens really care about who was going to be the next TV celebrity (at least one should hope so!).

The evidence assembled in this book is somewhat mixed. As Thomas Zittel argues in his introductory chapter, it was to be expected that minimal reform strategies would be particularly likely because they do not really threaten the control of politicians. A telling example is that referenda are far more often used as plebiscites initiated by party politicians rather than as instruments providing a channel for popular initiative. Nevertheless, it is evident that the concern about the lack of popular involvement has led to institutional engineering in many countries. In most cases, this does not aim at a fundamental reform of democracy. Rather, it tends to be cautious, piecemeal and sometimes has unintended side effects. Given that democracy is inconceivable without citizens' participation, it is certainly a worthwhile effort – and deserves the attention of our discipline.

Thomas Poguntke, Series editor

Acknowledgments

This book originated at a workshop entitled "Bringing Citizens Back in: Participatory Democracy and Political Participation," held as part of the 2003 Joint Sessions of the European Consortium for Political Research at the University of Edinburgh. That occasion brought together scholars from 12 different countries to discuss the question of whether the reform of democratic institutions can affect the quantity and quality of political participation in positive ways. Given the steady decline in traditional forms of political participation across most established democracies, this question is of pressing concern for the practical world of politics. Furthermore, the existing gaps between normative and empirical theories of democracy on the one hand and the macro- (political institutions) and micro- (political behavior) levels of analysis on the other raise considerable intellectual challenges in the search for an answer. The intellectual and practical relevance of the key question addressed at the workshop generated a level and intensity of debate that, we hope, will be reflected in the chapters that follow.

We are grateful to all participants in the workshop for contributing to this debate and for making it a stimulating experience for all of us. We are indebted to the ECPR for helping us to create such a congenial setting for this debate. We want to thank the Routledge team, Heidi Bagtazo and Harriet Brinton, for their guidance, patience and support throughout. Our special thanks are directed to Series Editor, Thomas Poguntke, and the two referees of the proposal for their helpful comments and advice. We also want to thank Rachel S. Folkes for copy editing most of the chapters of this book in a very thoughtful and timely manner. Finally, we would like to acknowledge the role of the Mannheim Center for Social Research (MZES) in actively supporting the preparation of the manuscript for this book.

Introduction

Democratic reform and political participation

Thomas Zittel and Dieter Fuchs

Downward trends in electoral participation, the decrease in organizational membership and survey data that signal waning trust in political institutions are prominent issues in public discourse in many established democracies. They are raised in various political arenas with different implications regarding their status on the political agenda. The spectrum ranges from individual statements by public officials to large-scale government-sponsored inquiries into the state of democracy, particularly in Scandinavian countries.[1] Despite differences in agenda status, elite concerns about downward trends in political engagement share a common understanding in terms of democracy. The all-encompassing assumption is that it indicates that citizens are turning their backs on democracy and that this system of government is in crisis.[2]

Political elites usually fail to acknowledge a crisis without having a solution ready at hand. Policies that would provide new opportunities for political participation are up on the political agenda as an answer to this perceived crisis of democracy. In Sweden for example, a commission on democracy deliberated between 1998 and 2000 on institutional reforms to increase political participation. It submitted a report which put a special emphasis on suggestions to strengthen the local basis of democracy (Swedish Ministry of Justice 2000). In Germany, the Red–Green government coalition introduced a bill in 2002 to change the country's constitution to allow for measures of direct democracy at the federal level. This bill was explicitly promoted as a means to revitalize the waning interest of German citizens in political affairs. It could not mobilize the necessary support of two-thirds of the members of the German Bundestag but the issue remains to be on the agenda for years to come (Keil 2004; Bannas 2004). A glance at the situation on the other side of the Atlantic reveals similar initiatives towards democratic reform. In Canada in 2004, Jacques Saada, then Government House Leader, tabled a reform initiative in the House of Commons that outlined parliamentary reform measures to remedy the "democratic deficit" (Seidle 2004). All these initiatives can be perceived as examples of *participatory engineering*. They reflect purposive attempts on the part of political elites to affect political participation positively via the reform of the institutions of democracy.[3]

This book confronts moves towards participatory engineering in practical politics with a set of questions that focus primarily on the effectiveness of this approach within the democratic system of government. The notion of effectiveness highlights the link between the macro- and the micro-levels of analysis. At the most general level, a particular reform measure can be rated as effective if it is able to increase or sustain political engagement. Confining ourselves explicitly to the democratic system of government places a special emphasis on the link between the normative and empirical levels of analysis. It stresses that our overall aim in this volume is to identify concrete strategies for reform at the institutional level that can be related to core normative models of democracy and that are compatible with such models. This does not mean that other types of reform efforts might finally not have a major impact on political behavior. At this point, it only defines the range of our analytical lenses which are rooted in democratic theory and which aim to identify relevant, major reform efforts not only with respect to political behavior but also with respect to the structural basis of democracy.

At the most fundamental level the contributors to this volume were confronted with one core question which was stated as follows: Is there any empirical evidence supporting the claim that participatory engineering can work as a means to increase the level of political participation? At a more specific level, the contributions to this volume are concerned with a number of follow-up questions such as: Which particular institutional or procedural measures increase the level of what types of political participation and why? How does the institutional and social context affect the relationship between specific institutional reforms and political participation? What are the politics of participatory engineering and how do politics affect the feasibility of certain types of policies? Can we increase the level of political participation without decreasing the quality of political participation? Is it possible to foster the goal of political participation through participatory engineering without compromising other values of democracy?

With its thematic emphasis, this volume goes well beyond the existing treatments of the subject. Those are either driven by normative concerns (Dryzek 2000), mainly emphasize the macro-level of analysis (Saward 2000) or are focused on a particular empirical model of participatory democracy (Fung and Wright 2003; McLaverty 2002). In contrast to this, our main concern is to explore systematically the range of relevant alternatives and strategies for democratic reform rooted in normative democratic theory and to analyze empirically their effects on participation within a given context. This is not only an academic endeavor but also aimed at informing political elites in their move toward democratic reform through the act of participatory engineering.

This edited volume is divided into five main parts. Part I is theoretical and consists of two chapters that discuss the issue of participatory engineering from distinct and different theoretical perspectives. Zittel, in Chapter 1, argues that participatory engineering is supported by sound theoretical arguments in the realm of normative democratic theory. According to his analysis, a broad reading of the theory of participatory democracy unveils concrete empirical strategies for reform along with mechanisms that link the institutional and behavioral level of politics in plausible ways. On this basis, Zittel distinguishes between three alternative empirical strategies for democratic reform that he labels expansive democratization, integrative democratization and cost-efficient democratization. Fuchs takes a skeptical stance in Chapter 2. He distinguishes between two major normative models of democracy: liberal and participatory democracy. His core argument is that the context of modern democracy does not allow the implementation of the model of participatory democracy that aims at comprehensive mass participation.

The remaining parts of the book are empirical. They are structured along crucial empirical models of democracy that flow from the normative models discussed in Part I of this volume. These models inform the debate on participatory engineering by mapping particular strategies of democratic reform within a broader systemic context. They can be labeled as responsive representative government, direct democracy, civil society and local democracy.

Responsive institutions are structured to take the interests of citizens into account in the process of policy making. The authors contributing to Part II concentrate on different means of increasing the responsiveness of representative institutions. Rahat and Hazan analyze the impact of party primaries on intra-party participation in the Israeli party system. McLaverty and Morris focus on the new Scottish Parliament that has been designed on the basis of a "participatory ethos" and with regard to the specific goal to increase the involvement of ordinary citizens in the parliamentary process and to render it more responsive. The authors in Part III direct our attention to direct democracy as a means for democratic reform. The model of direct democracy enables citizens to take policy choices rather than merely selecting political personnel. Baglioni conducts a comparative analysis of two Swiss cantons to learn more about the impact of different traditions and structures of direct democracy on participation. He also considers the impact of size as an intervening variable in this relationship. Moeckli analyzes the behavioral consequences of direct democracy in an international comparison. He pays close attention to the difference between what he calls minority direct democracy and majority direct democracy and he focuses on differences between direct and representative systems as well.

The authors in Part IV deal with various aspects of civil society. Proponents of civil society assume that the formal institutions and processes of democracy need to be embedded in vital group structures as a prerequisite for political engagement and empowerment. In their chapter, Maloney and Jordan ask why individuals join public interest groups that provide collective goods. In his chapter, Uslaner studies the foundations of general social trust that some have held to be a prerequisite for political and civic engagement. Carter's chapter deals with the concept of workplace democracy and the claim that the democratization of the workplace is crucial for the transformation of individuals into citizens. Classic authors such as John Stuart Mill have argued that small-scale local communities are best suited to fulfill the promise of mass participation. The authors in Part V direct our attention to this very level of government. Montin analyzes the Swedish government's large-scale efforts towards democratic reform that emphasized the need to strengthen local democracy. Aars analyzes a local democracy program in Norway initiated by the Norwegian Association of Local and Regional Authorities.

This edited volume closes with Zittel's Conclusion. It aims to synthesize the chapters of the book on the basis of our initial research questions that touch upon the policies, the politics and the behavioral impact of recent trends in participatory engineering. The Conclusion also aims to outline major challenges for further research on participatory engineering and democratic reform.

Notes

1 For an overview and further references see a listing at the OECD-website under www.oecd.org/document/42/0,2340,en_2649_33707_33617194_1_1_1_1,00.html (accessed 20 July 2005).

2 It is important to note that this book project does not aim to discuss actual trends in political participation. It rather takes the perception among political elites at face value and as a vantage point for its argument. Obviously, students of political participation unveil a more complex situation when it comes to trends in political participation. They argue, for example, that downward trends in electoral participation are far from dramatic (Franklin 2002), that the evidence across multiple types of political participation is mixed (Klingemann and Fuchs 1995) and that downward trends in traditional forms of participation are offset by new forms of political engagement (Skocpol 1999). However, one can hardly disagree with the argument that traditional forms of participation have decreased to a significant degree over the past decades (Stolle and Hooghe 2004) and that public opinion does signal dissatisfaction and frustration with democratic governments (Pharr and Putnam 2000). The current perception among political elites is thus not without any empirical basis.

3 For a most recent comprehensive overview on democratic innovations around the world see Smith 2005.

References

Bannas, G. (2004) "Es steht im Koalitionsvertrag. Koalition und Opposition wollen mit den Plebisziten Widersprüchliches auf die Reihe bringen," *Frankfurter Allgemeine Zeitung*, 29 October: 12.

Dryzek, J.S. (2000) *Deliberative Democracy and Beyond*, Oxford: Oxford University Press.

Franklin, M.N. (2002) "Electoral Participation," in L. LeDuc, R.G. Niemi and P. Norris (eds) *Comparing Democracies 2: New Challenges in the Study of Elections and Voting*, London: Sage.

Fung, A. and Wright, E.O. (eds) (2003) *Deepening Democracy*, London: Verso.

Keil, L.B. (2004) "Trotz Nein von Müntefering fordern SPD-Abgeordnete Volksentscheide," *Die Welt*, 18 December: 7.

Klingemann, H.-D. and Fuchs, D. (eds) (1995) *Citizens and the State*, Oxford: Oxford University Press.

McLaverty, P. (ed.) (2002) *Public Participation and Innovations in Community Governance*, Burlington, VT: Ashgate.

Putnam, R.D. and Pharr, S.J. (eds) (2000) *Disaffected Democracies: What is Troubling the Trilateral Countries?*, Princeton, NJ: Princeton University Press.

Saward, M. (ed.) (2000) *Democratic Innovation: Deliberation, Representation and Association*, London: Routledge.

Seidle, L.F. (2004) "Expanding the Federal Democratic Reform Agenda," *Policy Options*, October 2004: 48–53.

Skocpol, T. (1999) "Advocates without Members: The Recent Transformation of American Civil Life," in T. Skocpol and M.P. Fiorina (eds) *Civic Engagement in American Democracy*, Washington, DC: Brookings Institution Press.

Smith, G. (2005) *Beyond the Ballot. 57 Democratic Innovations from Around the World*, A Report for the Power Inquiry, London: The Power Inquiry.

Stolle, D. and Hooghe, M. (2004) "Emerging Repertoires of Political Action? A Review of the Debate on Participatory Trends in Western Societies," Paper presented at the 2004 ECPR Joint Sessions of Workshops, Uppsala, 13–18 April.

Swedish Ministry of Justice (2000) *Sustainable Democracy. Policy for Government by the People in the 2000s. Report of the Government Commission on Swedish Democracy*, Stockholm: Official Government Reports-SOU 2000: 1 (English translation of the recommendations made by the Government Commission on Swedish Democracy).

Part I

Democratic reform and political participation

Two theoretical perspectives

1 Participatory democracy and political participation

Thomas Zittel

Political institutions and political participation

This chapter addresses efforts in established democracies to reverse downward trends in political participation through *participatory engineering*. This concept indicates purposive attempts on the part of political elites to affect political participation positively via the reform of the institutions of democracy. German politics provides one recent example for this kind of democracy policy. In 2002 the Red–Green government coalition introduced a bill to change the country's constitution, allowing for measures of direct democracy at the federal level. This bill was explicitly promoted as a means of revitalizing the waning interest of German citizens in political affairs.

The concept of participatory engineering is linked to two core assumptions which form the basis of the following analysis. The first core assumption is that any policy to reform the institutional basis of democracy should be based upon empirical evidence regarding the effects of these reforms on political participation. It seems absurd to engage in far-reaching institutional reforms on an ad-hoc basis without taking systematic empirical research into account. The second core assumption of the paper is that the theory of participatory democracy provides a useful vantage point from which to consider the effectiveness of participatory engineering from a theoretical perspective. This means that participatory theory can serve as a basis to specify concrete institutional structures suited to stimulating participation, and that it can help link them to the behavioral level of politics in plausible ways. The aim of such theoretical reasoning should be to formulate hypotheses regarding the effectiveness of participatory engineering and to test them in the course of empirical research.

The main focus of participatory theory lies in the critique of the liberal conception of democracy as a competition for political power among responsible elites. This critique originated in the late 1960s and early 1970s in the midst of a larger cultural quest for more democracy and social equality. Participatory theory envisions citizens who engage into political decision-making in great numbers and who share a sense of collective responsibility. Its protagonists claim that this vision can be achieved by increasing opportunities to participate through institutional reform (Pateman 1970; Cook and Morgan 1971; Macpherson 1977;

Bachrach and Botwinick 1992). They argue that the institutional restraints impinging on political participation within the frame of liberal democracy lessen political engagement and spawn political apathy in the long term, while different institutional impulses are assumed to engender contrasting behavioral effects (Walker 1966).

Participatory theory faces many critics in various fields of the discipline. Liberal democratic theory views the preoccupation with private concerns and the hesitancy to participate in public affairs as quasi-anthropological constants at the individual level that can hardly be influenced by institutional frameworks (Sartori 1987; Kielmansegg 1977). This claim drew empirical support from students of political attitudes such as Dieter Fuchs (2000) and Jan van Deth (2000) whose analyses stress that politics takes a back seat in the minds of the citizens. Students of political participation tend to see differences in the degree of political engagement as explained by socioeconomic factors rather than by the institutional context. Their findings suggest among others that citizens with advanced educational background and above-average income are most likely to develop an interest in politics and to cope with the complexities of modern political life (Verba and Nie 1972). From this perspective, it is economic development rather than political institutions that makes a difference in terms of participation.

Critics of participatory theory argue, regardless of debates on alternative determinants of participation, that its proponents carry little theoretical ammunition to support their analytical claim regarding the impact of political institutions on participation and that this strand of democratic theory remains purely normative in character. Participatory theory is criticized for failing in three respects: first, its critics argue that it fails to tell us which particular institutions could have a positive effect on participation; second, it is criticized for being silent on the contextual conditions under which these institutions might affect political behavior; third, participatory theory is denounced for lacking a plausible explanation of how and why particular institutions foster which type of political behavior. All in all, critics of participatory democracy claim that it is solely driven by normative concerns without opening itself up to empirical inquiry and to empirical testing of its claims. Proponents of participatory theory are pictured as utopian dreamers obsessed with the question of how things should be rather than how things can be in real world settings (Offe 1997; Pieterse 2001).[1]

In contrast to its critics, this chapter perceives the theory of participatory democracy as a useful starting point to specify institutional options for democratic reform, to discuss theoretically their effectiveness at the behavioral level, and to develop hypotheses that can be tested empirically. My argument is that participatory theory does have potential as an analytical tool. To make this point I argue in particular that participatory theory should neither be reduced to those critical authors writing in the 1960s and 1970s who coined the original concept, nor simply to particular strands in this debate. Rather, I suggest an inclusive understanding of participatory democracy incorporating various as yet distinct strands of democratic theory. This encompasses among others the literature on direct democracy, secular models of democratic reform (Burnheim 1985) as well as the theory of deliberative democracy (Dryzek 2000; Fishkin 1991).

An inclusive and broad reading of participatory theory certainly offers a tapestry of conceptual discussions and empirical models of democracy. These models rely on a variety of scientific methods and are pitched at different levels of abstraction. No element of this mosaic manages to provide a model that could give an explicit and comprehensive answer on which particular democratic institutions affect which particular type of political behavior and why (Zittel 2003). However, this chapter argues that these different approaches share an institutionalist approach to political participation, as well as the basic tenet of participatory theory, namely that political participation can be positively affected by political institutions and that this should be the case. They thus can be seen as elements of a common debate that can be synthesized and reconstructed to serve as a theoretical basis to discuss, evaluate and inform a strategy of participatory engineering. This will be the task of the following analysis. It will be based on a simple organizing argument.

On the basis of a comprehensive reading and a synthesis of the theory of participatory democracy, the chapter distinguishes between three different strategies of participatory engineering that emphasize different linkage mechanisms related to different institutional options to be implemented in the course of democratic reform. I label these strategies as expansive democratization, integrative democratization and efficiency-oriented democratization. These different strategies are analytical constructs that cannot be equated with any single author. They rather follow from distinct lines of argumentation which are sometimes clumsily intertwined or which are frequently simply kept implicit within the debate on participatory democracy. They provide a comprehensive road-map to comparative and empirical research on participatory engineering and the question of its effectiveness. They also alert us to the existence of vital tradeoffs between the political feasibility and effectiveness of particular democracy policies and to a reform dilemma that I will outline in the course of this analysis.

Integrative democratization

The strategy of *integrative democratization* describes the relationship between individual actors and institutions in a distinct way. Institutions are seen as a factor that shapes the very goals and perceptions of individuals (Hall and Taylor 1996). With a view to increasing political participation, this notion is linked to the classical argument that people are not born as citizens. Rather, democracy must be learnt and this can be ensured only through relevant institutional frameworks that empower people by educating them.

The notion of individual growth and self-transformation triggered through institutional context is probably a dominant paradigm among theorists of participatory democracy (Warren 1992). At the same time, it is the most difficult aspect of participatory theory to deal with because the notion of citizen-education has been perverted by dictatorships across the globe. However, the decisive difference between a totalitarian concept of education and participatory theory lies in the interrelationship between education and political choice. Participatory theory does not substitute political choice with self-transformation as totalitarianism does. It argues rather that expanding citizens' rights to affect policy choices has to be paralleled by a process of political socialization and self-transformation to balance the pursuit of private interest with a sense of collective responsibility. Choice and education stand in a complementary relationship rather than being substitutes for each other.

The emphasis on political choice does not only distinguish participatory theory from totalitarianism. It also provides the crucial institutional principle to specify concrete institutional structures and to distinguish them from those structures that are related to liberal democracy. Participatory theory argues that participatory institutions maximize opportunities to affect policy decisions. This stands in contrast to liberal democratic theory that stresses the significance of institutions that allow only for the selection of political personnel. Having stated these crucial principles of participatory theory and the strategy of integrative democratization that flows from it, I will have to turn to several follow-up questions.

The strategy of integrative democratization raises first and foremost the question of which educational goals this perspective ought to address. In other words, it asks what are the individual characteristics of good citizens who are motivated and capable to participate. Participatory theory proposes various answers to this question. Carol Pateman points towards the notion of political efficacy that recognizes at the individual level a basic disposition in relation to the possibility of exerting political influence (Pateman 1970). Political efficacy is less about cognitive knowledge of political issues that are at the center of a decision and of constitutional rights to participate in decision-making. It is also not a behavioral concept that assumes that individuals actually participate all the time in any given situation. This concept rather points to the attitudinal level. It is about subjective faith in one's own ability to influence political decision-making and to make a difference in public life. As an alternative to the notion of political efficacy, Jane Mansbridge's concept of unitary democracy stresses the idea of a social urge, which means a focus on common interests and social cooperation on an equal basis as the most basic feature of the good citizen (Mansbridge 1980: ch. 3). Jürgen Habermas's concept of individual autonomy combines both notions of individual empowerment and social responsibility and can be perceived as a third vision of the democratic personality (Habermas 1962, 1992, 1998).

The Habermasian autonomous self is distinguished by a balance between self-referentialism and the capacity for internal and external reflection. The notion of internal reflection suggests that the self is critical toward his or her own impulses and motivations in the process of generating a preference. It touches upon the awareness that individual preferences have to be reconciled with the interests and preferences of other actors. According to Habermas, it is from this balance – which can be considered a psychological state of mind – that flows the ability to cooperate and to be part of a community that forms the basis of collective action.

One of Habermas's important hypotheses states that these characteristics are primarily related to neither anthropological constants nor techniques of behavior that can be learnt and strategically employed. Rather, the autonomous self seems much more to arise from a basic psychological predisposition that – drawing on theories of cognitive psychology – can be seen as a stage in the development of individuals whose formation is shaped by external environments and their effects (Warren 1993). This assumption raises questions regarding the nature of this environment and regarding the role that institutional reform could play in this respect.

While the theory of participatory democracy does not explicitly discuss problems of institutional design, it does make an important more or less implicit statement regarding this very aspect. It stresses that transformative environments, meaning environments that educate the self to become a good citizen, cannot be located at the level of constitutional structures. Quite the contrary; on this view, political apathy is a consequence of thin democracy that functions solely through procedures and formal institutions at the constitutional and sub-constitutional level and this has no residual effect on the subjective dimension of democracy (Barber 1984). The reason for this lack of impact on the part of constitutional structures is seen in the lack of microstructures that could be able to shape the daily experiences of citizens and to provide an infrastructure for political learning and political socialization.

Integrative democratization promotes a conception of democracy as social practice that can be seen as a crucial prerequisite for the process of self-transformation into a citizen. Social groups appear as the core building block of democracy here, since they appear as central agents of socialization. From this perspective the integration of individuals into the group is a central prerequisite for building citizen virtues that are in turn directly related to political participation.

This benevolent perspective on social groups is not uncontested in democratic theory. This is due to the fact that social groups, as long as they are voluntary, are characterized by high interest homogeneity and stark demarcation from their social environment. Accordingly, the history of political ideas was shaped until well into the nineteenth century by the conviction that organized social interests endanger the common good, fostering both instability and high-intensity conflict. This hypothesis made for strange bedfellows such as Jean Jacques Rousseau and James Madison. Their political theories differ in many respects, except in their very skepticism regarding social groups (Hirschman 1997). Both theorists subscribe to the notion that social groups are hardly suitable as socialization agents for transforming individuals into responsible citizens.

This gloomier picture of the impact of social groups has been recognized by proponents of the strategy of integrative democratization as well. It triggered a more differentiated picture regarding the type of social group which could support democracy. The concept of workplace democracy represents one crucial element of this picture. Advocates of this concept argue that organized interests, which primarily carry out linkage functions within the framework of representative democracy, hardly fulfill the role of a socializing agent. Instead they point to the importance of functionally defined group relationships in general and the workplace in particular. From this perspective, worker cooperatives are viewed as suitable agents of socialization in democracy because they are characterized by a greater heterogeneity of interests and are perceived to be grounded in the netherworld of daily life, raising real world problems of social cooperation (Pateman 1970: chapter 3; Bachrach and Botwinick 1992; Warren 1993).

The theory of deliberative democracy has been a recent alternative to the concept of workplace democracy. It also stresses political learning and opinion formation as a core feature of the democratic decision-making process (Dryzek 2000; Fung and Wright 2001: 20ff.). In contrast to the concept of workplace democracy, its focus is not primarily on the economic system as a basis for deliberative politics but rather on the notion of the public sphere. This concept is rooted in the works of Jürgen Habermas. The search for an equivalent of this sphere at the constitutional or even institutional level in Habermas's writings draws a blank. Habermas explicitly understands the public sphere as a practice carried out beneath constitutional practices and as embodying a specifically social bias (Dryzek 1987). As a result, we are directed to a sociological analysis which explores the social prerequisites of the public sphere from a historical point of view.

The concept of the public sphere developed by Habermas describes at a very abstract level the image of a social space shaped by a particular form of double autonomy. This form of autonomy is based on the idea of the absence of state-sanctioned hierarchical relationships, on the one hand, and societal – market-sanctioned – inequality on the other (Habermas 1962: 40ff.). He traces the reality of this social basis to the literary circles of the emerging bourgeoisie in the eighteenth and nineteenth centuries. According to Habermas, this social realm provided the basis for critical reasoning free of social and political pressures, and generated a form of public opinion that embodied moral authority and that could serve as a check on political decision-making (Habermas 1992; 1998: 383ff.). Habermas views modern democracy as shaped by a decay of the public sphere because of the influence of mass media and the economic imperatives they operate under. However, he perceives emancipatory movements as a fragile foundation for revitalizing the democratic public sphere and for providing a new basis for political socialization and opinion formation. The dominance of debate, discourse and the exchange of ideas are viewed as a safeguard towards the frenzy of particular interest that has been related to the group basis of politics among its critics.

Participatory theory stresses neighborhood groups in the local context as another basis for personal growth and self-transformation. In this context, the purpose of descending to the local level is to guarantee the social embeddedness of individuals in types of groups that are rooted in everyday practices as well as shared memories and traditions.

A further key question that must be asked of integrative democratization strategies relates to the degree to which political control can be exercised over social integration and resulting patterns of political attitudes. The existence of socialization agents necessary for this kind of integration, such as social groups, is seen by the proponents of integrative strategies themselves primarily as the result of historical, cultural or economic developments that would defy short-term control through political measures and participatory engineering. Indeed, the integrative strategy runs into problems if deficiencies in the subjective and social foundations of democracy can be established, and the question consequently arises of what short- to medium-term solutions are possible. According to Jane Mansbridge, unitary democracy makes formal and extends to the level of a polity the social relations of friendship (Mansbridge 1980: 8). But is it possible to engineer friendship once it has experienced serious setbacks? This question concerning the ability to control and engineer social integration has been answered by participatory theory in five ways that can be only briefly mentioned here.

The first response relates to the previously mentioned concept of workplace democracy. It advocates the democratization of this functionally defined social arena. This can be achieved through regulatory policies, among others (Warren 1993). More coordinated welfare-state economies such as those of Germany provide some faint examples in this regard (Streeck 1984; Hall and Soskic 2001).

The second answer relates to debates about the public sphere and the concept of civil society. It advocates strengthening emancipatory social groups through a transfer of resources and/or granting representation. This policy objective gained prominence during President Johnson's "War on Poverty" in the USA. In recent times, however, it has remained focused on new democracies in Eastern Europe via foreign policy efforts.

A third answer focuses on initiatives to revitalize local democracy. To become a broad-based strategy towards participatory engineering, rather than a project-driven approach, these initiatives have to be integrated in a national strategy, apply potent incentives for communities to implement participatory measures and stress politically meaningful and consequential opportunities to participate in local politics.

The fourth answer stresses structured communication as a means within a strategy of integrative democratization. This approach stipulates that microstructures that could serve as an agent for political socialization and self-transformation can be artificially created by way of structured communication. The model of the deliberative opinion poll proposed by James Fishkin offers an example that has been tested practically in numerous experiments. It encompasses a representative selection of citizens who are brought together to deliberate on a specific issue and to reach a decision at the end. According to Fishkin this decision will reflect a considered, collective will that differs from a decision that is based upon the mere aggregation of individual preferences (Fishkin 1991, 1995; Luskin *et al.* 2002).

A fifth response perceives the Internet as a new kind of public sphere that allows for autonomous deliberation and opinion formation in a spontaneous fashion. The assumption is that this will transform individuals into social beings (Rheingold 1993; Poster 1995; Zittel 2001). So-called cyber-optimists see the future of this development as being shaped to a large extent by regulatory policy that is considered to be the prerequisite both for universal access to the Internet and for shielding the autonomy of the medium from commercial imperatives and state intervention (de Sola Pool 1983; Kubicek 1996; Wilhelm 2000). Prudent regulation is seen as a prerequisite for the Internet to provide the vantage point for a new age of digital reasoning and a reincarnation of a critical public sphere in the Habermasian mould.

Expansive democratization

The debate on participatory democracy entertained among others the notion of political apathy as a rational decision. This is taken to be based on the belief that established participation rights within the framework of liberal democracy offer no real opportunity to exercise political influence and thus no actual benefits. It is furthermore assumed to be based on the fact that individuals are short of resources such as time and energy. Given the assumption that individuals aim at positive utility functions – meaning that they behave rationally – under these conditions they will draw back to the private sphere because it guarantees greater returns to the investment of scarce resources. From this perspective, the assertion of the liberal-democratic theory that individuals value their private life more than politics is not wholeheartedly disputed, but it is unmasked as an artefact of a specific institutional context rather than being an authentic goal. The strategy of *expansive democratization* aims to increase the utility of political participation by expanding rights to participation.

Claims regarding the positive effect on political participation of expanding rights to participate have hardly been elaborated on by advocates of participatory democracy in terms of theoretical plausibility. Theories of participatory democracy make no mention of those mechanisms that link the institutional and behavioral levels of politics. I argue in this chapter that one particular reading of participatory theory suggests a utilitarian motivation on the part of individual citizens based upon specific goals and a particular relationship between institutional context and political behavior. Regarding individual goals, it is clearly based on the assumption that having political impact is at least of some importance in the mind of each individual. One could argue that even in a more participatory frame, citizens might decide not to participate either because they are ignorant of the goal to participate or because they value other goals more, and thus abstain from participation. Theorists of participatory democracy obviously do not side with this assumption but regard political influence as one important goal among others. A second crucial assumption is that institutional structures pattern the behavioral strategies of each citizen in light of the goal of having political impact. It is assumed that in some way opportunities to participate are adequately perceived and evaluated among citizens in terms of political impact and thus provide behavioral incentives at the individual level.

What does it mean to expand rights to participate at the institutional level? The particular institutions of expansive democratization are rooted in Carole Pateman's book *Participation and Democratic Theory*. In this book, Pateman sees the concept of participatory democracy as the product of an intellectual development over time with Jean Jacques Rousseau as its founding father. Looking through these intellectual lenses, she specifies what participatory democracy is not in terms of political institutions. According to Pateman, it ought not to be based on representative institutions which Rousseau considered incompatible with the principle of public sovereignty. This is most clearly stated in Rousseau's famous verdict about English citizens whom he considers free while they elect their representatives, but whom he considers slaves immediately in the aftermath of the election because they hand over their political authority to elected representatives (Rousseau 1994: 3rd Book, chapter 3). As Pateman stresses, participation for Rousseau is participation in the making of decisions (Pateman 1970: 24ff.). This observation points to a positive definition of the institutional basis of participatory democracy. It can be rephrased in terms of an institutional principle by stating that institutions of participatory democracy should allow for participation in decision-making in contrast to participation in the selection and election of political personnel.

In participatory theory, expanding rights to participate clearly has qualitative rather than quantitative connotations. It cannot be increased solely by increasing the number of opportunities or channels to participate. It is rather increased by allowing for certain forms of participation in contrast to others. According to participatory theory, the criteria here is access to policy decisions and the ability to influence these decisions. In contrast to this, any form of participation that is linked to the selection of political candidates can be seen more or less as a source of legitimacy for governing elites (Salisbury 1975).

In the aftermath of Pateman's book and in line with the principle stated above, the concept of participatory democracy has been related closely to the empirical model of direct democracy (cf. Mather 1995; Saward 2001). Some students of participatory democracy even use both concepts as synonyms (Becker 1981). This is certainly not in the mold of Pateman's further treatment of the concept. She clearly stresses other institutional means to implement the notion of participatory democracy rather than paying attention to direct democracy. But from a purely utilitarian point of view, direct democracy as a specific instrument of expansive democratization makes perfect sense for various reasons.

In the model of direct democracy, Pateman's general notion of participating in policy decisions is further specified at the conceptual level of analysis. It is specified in the sense of taking binding policy decisions rather than merely having an influence in this very process. The model of direct decision-making thus prescribes that binding decisions within a political community are taken by all its citizens. This empirical model can be considered as a natural element of participatory democracy. From a logical point of view, it stands in direct contrast to representative democracy and it has been discussed in this sense quite extensively in modern democratic theory. From the perspective of an expansive strategy of democratization, the institution of direct democracy is most relevant and most closely related to the notion of participatory democracy. This is because it defines the most far-reaching way to participate in the making of decisions and to have an effect in this regard. It therefore can be assumed that it also provides the most far-reaching incentives to citizens to actually participate. Political scientist Ted Becker (1981: 6), a strong proponent of participatory politics, is convinced that "people are eager to get involved in politics when they believe their decisions . . . directly affect their futures."

Direct democracy as a means of expansive democratization raises several follow-up questions regarding its actual institutional design that need to be discussed in detail. The scope and comprehensiveness of direct decision-making and the level of jurisdiction are among them and shall be subject to some further remarks.

An expansive strategy of democratization is confronted with the objection that a single individual vote is insignificant for the overall outcome of decision-making on account of the size of modern democracy. From the individual's perspective there is no further benefit of political participation in this situation to outweigh its costs. One relevant type of cost here would be so-called opportunity costs, meaning the cost of something in terms of an opportunity foregone (and the benefits that could be received from that opportunity). The theory of participatory democracy has given little attention to this objection so far. However, a similar problem has been debated in the theory of the rational voter. The conclusions of this debate should be of interest for a utilitarian approach to participatory democracy as well.

The fact that a large number of people bothers to vote despite a negative utility function has been explained in classical studies on the rational voter in various ways. The notion of procedural utility that is attached to the act of voting plays a prominent role in this respect. By this it is meant that voters benefit from the act of voting itself, independent of the advantages they may get from realizing a specific type of policy outcome (Downs 1957; Riker and Ordeshook 1968). For example, the act of voting allows for self-expression and it can also be perceived as a core feature of democracy which has to be supported in order to secure the stability of democratic government. This means that the goal to affect public decision-making directly is authentic rather than strategic and indirectly derived from the assumption that public policies have a serious impact on one's personal affairs.

The support for direct democracy documented by opinion polls suggests that similar considerations of procedural utility might be attached to this institution. Eurobarometer data from 1997 show that in the majority of European Union states solid majorities of the population support direct democracy along the lines of the "Swiss Model" (Dalton *et al.* 2001). The most recent practical experiences with direct democracy facilitate similar conclusions. David Butler and Austin

Ranney point to a significant increase in the use of direct democracy, although they have to admit that these trends are limited to a few cases (Butler and Ranney 1994). According to Susan Scarrow, public support for direct democracy becomes more visible when measured along the lines of actual institutional change. On the basis of this criterion, she observes a comprehensive cross-national trend towards the implementation of means of direct democracy (Scarrow 2001). These empirical indicators suggest that citizens in many countries value the process of direct democracy and that they might therefore participate in it in greater numbers as soon as this option becomes available to them.

Specific forms of implementing direct democracy might also increase the individual benefits attached to this tool of participatory democracy, despite the size of modern democracy. The weight of individual votes in the process of direct decision-making is affected by the particular design of direct democracy in a threefold way. First, the comprehensive implementation of all available measures of direct decision-making increases the weight of strong preferences by opening up opportunities to shape the governmental agenda. The citizens' initiative as the most far-reaching measure of direct democracy enables citizens to shape both the issues and the alternatives on the governmental agenda, rather than just reacting to proposals submitted by political elites. It gives those with intense preferences on an issue the opportunity to promote their concerns and to bring them up for vote if enough public support can be mobilized. This is not an option if the implementation of direct democracy restricts itself to the referendum process. In a referendum, the initiative lies with political elites, not with ordinary citizens. They may pursue this initiative voluntarily or as a result of legal requirements. However, in any of these versions of the referendum, political elites will be able to control the range of alternatives that are up for decision. Ordinary citizens are restricted to casting their vote on given alternatives in the context of given issues. In this case, citizens with strong preferences on a particular issue will not have an "extra incentive" to participate by being able to influence the political agenda.[2]

The second institutional factor that affects the weight of individual votes in a process of direct decision-making is related to the number of decisions. A large number of policy positions taken by popular vote will most likely have a reverse effect on turnout per single ballot vote. Turnout should decrease with a large number of direct votes because citizens will not be ready to bear the costs of constantly taking a trip to the voting booth. If we assume that turnout in a referendum has to be perceived as a function of political interest, voters will bother to participate only in those issues they care most about. Low turnout obviously has a positive effect on the weight of an individual vote: the lower the turnout, the higher the weight. This compares in positive ways to the representative mode of decision-making which is characterized by one popular vote every two to six years. The turnout in such elections is comparatively high, but the weight of individual votes rather weak.

Critics of direct democracy stress the relatively low turnout in single ballots as an argument against this mode of decision-making and as an indicator that it is not suited to increasing the level of political participation. This negative conclusion rests on a direct comparison between turnout in single ballot measures and turnout during one parliamentary or presidential election at a time. However, these critics tend to forget that compared with representative systems and the electoral process, the number of citizens participating in the aggregate across all ballot measures is far higher during one legislative cycle in direct democracies. Direct democracy moreover optimizes the weight of an individual vote in matters most dear to the individual participants. We have to note that this holds true only if a large number of issues are decided by popular vote, because only in this case will citizens concentrate on the issues they care most about and they will not bother to vote on other cases. The institutionalization of direct democracy as a routine procedure in a given polity is a prerequisite for this very fact. One could speak of such a routine procedure to exist once a full-blown system of autonomous direct decision-making had been fully incorporated as an integral component of the political process (Gebhardt 2000: 16).

The level of jurisdiction of direct democracy is a third institutional feature that affects the impact of individual votes in the aggregate decision. Direct democracy at the local level features the reduction in the number of decision makers and thus the increase of the political weight of each individual vote with respect to the overall result. Many advocates of participatory democracy who stress direct decision-making as a core characteristic of this model of democracy are simultaneously supporters of local democracy. This suggests that they comprehend the low impact of individual votes on a national scale and that they acknowledge local democracy as a feasible solution (Wolfe 1985).

However, in the context of an expansive strategy of democratization, strengthening direct democracy at the local level begs the question of the distribution of competencies between the levels of the state. If the local arena enjoys only marginal power of collective self-determination, then democratization at this level remains symbolic from the perspective of an expansive strategy. In this connection, local democracy presupposes the decentralization of policy competency. Only under these circumstances will a sufficient degree of political influence be achieved to offer a positive incentive – and thus a rational basis – for political participation. Strengthening direct democracy at the local level also raises questions regarding the comprehensiveness of this approach. As stressed above, I take issue with a project-based, piecemeal approach to participatory democracy. As a consequence, local democracy as a means of expansive democratization presupposes institutional guarantees at the federal level that restrict the discretion of communities to implement these measures.

Some theorists of participatory democracy suggest far-reaching reforms of the representative system as an alternative solution to the problem of the marginal impact of individual votes and its negative consequences for rational political participation. These reform schemes aim to form functional equivalents of direct democracy in the guise of representative structures. According to one strand of participatory theory, functional equivalence is reached when representatives retire as autonomous decision makers and instead adopt the role of delegates or deputies who act on behalf of their constituencies (Pitkin 1967). Reform measures such as the option to recall individual MPs by popular initiative are perceived as concrete means to achieve this aim (Cronin 1999). Another strand of participatory theory promotes the random selection of ordinary citizens as members of representative decision-making bodies to achieve the goal of functional equivalence. According to its advocates, this alternative scheme of recruitment minimizes the elitist bias of representative assemblies and ensures a perfect congruence between social interests and political decision-making. From this perspective, elections breed oligarchies, and broad-based political engagement and responsive government is only possible if the decision makers are a representative sample of the people concerned (Burnheim 1985).

Efficiency-oriented democratization

The strategy of *efficiency-oriented democratization* stresses a conception of political institutions as incentive systems that pattern actors' strategic behavior (Ordeshook 1995). This strategy accepts the basic assumption of expansive democratization that views political apathy as the result of a negative cost–benefit calculus and thus as "rational ignorance." Yet, in contrast to expansive democratization the strategy of efficiency-oriented democratization sees the solution as lying not in increasing the benefits of participation, but rather in lowering its costs.

The costs of political participation can be captured theoretically via the concept of transaction costs. This concept is rooted in an essay by economist Ronald Coase, which concentrates on the question of why we end up seeing the establishment of firms in free markets and thus a restriction of the free market principle. Coase believes that the answer to this question lies in the point that firms carry out the function as a means of reducing transaction costs (Coase 1937). This concept essentially incorporates three types of costs that individual actors incur in market processes: information costs, costs accruing during negotiation and coordination, and the costs of implementing the outcome of negotiations. Coase saw firms as a means of lowering each of these types of costs and thus as contributing to an increase in the efficiency of market processes.[3]

Rational choice theorists in politics have in the past applied the concept of transaction costs to the political sphere to explain political organizations. The work of Weingast and Marschall on the committee system in the American Congress is one such example (Weingast and Marschall 1988). The concept has also been used in efforts to explain the voting paradox alluded to earlier. In this context, political parties are seen as organizations whose existence can be explained by the function they perform of reducing information costs. On this view, the existence of parties dramatically reduces the information costs for each individual voter via the creation of party ideologies that offer voters general cues regarding a party's position across multiple political issues (Wittman 1989; Jones and Hudson 1998; Müller 2000).

Within the realm of participatory democracy, the idea of increasing participation by lowering transaction costs has attracted considerable attention in the most recent stage of the debate. This basic intention has shaped a range of specific proposals related to the concept of electronic democracy, which promotes the use of the Internet in order to increase opportunities for political participation (Zittel 2001). The reduction of information costs through the spread of political information via the World Wide Web (WWW) is in this context an important, but not necessarily the most consequential, development in an increasingly networked society. Demands for utilization of the Internet as a means of reducing negotiation and coordination costs may be of greater significance from a democratic theory perspective.

Demands for elections on the Internet and the concept of online-consultation have attracted the most attention in public as well as academic debates. Remote elections on the Internet would allow voters to cast their vote from home at any given moment during a fixed period of time. This opportunity cuts the amount of time needed to travel to a poll station in order to cast a vote in public. Online-consultations organize an electronic debate on policy issues between political representatives and citizens. They greatly decrease the resources that are customarily needed to get into contact with elected officials and to voice one's opinion.

The issue of Internet elections continues to present unresolved questions against the backdrop of core principles related to democratic elections and the need for a secure voting process. Regarding security, it is difficult to ensure that votes are authentic and that voting results will not be manipulated by third parties in a medium fundamentally based on openness and a decentralized structure. The search for a technological solution to this particular problem is central to numerous pilot programs currently being carried out in Europe and North America (Buchstein and Neymanns 2002; Gibson 2001). At the level of democratic principles, e-voting causes among others questions regarding the public nature of political participation and the secrecy of the vote. Voting in elections is not a private act. Rather, it puts a special burden on us to consider the social implications of our decisions. Privatizing public participation via e-voting downplays the public nature of participation at a symbolic level and thus might compromise our ability to remember this very fact during the act of voting. Voting in our living room also opens up this process to coercion and influences from third parties that ought to be neutralized by the secret nature of the vote.

Compared with Internet elections, the concept of online-consultation poses considerable structural and organizational problems. The question here is how a system of electronic debates between citizens and the state based on specific political issues can be incorporated into existing processes of decision-making that are primarily based upon the electoral connection and the notion of party government. So far, developments in the UK provide the most extensive experience dealing with this question, as the lower chamber has undertaken several experiments with Internet-based consultations in cooperation with the *Hansard Society* (Coleman 2000; Needham 2001). In the US Congress the idea of online-consultation has been realized within the framework of the existing procedure of committee hearings. Here, the physical presence of witnesses is increasingly abandoned and they instead give testimony and participate in the hearing via digital means.

This strand of electronic democracy exhausts by no means the agenda of an efficiency oriented approach to participatory engineering. One alternative measure for example has been debated and implemented in the context of the so-called motor voter legislation in the US that was designed to decrease the costs of registering to vote (Franklin and Grier 1997). However, electronic democracy is one important feature of efficiency-oriented democratization that shall serve as an example to clarify the core assumptions of this approach.

Efficiency-oriented democratization does in no way aspire to transforming established liberal democracy. In some cases the focus is simply on reducing negotiation and cooperation costs within the framework of established forms of political involvement. It can therefore be emphasized that this approach is not wholeheartedly affiliated with the participatory democracy paradigm, which has been characterized as an alternative to liberal democracy at the institutional level. However, these reforms are debated with regard to their effects on the level of political participation and they could have considerable effects if their theoretical assumption holds. For this very reason cost-efficient democratization can be perceived as a third approach to participatory engineering.

Conclusion and discussion

The chapter develops a theoretical basis to analyze empirically as well as to inform political moves to engineer participation through democratic reform. It argues that theories of participatory democracy can be synthesized and reconstructed along three different mechanisms that theoretically link democratic institutions and political behavior in plausible ways. These three mechanisms point to different concrete instruments and institutions of participatory democracy that affect political behavior through different types of stimuli in different ways. In the following concluding remarks, I will sketch three problems that emerge from this analysis and that define the agenda for further research.

A first problem concerns the research hypotheses that can be drawn from the strategies sketched above – it addresses the notorious "so what question." I argue in this respect that the three strategies sketched above raise a reform dilemma for democracies in light of two basic evaluative criteria, namely effectiveness and feasibility. Let me briefly outline this dilemma.

The integrative approach to democratization should ideally be the most effective one in simultaneously increasing the quantity and quality of participation. It stresses measures for democratic reforms that promote various types of participation alongside taking policy choices. Taking part in social meetings or discussing community problems are assumed to have educative (transformative) effects at the attitudinal level that will enable individuals to strike the difficult balance between private interests and the common good, as well as between voice and loyalty. Compared with integrative strategies, expansionist and cost-efficient strategies are more susceptible to the risk that an increase in the quantity of participation will actually endanger other values of democracy such as individual rights. This is because they do not allow for inherent mechanisms which ensure the quality of participation.

A reform dilemma arises because the strategy most effective is politically the least feasible. A reform of liberal democracy has to be implemented by political elites through law making and constitutional reform, so they must be understood and accepted at the elite level. The expansive and efficiency-oriented approaches are the most straightforward and direct in terms of their instruments and the way they are assumed to affect individual behavior.

In contrast to the expansive and efficiency-oriented approaches, the instruments proposed by the integrative approach are much less specific. For example, the concept of discursive or deliberative democracy is not easily applicable within the political world. There is a remaining gap between normative and empirical theory despite the recent empirical turn in deliberative theory for two reasons. First, empirical approaches to participatory democracy suffer from confusion between projects and institutions. They focus on participatory events such as deliberative opinion polls and their design, and disregard the connection with a given decision-making system and the institutions that need to be adopted to establish this connection. Further developing this process as a serious option for democratic reform would presuppose an answer to the question of how deliberative opinion polls can be adapted to fit into constitutional decision-making structures. Second, the integrationist approach is focused on small-scale institutions at the local level without asking about their institutional basis at the federal level of government in terms of guaranteed jurisdiction and enabling incentives to foster their diffusion across the whole system (Fung and Wright 2001, 2003, McLaverty 2002). Moreover, the causal mechanisms by which strategies of integrative democratization are seen to exert effects on participation are far less direct, since they stress the attitudinal level as a crucial linkage between political institutions and political behavior. Owing to the lack of specificity and the indirect causal mechanism promoted by integrative democratization, it can be assumed that this strategy will be the one which is the least feasible in political terms.

One reservation ought to be raised with regard to the hypothetical reform dilemma outlined above; feasibility is, of course, not solely dependent upon the nature of the measure itself but also upon the particular political context in which the measure is applied. A similar argument holds true for the notion of effectiveness which should be affected in its impact at the behavioral level by a complex web of cultural, political and individual factors as well. The politics of democratic reform as well as the actual effects of participatory institutions and their contextual prerequisites should be subject to further empirical inquiry. Ideally, this research should be comparative, including a range of most different systems to aid understanding of the dilemma of democratic reform and to search for possible resolutions.

The second question concerns the process of researching participatory engineering and the reform dilemma that we have associated with such efforts. It is obvious that this research ought to be comparative, covering a large number of cases, i.e. countries. The collection of the broad basis of data would clearly overburden an individual researcher in terms of skills (language) and time. The development of a research network provides a solution to the problem but needs to avoid one pitfall. These kinds of endeavors end up all too easily with a selection of case studies that are based on very different concepts and ideas and that can thus not be accumulated. What is needed is an integrated research network based on similar concepts and research objectives.

A third and final question concerns the relevance of participatory democracy for future democratic reform efforts. One possible resort to avoid the reform dilemma outlined above would be to pursue marginal reforms in the context of the established order of representative democracy. There can be little doubt that this system was most successful in the past in securing the quantity and quality of participation at the same time and in balancing conflicting values. I close with the argument that marginal reform short of participatory institutions is the least likely option in the long run. This is not primarily because of the empirical fact that citizens are disaffected with the current structure of democracy. It is primarily because of reasons that account for this dissatisfaction. Due to social change representative institutions are to a lesser and lesser extent able to aggregate interests and link them to the system of government. The growing fragmentation and individualization of advanced societies results in the fact that either more and more individuals no longer feel represented in the political process or that more and more individuals feel that crucial interests of theirs are no longer represented. If the worst comes to the worst, these individuals feel so cross-pressured by multidimensional issue spaces that they leave the political arena out of frustration and despair. This frustration and despair will accelerate the pressure towards reform in the future and it gives way to the pressing need to find a way out of the reform dilemma outlined in this chapter.

Notes

1 See Fuchs in Chapter 2 in this volume for this position.
2 For a more detailed account on different types and measures of direct democracy see Gebhardt (2000), Moeckli (1994) and Butler and Ranney (1994).
3 For a further discussion of the concept of transaction costs in microeconomics see especially Williamson and Masten (1999).

References

Bachrach, P. and Botwinick, A. (1992) *Power and Empowerment. A Radical Theory of Participatory Democracy*, Philadelphia, PA: Temple University Press.

Barber, B. (1984) *Strong Democracy. Participatory Politics for a New Age*, Berkeley, CA: University of California Press.

Becker, T.L. (1981) "Teledemocracy: Bringing Power Back to the People," *The Futurist*, December: 6–9.

Buchstein, H. and Neymanns, H. (eds) (2002) *Online-Wahlen*, Opladen: Leske & Budrich.

Burnheim, J. (1985) *Is Democracy Possible? The Alternative to Electoral Politics*, Berkeley, CA: University of California Press.

Butler, D. and Ranney, A. (eds) (1994) *Referendums Around the World – The Growing Use of Direct Democracy*, Washington, DC: AEI Press.

Coase, R. (1937) "The Nature of the Firm," *Economica*, 4: 386–405.

Coleman, S. (2000) "Parliament in the Information Age: The Case of Westminster and Holyrood," in R. Gibson and S. Ward (eds) *Reinvigorating Democracy? British Politics and the Internet*, Aldershot: Ashgate, pp. 67–79.

Cook, T.E. and Morgan, P.M. (eds) (1971) *Participatory Democracy*, San Francisco, CA: Canfield Press.

Cronin, Th.E. (1999) *Direct Democracy. The Politics of Initiative, Referendum, and Recall*, San Jose, CA: to Excel.

Dalton, R.J., Bürklin, W. and Drummond, A. (2001) "Public Opinion and Direct Democracy," *Journal of Democracy*, 12: 141–153.

Downs, A. (1957) *An Economic Theory of Democracy*, New York: Harper.

Dryzek, J.S. (ed.) (2000) *Deliberative Democracy and Beyond*, Oxford: Oxford University Press.

—— (1987) "Discursive Designs: Critical Theory and Political Institutions," *American Journal of Political Science*, 31: 656–679.

Fishkin, J. (1995) *The Voice of the People*, New Haven, CT: Yale University Press.

—— (1991) *Democracy and Deliberation*, New Haven, CT: Yale University Press.

Franklin, D.P. and Grier, E.E. (1997) "Effects of Motor Voter Legislation – Voter Turnout, Registration, and Partisan Advantage in the 1992 Presidential Election," *American Politics Quarterly*, 25: 104–117.

Fuchs, D. (2000) "Demokratie und Beteiligung in der modernen Gesellschaft: Einige demokratietheoretische Überlegungen," in O. Niedermayer and B. Westle (eds) *Demokratie und Partizipation. Festschrift für Max Kaase*, Wiesbaden: Westdeutscher Verlag, pp. 250–280.

Fung, A. and Wright, E.O. (eds) (2003) *Deepening Democracy*, London: Verso.

—— (2001) "Deepening Democracy: Innovations in Empowered Participatory Governance," *Politics & Society*, 29: 5–41.

Gebhardt, J. (2000) "Das Plebiszit in der Repräsentativen Demokratie," in H.H. von Arnim (ed.) *Direkte Demokratie*, Berlin: Duncker & Humblot.

Gibson, R. (2001) "Elections Online: Assessing Internet-Voting in Light of the Arizona Democratic Primary," *Political Science Quarterly*, 116: 561–583.

Habermas, J. (1998) *Faktizität und Geltung. Beiträge zur Diskurstheorie des Rechts und des demokratischen Rechtsstaates*, Frankfurt am Main: Suhrkamp.

—— (1992) "Drei normative Modelle der Demokratie: Zum Begriff deliberativer Politik", in H. Münkler (ed.) Die Chancen der Freiheit. Grundprobleme der Demokratie, München: Piper.

—— (1962) *Strukturwandel der Öffentlichkeit*, Neuwied: Luchterhand.

Hall, P.A. and Soskic, D. (2001) "An Introduction to Varieties of Capitalism," in P.A. Hall and D. Soskice (eds) Varieties of Capitalism: Institutional Foundations of Comparative Advantage, Oxford: Oxford University Press, pp. 1–68.

Hall, P.A. and Taylor, R.C.R. (1996) "Political Science and the Three New Institutionalisms," *Political Studies*, 44: 936–957.

Hirschman, A.O. (1997) *The Passions and the Interests. Political Arguments for Capitalism Before its Triumph*, Princeton, NJ: Princeton University Press.

Jones, P. and Hudson, J. (1998) "The Role of Political Parties: An Analysis Based on Transaction Costs," *Public Choice*, 94: 125–181.

Kielmansegg, P. Graf (1977) *Volkssouveränität*, Stuttgart: Klett.

Kubicek, H. (1996) "Allgemeiner Zugang und informatielle Grundversorgung," in J. Tauss, J. Kollbeck and J. Mönikes (eds) *Deutschlands Weg in die Informationsgesellschaft. Herausforderungen und Perspektiven für Wirtschaft, Recht und Politik*, Baden-Baden: Nomos.

Luskin, R.C., Fishkin, J.S. and Jowell, R. (2002) "Considered Opinions: Deliberative Polling in Britain," *British Journal of Political Science*, 32: 455–487.

Mather, J. (1995) "What are the Democratic Impediments to Participatory Democracy," *Politics*, 15: 175–182.

Macpherson, Crawford B. (1977) *The Life and Times of Liberal Democracy*, Oxford: Oxford University Press.

Mansbridge, J.J. (1980) *Beyond Adversary Democracy*, New York: Basic Books.

McLaverty, P. (ed.) (2002) *Public Participation and Innovations in Community Governance*, Aldershot: Ashgate.

Moeckli, S. (1994) *Direkte Demokratie. Ein internationaler Vergleich*, Bern: Haupt.

Müller, W.C. (2000) "Political Parties in Parliamentary Democracies: Making Delegation and Accountability Work," *European Journal of Political Research*, 37: 309–333.

Needham, C. (2001) "Electronic Consultation in the UK and the USA – Electronic Democracy Beyond the Vote," Paper presented at the 2001 ECPR Joint Sessions of Workshops, Grenoble, 6–11 April.

Offe, C. (1997) "Micro-Aspects of Democratic Theory: What Makes for the Deliberative Competence of Citizens?," in A. Hadenius (ed.) *Democracy's Victory and Crisis*, Cambridge: Cambridge University Press.

Ordeshook, P.C. (1995) "Institutions and Incentives," *Journal for Democracy*, 6: 46–60.

Pateman, C. (1970) *Participation and Democratic Theory*, Cambridge: Cambridge University Press.

Pieterse, J.N. (2001) "Participatory Democratization Reconceived," *Futures*, 33: 407–422.

Pitkin, H.F. (1967) *The Concept of Representation*, Berkeley, CA: University of California Press.

Poster, M. (1995) *The Second Media Age*, Cambridge: Polity Press.

Rheingold, H. (1993) *The Virtual Community. Homesteading on the Electronic Frontier*, Reading, MA: Addison-Wesley.

Riker, W.H. and Ordeshook, P.C. (1968) "A Theory of the Calculus of Voting," *American Political Science Review*, 62: 25–43.

Rousseau, J.J. (1994) *Vom Gesellschaftsvertrag oder Grundsätze des Staatsrechts*, Stuttgart: Reclam.

Salisbury, R.H. (1975) "Research on Political Participation," *American Journal of Political Science*, 19: 323–341.

Sartori, G. (1987) *The Theory of Democracy Revisited*, 2 vols, Chatham, NJ: Chatham House.

Saward, M. (2001) "Reconstructing Democracy: Current Thinking and New Directions," *Government and Opposition*, 36: 559–581.

Scarrow, S.E. (2001) "Direct Democracy and Institutional Change. A Comparative Investigation," *Comparative Political Studies*, 34: 651–665.

Sola Pool, I. de (1983) *Technologies of Freedom. On Free Speech in the Information Age*, Cambridge, MA: Harvard University Press.

Streeck, W. (1984) "Co-determination: The Fourth Decade," in B. Wilpert and A. Sorge (eds) International Yearbook of Organizational Democracy, Vol. II: International Perspectives on Organisational Democracy, Chichester: Wiley, pp. 291–314.

van Deth, J. (2000) "Interesting but Irrelevant: Social Capital and the Saliency of Politics in Western Europe," *European Journal of Political Research*, 37: 115–147.

Verba, S. and Nie, N. (1972) *Participation in America: Political Democracy and Social Equality*, New York: Harper Row.

Walker, J.L. (1966) "A Critique of the Elitist Theory of Democracy," *American Political Science Review*, 60: 285–295.

Warren, M.E. (1993) "Can Participatory Democracy Produce Better Selves? Psychological Dimensions of Habermas's Discursive Model of Democracy," *Political Psychology*, 14: 209–234.

—— (1992) "Democratic Theory and Self Transformation," *American Political Science Review*, 86: 8–23.

Weingast, B.R. and Marschall, U.J. (1988) "The Industrial Organization of Congress: Or Why Legislatures, like Firms, are not Organized as Markets," *Journal of Political Economy*, 96: 132–167.

Wilhelm, A. (2000) *Democracy in the Digital Age*, New York: Routledge.

Williamson, O.E. and Masten, S.E. (eds) (1999) *The Economics of Transaction Costs*, Cheltenham: Elgar.

Wittman, D. (1989) "Why Democracies produce Efficient Results," *Journal of Political Economy*, 97: 1395–1428.

Wolfe, J. (1985) "A Defense of Participatory Democracy," *Review of Politics*, 47: 370–389.

Zittel, Th. (2003) "Participatory Democracy and Political Participation," Paper presented at the 2003 ECPR Joint Sessions of Workshop, Edinburgh, 28 March–2 April.

—— (2001) "Elektronische Demokratie – Planskizze für eine Demokratie des 21. Jahrhunderts?," *Neue Politische Literatur*, 46: 433–470.

2 Participatory, liberal and electronic democracy

Dieter Fuchs

Introduction

The reluctance of citizens in present-day democracies to participate in politics is a matter of considerable concern to many observers. Their concern is fed by two sources: first, this reluctance is understood to reflect an erosion of the legitimacy of these democracies; and second, it is set against the background of a normative understanding of democracy, according to which political participation is a constitutive characteristic. This understanding is implicit in the democracy concept, for government by the people, however it may operate in detail, and is quite simply inconceivable without the political participation of the citizens. However, there are widely differing ideas about the necessary extent and type of participation. They depend on the normative model that serves as our point of reference. The issue of political participation by the citizen can accordingly not be discussed in isolation; it can be meaningfully addressed only in the framework of normative models of democracy.

The first goal of the following analysis is to outline the most important democracy models and the status they confer on political participation. Our account is simplified: we restrict ourselves to a few fundamental models.[1] We proceed in three steps. First, antique democracy is described. There are several reasons for taking this as our point of departure. It was the first democracy in history and also a form of democracy in which the people literally governed themselves. It is therefore archetypal and exemplary for many modern models of participatory democracy. In addition, taking this point of reference can avoid the frequent overburdening of the democracy concept with almost arbitrary content and criteria (Eder 1998). Finally, the democracy of antiquity can provide insight into the conditions under which participatory democracy can be realized.

The second step is to describe modern democracy, generally referred to as liberal democracy, and which, from an institutional point of view, is representative democracy. We are interested not so much in providing yet another compilation of its characteristics but in comparing it with antique democracy. The intention is to demonstrate that, although both models can be understood as democracy, they imply quite different meanings of the term.

In the third step we turn to participatory and electronic democracy. The two terms can subsume a multitude of approaches. With regard to participatory democracy, we concentrate on what is presumably the most important variant under discussion in contemporary democracy, namely deliberative democracy. As regards electronic democracy, we consider only ideas that are committed to the ideal of participatory democracy. Proponents argue that participatory democracy can be realized under the conditions of modern societies thanks to technological innovations in information and communication media: "The new challenge of direct democracy lies in the startling fact that it is now technically possible" (Budge 1996: 1). The subject of this third step of analysis is therefore participatory democracy as electronic democracy or electronic democracy as participatory democracy.

The second goal of our chapter is to discuss how realistic it is to uphold the ideal of participatory democracy under present-day circumstances, and the extent to which it can be realized even approximately. It is, of course, beyond the ambition of this paper to settle this controversial issue, but theoretical plausibilities and scholarly findings can contribute to the discussion. Without engaging in this discussion the postulate of "bringing citizens back in" can come to nothing.

Antique democracy

The antique democracy is perceived as a model in a double meaning of the word. First, in the sense that it is a descriptive model that gives a simplified account of the complex reality of Athenian democracy in antiquity and which is restricted to identifying essential characteristics. Second, in the sense of a normative model, since for many modern theoreticians and practitioners, this antique democracy has been a natural example to be emulated. In describing antique democracy we are guided by both components of the democracy concept. What are the essential characteristics of the *demos* and the *kratos* in the original form of democracy? We begin with a formal definition of the demos, going on to deal with the kratos. Certain normatively relevant characteristics of antique democracy are then discussed in greater detail, and in this context we return to a consideration of the demos.

In the democracy of antiquity, the demos included all citizens, i.e. all male inhabitants of Attica with political rights. When in antiquity it was said that the demos rules, two meanings have to be distinguished: first, it meant rule by the mass (*plethos*), the many (*polloí*) or the people (demos) and not by the few, let alone an individual. Second, the equality (*isótes*) of citizens was emphasized. Poor and rich citizens, less well and well-educated citizens had equal part in government regardless of class and education. In the antique understanding of democracy, political equality between citizens is of decisive importance, and historically the isonomy concept (*isonomía*) to denote the system of government based on the equality of citizens precedes the democracy concept (Meier 1993; Bleicken 1994; Eder 1998; Raaflaub 1998).

If the notions that the people should rule and that all are equal in the system of rule are considered fundamental to democracy (Bleicken 1994), it begs the question of how they have been institutionalized. And the question of institutionalization concerns the "kratos components" of the democracy concept. The structure of the democratic system of government in antique Athens was based on four institutions: the assembly of the people (*ekklesía*), the council of the five hundred (*boulé*), the magistrates (*archaí*) and the people's courts (*dikasteria*).[2] The basis institution and center of government was the ekklesía. Every Athenian citizen had the right to attend and speak. And the vote of every citizen had equal weight. The ekklesía made all important decisions concerning the common affairs of the polis, and which were binding on the polis. The ekklesía met at least thirty times a year for this purpose. The number of participants presumably varied between a tenth and a fifth of the citizenry. Although only part of the citizenry was ever present in the ekklesía, it was also regarded as being the demos as a whole (Welwei 1999). This is expressed in the formula with which the decisions on the ekklesía were introduced: "demos and *boulé* have decided."

The council of the five hundred (boulé) had a double function (Hansen 1991; Bleicken 1994). In the first place, it was to ensure the efficient functioning of the ekklesía. It achieved this, for example, by preparing every matter to be put to the ekklesía, drawing up a "preliminary decree" (*proboúleuma*) which provided the basis for debate in the ekklesía. Second, the boulé directed and supervised the entire activities of the magistrates (archaí). In order to perform these functions, at least part of the boulé was in permanent session, thus ensuring government by the demos even when the ekklesía was not meeting. This naturally presupposed that the boulé was a direct expression of the demos and could not dissociate itself from the latter in its activities. This was ensured by a number of arrangements. All councilors (*bouleutés*) were replaced each year by lot, no citizen could belong to the boulé for two years in a row or more than twice in his life. The boulé was therefore a committee randomly selected from among the demos, and there was no possibility of it giving rise to a governing elite with corresponding ruling knowledge (Meier 1993; Welwei 1999).

We will not go into detail about the magistrates (archaí) and people's courts (dikasteria), but it should be noted that the archaí and the judges (*dikastai*) of the dikasteria were newly appointed each year and were also chosen by lot.[3] These institutional arrangements ensured that the demos itself did literally rule. In a famous passage from his *Politics* (1317a40–1317b7, see also 1261a31ff.), Aristotle described taking turns at ruling and being ruled as the essential feature of democracy.

The permanent rotation of rulers and ruled, the choice of office-holders by lot, the mass magistracy with relatively few powers (Bleicken 1994) and, especially, the concentration of the power to make binding decisions for the polis in the ekklesía realized what modern democracy theory calls the identity of rulers and ruled.

Finally, we look at certain aspects of the reality of antique democracy that are very important for current participatory democracy theories: (a) the extent of participation by citizens, (b) the nature of political opinion-building, (c) the nature of the decisions made, and, (d) the demos as a collective subject.

If Athenian democracy was to function at all, an extraordinary level of political participation by citizens was needed, and was, in fact, given. Every year 500 councilors and about 700 magistrates were required, and a further 700 or so magistrates were active for the Maritime League. If we include the 6,000 citizens from among whom the officers of the courts of justice were chosen by lot, we have a total of about 8,000 citizens who held and exercised public office in the polis each year. Given an approximate total of 35,000 citizens this amounts to almost a quarter. This list does not include participation in the ekklesía and activities in the communities (*demoi*). The enormous extent of political engagement on the part of Athenian citizens is incontrovertible. According to Meier (1993: 491f) "the expenditure of effort by the Athenians is almost incomprehensible," and "it is a mystery how political life concretely related to work." Hansen (1991: 313) takes a similar view: "The level of political activity by the citizens of Athens is unparalleled in world history, in terms of number, frequency and level of participation."

One of the most characteristic features of the reality of Athenian democracy was the extensive discussion on polis affairs by citizens in public places. This includes conversations in the marketplace (*agora*), and especially oratory and deliberation in the institutionalized meetings like the ekklesía and the boulé. Bleicken (1994: 341) even describes the freedom of speech in assemblies, *isegoría*, as the "key element of democracy" (see also Hansen 1991; Raaflaub 1998). This practice of participation in oratory and deliberation also determines the type of opinion-building by the demos and the type of decisions made. The will of the demos was formed through joint deliberation by the physically present demos in the ekklesía. To this extent one can indeed speak of a collective will of the demos that is more than an aggregation of individual opinions. A decision adopted by the ekklesía was an outcome of the deliberations and accordingly constituted an authentic expression of the collective will.

The principle that guided deliberations was the common good of the polis. This is shown, for example, by a passage in Euripides (1970: 435 ff.), which cites the following introductory formula for discussion in the ekklesía: "Who wishes to bring a proposal before the assembly that is useful for the polis?" In surviving records of discussions in the ekklesía, the contribution of a speaker is repeatedly justified in terms of the utility (*sympheron*) for the polis, and this utility for the polis is valued more highly than utility for the individual. What is useful for the polis is also seen as equitable. If we express these notions in the language of contemporary democracy theory, contributions by speakers were legitimate only if they appealed to the common good and were therefore non-particular in nature.

The institution of the ekklesía and the opinion-building that takes place there had another far-reaching consequence. From the perspective of each and every participant, the communal and public nature of deliberation in the ekklesía involved a limited and observable number of actually present citizens. He could ascribe every spoken contribution to a specific citizen and attribute every decision to the present gathering of citizens including himself. The demos of

Athenian democracy was thus constituted not as an imagined collective subject as is the case in modern nation states but as a tangible collective subject. And this satisfies a demand associated with the democracy concept. The subject of government should not be merely an aggregate of single citizens but the demos as a whole.

The experience of commonality was not limited to the ekklesía. Political discussions were conducted in other public places, the marketplace, gymnasiums, etc. If one considers the relatively small number of citizens, it is highly probable that people came across acquaintances on public occasions and in the exercise of public offices. This commonality experienced in public places was underpinned by the marked ethnic-cultural homogeneity of the citizenry. This homogeneity was grounded in a long, organic and unquestioningly accepted tradition which was highly valued as such by Athenians.

Modern democracy

Institutional and procedural characteristics of modern democracy

Modern democracy – generally termed liberal democracy – differs fundamentally from the antique democracy. Before we address these differences, some of its characteristics shall be considered. This can be done rather succinctly. According to Dahl (1989) it is the result of the "second democratic transformation," initiated by the extraordinary change of scale (territorial space, number of citizens). As a result, the principle of democracy merged with the principle of representation. And this had profound institutional and procedural consequences. Whereas in antique democracy the *ekklesía* was the institutional focus, in modern democracy it is the parliament and the government. In both institutions representatives perform the business of governing. Since the representation principle is not a democratic one per se, it gains its democratic character only through the specific selection of the representatives of the people by the people. This is done through elections, and elections are democratic only if the voter has alternatives, if all citizens who wish to take part can indeed do so, and if every vote has equal weight. These criteria are met in liberal democracy by the institution of periodic and competitive elections, generally implemented by the constitution.

The institutionalization of modern democracy through elections and through parliaments and governments has a far-reaching impact on what democracy means, transforming it dramatically. Sartori (1987: 86) puts it tersely and almost cynically: "Since in order to have democracy we must have, to some degree, a government of the people, let us immediately ask: When do we find a 'governing people,' the demos in the act of the role of governing? The answer is: at elections."

The mere fact that the demos elects representatives who take on the business of governing is, however, insufficient to satisfy a reasonably demanding understanding of democracy. If, after election, these representatives were willing and able to govern only according to their own wishes without any regard for the demos, the idea of government by the people would be completely devoid of sense. It must therefore be ensured with the institution of elections that representatives rule in accordance with the will of the demos. The concept of responsiveness (Dahl 1971; Fuchs 1998) has become established to describe this state of affairs. According to the theory of liberal democracy, responsiveness is to be structurally generated through the periodicity of elections and the possibility of a change in government. The prospect of the next elections obliges the rulers to take heed of the opinion of the demos in their own interest.

The responsiveness of rulers to those ruled introduces a completely new criterion to the semantics of democracy. It played no role in antique democracy. If there is identity of ruler and ruled, there can perforce be no difference between them. But where elected representatives are in government, such a difference is almost structurally inbuilt. The situation between rulers and ruled thus changes fundamentally in modern democracy. This change naturally affects the meaning of political participation by citizens. Politics is concerned with regulating the common affairs of a polis or a state through generally binding decisions. If in liberal democracy this decision-making activity is performed by representatives – even though elected by the people – this must drastically modify the concept of popular sovereignty. Popular sovereignty can no longer consist in the participation of the demos in governing but only in the control of government action by the demos, or – which is the same seen from another angle – the responsiveness of the rulers to the will of the demos. The institution that is to generate this responsiveness structurally is, as we have seen, periodic and competitive elections. This considerably reduces the standing of political participation by the citizens, which assumes quite a new character. Whereas in antique democracy participation by the citizens in government was both means and end, in liberal democracy it is now only a means to an end. Under the second democratic transformation popular government is thus no longer direct participation in government by the people but the choice of rulers by the people and the responsiveness of the rulers to the people.

Comparison between antique and modern democracy

Some important differences between antique and modern democracy have been dealt with in the preceding section. They include the nature of participation by the demos in government. In antique democracy, the demos was directly involved, one could even say that through annual and mass rotation in ruling and being ruled and through the institution of the ekklesía, the demos not only participated in government, but governed itself. In modern democracy, in contrast, which is representative democracy, there is only indirect participation in government, in that the demos chooses representatives to govern, and – through the institution of periodic and competitive elections – imposes more or less strong constraints on the latter to act in accordance with the will of the demos.

The type of participation in government partly determines the extent of participation. Since elections do not take place very often and are concerned not so much with policy content than with the selection of representatives, political participation by citizens in modern democracies can be described as occasional and limited. But participation in elections does not exclude engagement on the part of citizens in political parties and collaboration in civil society voluntary associations. In fact, however, only tiny minorities are involved. Precisely this state of affairs together with the declining participation in elections to be observed in many countries is the source of concern for many observers mentioned in the introduction and which has led to the postulate of "bringing citizens back in."

Another important difference between antique and modern democracy lies in the nature of opinion-building. In modern democracies, on account of the scale involved, no joint deliberation by the demos in assemblies occurs. For the individual citizen, political opinion-building is largely monologistic, or takes place in very restricted communication in the primary life-world. The demos as a whole can at best be reached through the mass media. And something like a discussion occurs there. But it is not discussion among citizens but advocatory discussion among journalists and representatives that is conducted in public and, perhaps, for the public. Through this type of political opinion-building, anything resembling a deliberatively constituted will of the demos can scarcely come into being. The will of the demos in a liberal democracy is accordingly a factor calculated on the basis of procedural rules – primarily the majority rule. The basis for applying this procedure is the preferences and interests of individual citizens, factors largely exogenous to the democratic process. Anything in the way of a common good can therefore hardly be the outcome of these processes and is reduced to a non-binding, rhetorical formula.

In what sense can we speak of a demos at all in a modern democracy? The demos is a political community and, like every community, it constitutes itself through two mechanisms (Fuchs 2000b). First, by drawing a boundary that decides who belongs and who does not; and, second, through commonalities among those who belong, which provide a starting point for more or less strong identification of members with the community. In both antique and modern democracy, boundary drawing is very exclusive. Since Pericles' 451/450 BC citizenship law, only a male resident of Attica whose parents were born Athenians could be an Athenian citizen. In modern democracy the boundary is drawn by the law relating to nationality.

In antique democracy there was further exclusion within the population of Attica. Citizenship was denied to women, slaves and so-called metics (*metoikoi*). The latter were free foreigners living and working in Attica. This internal exclusion is one of the main points of criticism extended by contemporary analysts of antique democracy, and in this regard the modern understanding of democracy differs considerably from the view taken by antiquity. Dahl (1971, 1989) considers the inclusion of all members of the social community in the demos as one of the most important criteria of a fully developed democracy. This is likely to be one of the few aspects where modern democracy can be regarded as being "more democratic" than antique democracy.

A crucial difference between the demos in antique and modern democracy has already been mentioned in discussing political opinion-building. The demos of antique democracy was a real community formed through interaction between physically present citizens in public places. This interaction was based on an extraordinarily homogeneous culture with shared values and modes of behavior. These commonalities were permanently manifested in interaction, thus stabilizing the political community. This real community was one of the preconditions for the demos to be able to constitute itself in actuality as the collective subject of government. Because every single citizen had the experience of being a member of a demos he could comprehend what it means to be involved in discussing and determining the affairs of the polis together with the other members.

In modern societies these preconditions are not met or, at best, are met only in a very diluted form. The community of modern societies is characterized by pronounced ethnic-cultural plurality, and its members are spread over the extensive territory of a state. For the individual, other citizens are therefore necessarily strangers; he knows only that they exist. This knowledge is underpinned by extremely selective encounters in public situations and by reports about other citizens in the mass media. But if they are to be understood as citizens and thus classed as belonging to a political community, this community must exist. And it can exist only as an imagined community, not a real one as in antique Athens. But such an imagined community, too, must be moored to something substantial that, first, embraces ethnic-cultural plurality and, second, draws a boundary. In European nation states this is achieved by the idea of the nation, and the nation is characterized above all by factors like a shared language, history, tradition and territory (Smith 1991; Fuchs 2000b). Such a political community, whose collective identity is that of a nation, is a cognitively and affectively highly contingent construction. And it is questionable whether this construction can be maintained under the conditions of globalization (see final section).

The comparison between modern and antique democracy undertaken in the previous section makes one thing clear: if antique democracy is seen as the ideal, modern democracy is indeed a pale imitation of this model. Instead of actual self-government, there is only choice of the rulers by the ruled and more or less effective control of government action by the demos. Instead of joint and deliberative opinion-building by the demos, there are at best advocatory discussions in the mass media limited to a small selection of subjects that need to be decided. Instead of an authentic popular will that substantively constitutes a common good, the decisions made in liberal democracies are a procedural aggregation of particular group interests. In modern democracy the demos is not a collective subject but a collection of individual subjects, and, at best, an imagined, i.e. abstract community. Because of these considerable differences, Meier (1993: 478) asks the skeptical question: "In all, it [Athenian democracy] was so characterized by peculiarities that we must question whether our democracy deserves this name at all when compared with the antique model." We will take this skepticism a step further with the postulate that modern democracy is undemanding in comparison with the antique ideal.

This matter of fact can occasion different responses. One possibility is to problematize the antique democracy as a normative reference point and to claim normative independence or even superiority for liberal democracy. Another possibility is to uphold the normative ideal of a participatory democracy. This does not necessarily mean confronting the reality of liberal democracy with a fundamentally unrealizable ideal and thus adopting a resigned stance. Some proponents of participatory democracy seek to show what it means under modern conditions and how it can possibly be realized. This is the perspective that is interesting in the context of our analysis and one we will return to. First of all, however, we must recall certain restrictions that are imposed on greater political participation by citizens in a modern society.

The complexity of society and restrictions on political participation

The normative question of how a political system should be designed can never be answered with any finality by referring to realization problems. One can stand by normative ideas, even counterfactually, for very good reasons. However, such realization problems cannot fail to affect the justification of normative positions.

The second democratic transformation, which led to the formation of liberal and thus representative democracy, was not the chance outcome of a historical process. As we have already described, it was made necessary by a change in scale (states covering large territories, a public amounting to millions) (Dahl 1989). This change in scale does not limit the possibility of political participation per se. But if it is not a matter of some participation or other but of self-government, we have quite a different state of affairs. Self-government means that the demos itself actually rules, and, by definition, this means not via representatives. And such self-government by the demos presumably requires the presence of citizens in assemblies all the more if opinion-building is to proceed in the form of deliberations. However, the bigger the territory and the greater the number of citizens, the more implausible ruling without representatives and ruling in assemblies becomes.

In Dahl's (1989) concept of the second democratic transformation, one decisive characteristic of modern societies has not yet been taken into account: societal complexity. A modern society is a functionally differentiated society, in which the primary societal subsystems have to perform specific services for the others. The political system, as we know, is responsible for controlling functions, for providing infrastructure, for ensuring internal and social security, etc. This is associated with a decision-making activity that can no longer be compared at all with antique democracy as regards the complexity of problems. If these services are to be performed, the political system needs to be differentiated into professionalized roles. And if this is the case, self-government is no longer possible unless one is prepared to accept dedifferentiation and to renounce the gains in effectiveness and increases in options associated with the growth in complexity. It is questionable whether this would be in keeping with the will of the demos. In accordance with Sartori (1987: 65), the argument can be summed up and formalized in the following proposition: the intensity of self-government attainable stands in inverse relation to (a) the extent of the territory, (b) the number of citizens, (c) the quantity of decisions, and, (d) the complexity of the problems.

We now shift our perspective from the systemic to the individual level and consider the rationality of political participation under the conditions of modern societies. As argumentative background we draw on rational choice theory. This theory assumes that, in an action situation, an actor chooses the alternative which he expects to bring the greatest benefit at the lowest cost. These choices are made under situational and structural constraints. At least three constraints can be distinguished. Identifying a benefit of one's own political participation involves information costs, and in complex societies the corresponding expenditure of time and energy is systematically insufficient (Downs 1957). If a benefit can nonetheless be identified, the problem arises as to the significance of personal participation. In elections, for example, the weight of an individual's vote in an electorate of millions is infinitesimal. The probability of actually bringing the preferred party to power through personal participation in the election and, by this means, to realize the perceived benefit, is accordingly almost zero.

But this raises the question of opportunity costs, i.e. of lost benefits owing to action alternatives not taken. In a modern society, the realization of personal life plans and action goals and the achievement of the highest possible social status depend much more strongly than in antique society on subsystems other than politics. Investing the scarce resources of time and energy in actions in other subsystems would therefore be more rational for the majority of citizens. There is empirical evidence to support this theoretical assumption. In the analysis by Verba, Schlozman and Brady (1995: 129), the three most important reasons stated by American respondents for their political inactivity were the following: "I don't have enough time" (39 percent), "I should take care of myself and my family before I worry about the community or nation" (34 percent), "The important things of my life have nothing to do with politics" (20 percent). The findings of the comparative World Values Survey point in a similar direction. In comparison with other spheres of life, the subjective importance of politics is lowest in all Western countries (the data are not provided here; see Fuchs 2000a; van Deth 2000). Most important were family, friends and work. From a normative point of view it is a matter of concern that leisure time is seen as much more important than politics. This alone indicates that it is likely to be difficult to mobilize time resources invested in leisure activities for political participation.

Participation in self-government by the demos would mean comprehensive and everyday engagement on the part of citizens. And, as we see it, reality imposes restrictions in modern societies that are difficult to overcome. But if participatory democracy theory wishes to do more than uphold an ideal without consequences, it cannot entirely eschew discussion on how such participation can be motivated and institutionalized under contemporary societal conditions.

Participatory and electronic democracy

Participatory democracy

Unlike the models of democracy discussed so far, participatory democracy is a purely normative model. Of the wide spectrum of approaches that can be classed under this heading, we concentrate on those that have played a prominent role in the democracy theory discussion over the past two decades, and which focus on the notion of deliberation. Specifically, we will be looking at the theory of strong democracy put forward by Barber (1984), at Habermas's (1992) theory of discoursive democracy, and at the directly-deliberative polyarchy theory of Cohen and Sabel (1997). The three theories overlap in important aspects.

Their starting point is criticism of existing liberal democracy. It proceeds from two perspectives, normative and practical. From a normative point of view, they object that liberal democracy is now hardly in keeping with a reasonably demanding interpretation of the democracy principle. From a practical point of view they presume that liberal democracy confronts problems no longer amenable to solution within its institutional framework and by its procedures alone. The most important problem they see is the unquestioned dominance of particular interests in politics, which in the long run erode the foundations of the democratic process itself:

> Liberal democracy is based on premises about human nature, knowledge, and politics that are genuinely liberal but that are not intrinsically democratic. Its conception of the individual and of individual interest undermines the democratic practices upon which both individuals and their interests depend.
>
> (Barber 1984: 4)

Habermas (1992) stresses that the social and political integration of modern societies can no longer be effected only by systemic mechanisms and the bargaining of particular interests, but needs also to be placed on a communicative basis. According to these approaches, participatory democracy is thus the normatively desirable and the practically necessary form of democracy; it is: "desirable both in itself and as a problem solver" (Cohen and Sabel 1997: 314). The extent to which it is also possible, that is to say, actually implementable, is a moot point. We will leave this question to one side for the moment and turn to the normative dimension.

It has been indicated that the two central characteristics of all three variants of participatory democracy are the directness of participation by citizens in governing and deliberation in political opinion formation. Another common feature is the attempt to adapt the model to the conditions of modern societies. This is shown in the following three definitions by Barber. The first describes unrestricted participatory democracy:

> Participatory democracy [. . .] denotes the form in which the people literally rule themselves, directly and participatorily, day in and day out, in all matters that affect them in their common lives [. . .] To its advocates [. . .] participatory democracy involves extensive and active engagement of citizens in the self-governing process; it means government not just for but by and of the people.
>
> (Barber 1995: 921).

The correspondence between this definition and antique democracy is obvious. The contrasting form of democracy is the liberal democracy of modern society: "A form of government in which some of the people, chosen by all, govern in all public matters all of the time" (Barber 1984: XIV). Barber concedes that liberal democracy can no longer be replaced by a participatory democracy in the unconditional form, and therefore weakens his normative requirements, using the term "strong democracy" to denote a realistic model of participatory democracy: "A form of government in which all of the people govern themselves in at least some public matters at least some of the time" (Barber 1984: XIV). We will be looking at the implications of this normative dilution of the ideal of pure participatory democracy as it existed in antiquity at a later point. It is not quite so clear how we are to understand direct participation by the citizens in Habermas' (1992) and Cohen and Sabel's (1997) variants. Their argumentation tends to remain on a fundamental and normative level.

After directness, the second focus of the three theoretical approaches under consideration is deliberation. Two basic justifications are offered. The first is purely normative. With explicit or implicit reference to the ideal of participatory democracy in antiquity, it is postulated that a collective decision by representatives and, above all, a collective will of the demos should be brought about by deliberation. The aggregative procedure of liberal democracy is thus to be confronted by the deliberative procedure. The other justification is a combination of normative and practical arguments. On the one hand it is stated that democratic politics are controlled by a collective will of the demos and that its purpose ought to be the pursuit of common goods. On the other hand, it is realistically stated that modern society is characterized by a plurality of particular interests and that there is no going back on this "fact of pluralism" (Rawls 1993). The conclusion is that the multiplicity of particular interests is only the starting point for the democratic process and that they are to be transformed by joint deliberation. Barber (1984: 119, 173) states accordingly: "The stress on transformation is at the heart of the strong democratic conception of politics [. . .] at the heart of strong democracy is talk." Through this strong democratic talk,[4] the isolated citizens of liberal democracy are once again to form a community and thus restore the demos as a collective subject of self-government. Habermas (1992) goes a step further, defining democracy as the legal institutionalization of discursive opinion and will-formation by the citizens. Cohen (1989) offers a similar definition. He sees a democracy as an association whose affairs are governed by the public deliberation of its members.

The status of deliberation is thus extraordinarily high, and we must ask what exactly it means and how it can effect the claimed transformation. Barber (1984: 173) starts with a negative definition: "talk is not mere speech." Although he is referring to modern liberal democracy, the reduction of talk to speech can in a certain fashion be said to be a problem of antique democracy, too. The assembly of the people included up to 6,000 citizens, and no real discussion was therefore possible. In actual fact, it consisted of a series of speeches that did not interrelate in any great measure. It was more a matter of convincing those citizens present to adopt a certain view than of reaching agreement among the citizens. And deliberative procedures are concerned with the latter. The basic postulate is that deliberations proceed in argumentative form, which means the systematic exchange of information and reasons between the parties (Cohen 1989). A further postulate is that deliberations are inclusive and have to be public: no-one must be excluded and everyone who may possibly be affected by the decisions to be taken must have the same opportunity of access to the deliberations.[5] Habermas (1992) concurs with this characterization of deliberative procedures, adding another aspect: in deliberative procedures reasons are legitimate only if they are impartial and can therefore, in principle, be accepted by everyone. According to Habermas, it is this criterion of impartiality that distinguishes the discourse from bargaining. He sees bargaining as a procedure of compromise formation between particular interests, which as such are not at all transformed through the procedure.

This understanding of deliberation shows an interesting situation. In the present-day variant of participatory democracy as compared with the antique variant, directness is normatively weakened whereas deliberation is strengthened. This makes it all the more necessary to enquire into the realization and implementation of participatory democracy as deliberative democracy. We will deal with this issue and then go on to look at electronic democracy.

Cohen and Sabel (1997: 334–337) devote a separate section to the question. In their model of a directly-deliberative polyarchy, collective decisions are made through public deliberation in public arenas open to all citizens. However, they do not explain exactly what these public arenas are and how they can be set up. The institutional proposal made by the authors is primarily a change in the role of existing institutions like legislatures, courts, executives and administrative agencies. This change in role consists of the enablement of directly-deliberative arenas and provision of an infrastructure for the exchange of information between these arenas and political units at various levels. We see this not so much as a proposal for the implementation of deliberative democracy but as a further postulate.

Although Habermas (1992) takes the institutionalization of discursive opinion and will-formation as the central criterion of his democracy concept, his definition of this institutionalization remains curiously vague. He works with the figure of a complex communication cycle between institutionalized deliberations, elections and informally formed public opinions. This communication cycle is ultimately to lead to decisions made in the politico-administrative system being linked back to the "communicatively generated power" (Habermas 1992: 362). This communicative power is generated in an autonomous public sphere through deliberation. The autonomous public has its basis in a civil society equally distant from state and market. Its structure is composed of a network of voluntary associations. The important point for our context is that the autonomous public and its civil-society basis can be institutionalized through legal norms only to a very limited degree. Habermas (1992: 366) therefore logically has recourse to an accommodating political culture and socialization: "Precisely deliberatively filtered political communications have to rely on a liberal political culture and on an enlightened political socialization, and especially on the initiatives of opinion-building associations, which to a large extent constitute and regenerate themselves spontaneously." But at least a political culture cannot be deliberately institutionalized.

The relatively most concrete proposals for the institutionalization of deliberative democracy are made by Barber (1984). He suggests an institutional framework for strong democracy, and one of the criteria for the institutions is that they should be "realistic and workable" (Barber 1984: 202). At this point we will not deal in great detail with the entire institutional setting but consider only the most important elements. With reference to Arendt and Tocqueville, Barber regards it as absolutely essential for strong democratic talk to be institutionalized at the level of small local units. This is where citizens can deliberate in direct interaction about matters that directly concern them, thus acquiring and practicing civic competence. For this purpose he proposes so-called neighborhood assemblies. In these assemblies not only local problems could be discussed; they could also provide forums for the discussions of regional and national referendums and initiatives. Such neighborhood assemblies can be established purposefully and to this extent they are a realistic proposal. But Barber (1984: 273) himself points to a serious problem: "Neighborhood assemblies offer vital forums for ongoing political talk, but they reach only local constituencies and can divide and parochialize both regions and nation as a whole." For this reason, strong democratic institutions are also needed at the regional and, especially, at the national levels. Only they can ensure that the demos participates in discussions and decisions that affect all equally. Barber (1984: 273ff., 281ff.) proposes electronic town meetings and national referenda and initiatives as such institutions. The latter two institutions play an important role in the discussion on electronic democracy, and we will be dealing with them in that context. The problem of motivation, extremely important for the institutionalization of a deliberative democracy, has already been discussed.

The concept of electronic democracy

Expectations for electronic democracy

The concept of electronic or digital democracy subsumes a multiplicity of different approaches and analyses concerned with how the new information and communication media affect modern democracies and what opportunities they offer for it.[6] For our purposes, we can reduce the complexity of this discussion to two criteria. We first limit ourselves to the aspects that are relevant for the model of participatory democracy, and second, we follow Kaase (2002: 268) in assuming that the technical, political and economic problems involved in implementing an electronic democracy have largely been resolved. This assumption is prerequisite to any consideration of the participatory potential of electronic democracy.

Owing to the technological focus of electronic democracy, it cannot be an independent model. The technological innovations are of value only in the framework of traditional models of democracy (Bellamy 2000; van Dijk 2000). Our point of reference is the model of participatory democracy. This model repeatedly confronts the objection that it cannot be realized under the conditions of modern society. And despite the claim by some proponents of this normative model that it can indeed be put into practical effect, this has, in my opinion, yet to be convincingly demonstrated. This is the case with regard to institutionalization at least.

Now technological developments in the information and communication media seem able to eliminate or at least considerably reduce structural obstacles to the realization of a participatory democracy in modern societies. There are at least high expectations in this direction. In the introduction we quoted Budge (1996), who claims that, with the new media, we face the startling fact that direct democracy is now technically possible. Barber argues in the same vein, albeit more cautiously:

> new telecommunications technologies have offered the possibility of interaction among widely dispersed citizens across space and time in a fashion that encourages new experiments with participation. Aristotle had argued that the ideal republic was small enough that a man could walk across it in a single day, thus ensuring regular participation in the assembly by all citizens. Interactive telecommunications technologies, which in effect permit the hundreds of millions of citizens of a mass society to be in touch without leaving their television screen, raise the possibility of "teledemocracy" and "virtual communities."
>
> Barber (1995: 922)

Grossman (1995: 33) has the most ambitious expectations: "Today's telecommunications technology made it possible for our political system to return to the roots of Western democracy as it was first practiced in the city-states of ancient Greece. Tomorrow's telecommunications technology almost certainly will." Can participatory democracy be restored in modern times in the form of electronic democracy? Before discussing this question, we need to systematize the most important expectations for electronic democracy that technology has fostered.

Dahl (1989) has described the change in spatial dimensions as one of the causal factors in the development of representative democracy. And this factor space becomes relative because of rapid and direct communication via computer networks (Zittel 2001). A virtual space comes into being that overcomes the restrictions of real space (Abramson, Arterton and Orren 1988; Negroponte 1995). Space loses its physical quality and becomes merely a metaphor for a "place" of electronic communication among dispersed individuals. This relativization or perhaps even the death of space can, in conjunction with other technological properties, fundamentally change modern democracy. These properties include the multiplication and decentralization of information stocks which citizens can access rapidly and almost at will. But perhaps the most important is the possibility of interactive communication between citizens in virtual space.

The two following expectations for electronic democracy as participatory democracy can be formulated on the basis of these technological possibilities. The first is concerned with the criterion of directness and the second with the criterion of deliberation in the model of participatory democracy we have been discussing:

1 Through technologically facilitated referendums, citizens can again be comprehensively and permanently involved in government (kratos component).
2 Through interactive communication between citizens in virtual space, a common will of the demos can be formed deliberatively (demos component).

The following two sections discuss how plausible and realistic these two expectations for electronic democracy are.

Direct participation by citizens in government

Barber (1984) describes referendums at the national level as one of the most important forms of institutionalization for participatory democracy in modern society. There were, of course, referendums before the innovations in the electronic media. In the discussion on electronic democracy, these media have certainly quite rightly been considered a particularly effective means for conducting such referendums (Slaton 1992; Budge 1996). At the press of a button or the click of a mouse, citizens scattered over a wide area can take part in referendums and thus in political decision-making. For the citizens themselves, this participation is low-cost, and the organization of such referendums requires comparatively little effort. In principle, this permits comprehensive and lasting participation by citizens in government. But the technological facilitation of referendums changes nothing in the nature and implications of this instrument. This is already the subject of ongoing discussion. We will look at a number of aspects important for the normative benchmarks of participatory democracy.

One aspect is a problem caused by societal complexity and the associated fact that the political system has to perform a broad range of services for society. This means that the quantity of generally binding decisions that have to be made has reached enormous proportions. Previously, we formulated the postulate that the intensity of achievable self-government by the demos is inversely proportional to the quantity of decisions. Barber (1984: XIV) ultimately accepts this, defining his strong democracy "as a form of government in which all of the people govern themselves in at least some public matters at least some of the time." He has thus adapted his model of participatory democracy to reality. On the other hand, this normative weakening means that the idea of self-government is largely abandoned and reduced to a greater or lesser degree of citizen participation in decision-making processes, which are largely carried out by elected representatives. The possibility of increasing the quantity of referendums through the use of electronic media does perhaps reduce the problem somewhat, but not fundamentally. Budge (1996) suggests therefore that referendums be restricted to fifty important laws adopted by parliament. But from the point of view of information and discussion on the relevant issues, this number is still very high. Above all: since citizens have widely varying preferences, it is not possible to establish which problems and which laws are particularly important (Kaase 2002).

A second aspect has to do with societal complexity: the difficulty and interrelatedness of the problems with which politics has to deal. This calls for expert knowledge, the building of compromises between differing positions, and the development of policy packages. And it is for this reason that the political system has differentiated itself as a functional system. Referendums, however, are concerned with single issues and, in voting, citizens almost always have to rely on inadequate information, all the more so as the number of referendums increases. Budge (1996) answers this objection by pointing out that professional politicians have no "monopoly of expertise," and, as far as Switzerland is concerned, Kirchgässner *et al.* (1999) note that members of parliament and average citizens do not differ substantially in the level of their political information. We have some doubt whether this claim is empirically tenable, and its applicability in general terms would in any case have to be empirically demonstrated. But the point at issue is not a monopoly of expertise and the general political knowledge of representatives but the specific knowledge of political and administrative entities about certain issues and about the possibility of aggregating different policies through appropriate procedures to create meaningful packages.

A third aspect is motivation for participation in referendums. The normative postulate of self-government can be approached only if the institutional possibilities are available and if they are also used by citizens. As we have seen, there are systematic restrictions on the political participation of citizens in modern societies owing to factors such as information and opportunity costs and the relatively low status of politics. If this thesis is valid, it would also hold true for referendums. The astonishingly low average participation by Swiss citizens in referendums (Kirchgässner *et al.* 1999) certainly does not contradict this thesis. This state of affairs raises questions about the essential democratic postulate of equal weight for every vote, a postulate that is much more strongly redeemed when it comes to electing representatives. Sometimes very small minorities make binding decisions for correspondingly large majorities. This intensifies the nature of the decision as a zero-sum game (Sartori 1987), for compromise building between differing or opposing interests is not possible in referendums. The argument that every citizen can participate is, in my view, not sound. It forces the citizen to obtain costly information, for without it he has no way of identifying his own interest in the given issue, and his vote would then be senseless.[7] This is relevant above all against the background of the alternative of leaving the identification and enforcement of one's interests to elected representatives. The basis for this election is another matter that is not at issue here.

A fourth aspect is the blurring of the democratic logic of a representative system. Such systems are based on the clear accountability of elected representatives in the political decision-making system for their actions and the outcomes of these actions. The democratic mechanism of re-election or voting functions only through undiluted accountability. And it is primarily in this mechanism that the exercise of popular sovereignty in representative democracies is grounded. The more referendums are conducted, the more of a problem accountability becomes.

A fifth and last aspect leads us over to the demos component, which is to be discussed in the next section. According to Sartori (1987), referendum democracy is a direct democracy of isolated individuals and not of interacting citizens. But this interaction is the precondition for constituting a demos with a collective will, and it is a basic postulate of participatory democracy.

The interactive constitution of a common will of the demos

If a referendum democracy is a direct democracy of isolated individuals and not of interacting citizens, this does not satisfy the normative requirements of a participatory democracy. Emphatic advocates of the referendum instrument are aware of this problem and suggest linking votes on political issues in referendums to prior discussion (Kirchgässner *et al.* 1999). Switzerland can be cited as a practical example of this procedure, and the authors mentioned claim that, by a number of criteria, Switzerland performs better than purely representative democracies. We will not go into the validity of this assertion. But for the purposes of our analysis, this linkage involves a further inverse relationship: the more strongly referendums are tied to prior discussion, the fewer referendums can be held, and the less self-government by the demos can be realized by means of referendum. From a normative point of view, technologically facilitated referendums are thus almost without importance.

But regardless of how direct participation by the demos in making generally binding decisions is conceived and implemented, two questions first need to be answered: To what extent can electronic democracy contribute to the interactive constitution of a common will of the demos? And to what extent can it contribute to constituting the demos as a community? We will consider each in turn.

In antique democracy, the collective will of the demos was formed in joint discussion among its members in a real place. If one considers that only a minority of Athenians ever took part in discussion in the ekklesía, its structure can be characterized in brief as some-to-all communication in which all participants were physically present. The will of the demos constituted thus can be regarded as authentic and not as merely procedurally calculated. And it can be expected that those who took part also felt bound by it. The more strongly this collective will controls the decisions actually made, the more closely in keeping this is with the concept of self-government.

Owing to the problem of scale alone, will-formation in the democracy of modern societies is completely different. A discussion is conducted primarily in the conventional mass media – before the citizens and not by them. This type of discussion reaches very many, optimally almost all, citizens. In simple terms, it is very-few-to-almost-all communication in which the few are visually present and the many play no role. Nonetheless, conventional mass communication has two advantages: first, its reach, which means at least that the attention of a large part of the demos is occupied by the same issues at the same time, leading to a measure of communication in the private sphere and in public places in the primary life-world. Second, according to Gerhards and Neidhardt (1991), there is a code of communication in the general public sphere which requires arguments which can be generalized, rather than particular benefits to justify the views of a party. A certain degree of control or filtering of public discussion by the regulative idea of the common good can therefore by assumed, even if many actors appeal to it for primarily strategic motives.

In comparison with conventional mass communication, the Internet public sphere offers a different but highly ambivalent picture. In principle, "the Internet permits interactive communication by any number of participants at any spatial distance" (Zittel 2001: 433). Citizens can thus communicate with each other almost without restriction and no longer have to accept a largely passive role in hierarchically structured mass communication. Does electronic democracy then mean the restoration of the antique a-gora in the form of a virtual e-gora? There are at least two fundamental arguments against this hope.

In Internet communication, who communicates with whom is not determined a priori, but it is neither technically possible nor practicable for everyone to communicate with everyone on the same subject. On the Internet, a multiplicity of thematically focused communication communities forms. We can therefore argue that the Internet public sphere is fragmented (Wilhelm 2000) and as such, lacking one of the advantages of conventional mass communication. And a fragmented public can hardly contribute to interactively constituting a common will of the demos.

A second fundamental argument against the restoration of the antique agora in the form of a virtual e-gora lies in the character of "actors" communicating on the Internet. Partners in communication are neither physically nor visually present; they are mutually anonymous others. Basically, they remain concealed behind the communicated information. Each knows only that the source must be someone. But this someone can literally not take shape, except by fabrication in a completely unreal projection. This problem can perhaps be somewhat reduced but not solved by associating a picture with the message. The authenticity of pictures on the Internet is always subject to doubt, and a picture without action, gestures and facial expressions offers practically no additional information. In Internet communication, the anonymous other is thus not identifiable as a citizen belonging to the same demos as ego himself. Besides anonymity, the blurredness or even absence of boundary-drawing associated with Internet communication makes attributability to the demos more difficult. For these reasons, interactive will-formation by members of the demos through Internet communication generating a collective will is unlikely.

So far, we have been talking about the interactive constitution of a common will without clearly stating what is to be understood by this interactivity. The normative model of participatory democracy postulates not any sort of interaction or communication between citizens but deliberative interaction. It is only through deliberation that the transformation mentioned can be effected. The question is therefore how the specific properties of Internet communication relate to the deliberation requirement. Deliberation means the systematic exchange of arguments by persons present. This presence is doubly important. First, it alone permits the mutual ascription of arguments to specific persons, which is a precondition for the progressive process of building a common will. Second, it is only the fact that arguments are put forward by other people that generates the credibility that may induce a participant to change his opinion. Internet communication fulfills neither the criterion that communication takes place between identifiable persons nor that these persons be present in a physical or at least visual form. It is thus not very surprising that a number of studies conclude that Internet communication is primarily a superficial expression of views by anonymous sources and has little to do with deliberation (Rosenfield 1998; Galston 1999; Wilhelm 2000).

The virtual nature of Internet communication must necessarily affect the nature of the community it enables. And this can be interpreted positively. According to Poster (1995), it is precisely the anonymity and boundlessness of Internet communication that offer completely new freedoms. Everyone can present himself as he wishes, and everyone can communicate with whom he wishes. Biological, social and spatial constraints are abolished. A virtual community is thus the result of free decisions by individuals with multiple and decentralized identities that come together because they have common interests (Poster 1995). This interpretation is indeed possible. But from a democracy theory perspective another interpretation is more plausible. We share the view of other authors (Turkle 1995; Ravetz 1998; Galston 1999) that virtuality cuts the ground from under the feet of credible, serious and thus far-reaching cooperation between citizens in dealing with common affairs. If this is the case, then the finding of Galston (1999) that participation in virtual communities leads to withdrawal from traditional communities is normatively alarming.

In concluding our analysis, we return to the criterion of deliberation. It is of strategic importance for the variant of participatory democracy we have been considering (see also Cooke 2000). To effect the asserted transformation, deliberative procedures must be carried out in practice. This raises two problems: institutionalization and motivation. We have looked at both when discussing direct participation by citizens, but they are even more serious in relation to deliberative participation. One of the few concrete proposals for institutionalizing deliberative procedures has been put forward by Fishkin (1991, 1995). According to him, parliaments should be flanked by representative citizens' forums whose task it would be to supply the parliament with deliberatively grounded citizens' opinions. Once again, however, they would be representative bodies and would not provide for any notable direct participation by citizens. And if the problem of representativeness can be solved (Kaase 2002), we still have to ask why the vast majority of citizens, who have not taken part in deliberations, ought to accept the outcome as binding. Both – representativeness and the binding nature of decisions – are unsolved problems for all advocatory deliberations.

The structural restrictions on the political participation of citizens in modern societies have been discussed previously. But deliberative participation raises further problems. Every procedure has to be implemented by means of rules, and this is true in a special sense for deliberative procedures. A rule holds only if it is accepted and obeyed in fact. It will be accepted and obeyed only if there is a motive or an interest to do so (Alexy 1995). According to Habermas (1992: 141) this is, in the case of deliberations, an "interest in correctness." The question is the extent to which citizens in modern democracies can be assumed to have this interest. Habermas (1992: 142) is undecided: "It is certainly too optimistic to assume that every human being has an interest in correctness [. . .] But it is also too pessimistic to assume that no human being has an interest in correctness." Regardless of how one assesses the distribution of this interest, it is clear that a deliberative procedure as such cannot generate it. We must therefore count on the citizens possessing the appropriate virtues and on an accommodating political culture. To a certain degree, however, this presupposes what is supposed to be generated by deliberation, like the transformation of particular interests into general interests.

Summary and discussion

The system of government that has since been known as democracy came into being in antique Athens. For the first and only time in history, literal self-government by the people was realized. The notion of a democratic system of government was taken up again in the modern age. Under changed societal conditions, it was implemented not as direct democracy but as liberal, i.e. representative democracy. However, political thinking developed that upheld the ideal of self-government by the people, and confronted existing liberal democracy with this ideal. But the onus of proving how this ideal could be realized has always been on the theory of so-called participatory democracy. The alternative would be for it to remain an interesting but merely cerebral pursuit.

The versions of participatory democracy we have discussed stress deliberative forms of procedure and participation, and are accordingly referred to as theory of deliberative democracy. They assume that deliberative democracy is not only normatively desirable in modern society but also necessary to solve the practical problems of liberal democracy. If it is to do so, however, it must be possible in real terms. And to establish this, answers are needed to the questions of institutionalization and motivation. In our view, they have yet to be given, and can perhaps not be given at all. The structural restrictions of modern societies are presumably so strong that the ideal of participatory democracy cannot be realized even approximately.

The only really concrete proposal for institutionalizing direct participation by citizens in the making of generally binding decisions has been advanced by Barber (1984), who advocates the instrument of the referendum at the national level. But there is a fundamental mismatch between the quantity of decisions that have to be made in the politico-administrative system and the quantity of referendums that can be held. This state of affairs is exacerbated by coupling referendums to prior discussions or deliberations, indispensable for the theory of participatory democracy. In this regard, Barber (1984: XIV) adjusts to reality in describing his strong democracy as a form of government "in which all of the people govern themselves in at least some public matters at least some of the time." The number of decisions in which all citizens can participate directly, is, however, likely to be so small in relation to the total number of decisions to be made that this has almost nothing more to do with the normative postulate of self-government.

The more participatory a democracy is from an institutional point of view, the more strongly it has to rely on political participation by the citizens. It cannot be a question of only sporadic participation in demonstrations and the like. What is needed is optimally enduring and comprehensive engagement by citizens and commitment to the demands of deliberative procedures. This is highly contingent, and Barber (1984: 265) accordingly asks: "How then can we expect either the self-interested or apathetic to identify with a program of participation and civic renewal in which their most immediate interests would be ignored, at least in the short run?" His answer is as follows: "Through persuasion, through the self-education yielded by democratic participation itself [. . .] The taste for participation is whetted by participation: Democracy breeds democracy" (Barber 1984: 265). In view of the grounds we have given for the rational citizen to abstain from political participation, we must regard this argument as rather unconvincing wishful thinking.

What possibilities does electronic democracy offer for technologically overcoming structural obstacles in modern society and bringing us closer to participatory democracy? We have argued that coupling referendums with prior deliberations – indispensable for participatory democracy – deprives technologically facilitated referendums of any practical importance. But the production of a virtual public sphere and a virtual community abolishing the restrictions of space and scale is praised by the proponents of electronic democracy as one of its most important advantages. In this way, autonomous will-formation by the demos as a collective subject is to be restored under the conditions of modern societies. However, a number of studies conducted in the context of the discussion on electronic democracy have found the situation to be contradictory. Trends towards fragmentation of the public and the erosion of traditional communities are just as plausible. And these trends would be more likely to weaken than strengthen both the constitution of a common will of the demos in a general public sphere and responsible cooperation between citizens in a community of which they consider themselves members and with which they identify.

In the discussion on electronic democracy, we have abstracted from real problems posed by the new media. The intention has been, where possible, to probe the potential of electronic democracy for approximating to participatory democracy only on the basis of the technical properties of the media and the associated communication logic. Real problems like the complete commercialization of the Internet, the possibilities for monitoring Internet communication, the manipulation of voting via electronic media, etc., have naturally been left aside. Taking such real problems into account, Barber (1999) developed "three scenarios for the future of technology and strong democracy." Only one of them – which he calls the Jefferson scenario – was positive by the normative benchmarks for strong democracy. But this is precisely the one he describes as least realistic. It therefore seems that the possibilities for realizing a participatory democracy under the conditions of modern society by means of electronic democracy are to be regarded with skepticism for both "logical" and "realistic" reasons. From a normative point of view, it cannot be excluded that electronic democracy even falls short of the status quo of liberal democracy.

The dissemination and utilization of the new media is an irreversible development. The most optimistic proponents of an electronic democracy anticipate that the new media will trigger a "third democratic transformation" (Dahl 1989; Grossman 1995). This is expected to bring us back towards a participatory democracy under the conditions of a modern society. According to our analysis, however, it is more probable that it will tend rather to depart from this ideal. The most important reason has been stated to be the greater difficulty in forming a collective will and constituting a political community. And both are preconditions for the demos to govern itself as a collective subject.

If the predictions advanced in the globalization debate prove correct, the trend towards the dissolution of a collective subject through immigration and multiculturalism will strengthen. And nation states are tending to lose their capacity to control their own societies. They compensate this loss of control partly by implementing international and supranational regimes. In an attempt to address and positively interpret this development caused by virtualization and globalization, a further model of democracy is advanced: cosmopolitan democracy. In this model, the importance of democracy is more or less reduced to some sort of participation by some citizens of the world in decision-making by a multitude of national, international and supranational regimes. In other words, this means that the unambiguity of the demos, the kratos and of the relation between them begins to dissolve. This has hardly anything more to do with the idea of democracy that came into being in antique Athens about 2500 years ago and to which the models of participatory democracy are fundamentally committed.

Notes

1 See Held (1996) for a differentiated discussion of a wide range of democracy models.
2 At this point we disregard the legislative commission (*nomothétai*), which was set up only in 403/402.
3 One of the few exceptions was the office of military strategist.
4 Strong democratic talk, deliberation and discourse are different terms for largely identical concepts.
5 Other postulates on and conditions for deliberative procedures are to be found in the study by Cohen (1989).
6 For an overview on this discussion see Kamps 1999; Hacker and van Dijk 2000; Hoff, Horrocks and Tops 2000; Zittel 2001.
7 See Dahl's (1989) democratic criterion of "enlightened understanding."

References

Abramson, J.B., Arterton, F.C. and Orren, G.R. (1988) *The Electronic Commonwealth. The Impact of New Media Technologies on Democratic Politics*, New York: Basic Books.

Alexy, R. (1995) *Recht, Vernunft, Diskurs*, Frankfurt am Main: Suhrkamp.

Barber, B.R. (1999) "Three Scenarios for the Future of Technology and Strong Democracy," *Political Science Quarterly*, 113: 573–590.

—— (1995) "Participatory Democracy," in S.M. Lipset (ed.) The *Encyclopedia of Democracy*, London: Routledge, pp. 921–924.

—— (1984) *Strong Democracy. Participatory Politics for a New Age*, Berkeley, CA: University of California Press.

Bellamy, C. (2000) "Modeling Electronic Democracy: Towards Democratic Discourses for an Information Age," in J. Hoff, I. Horrocks and P. Tops (eds) *Democratic Governance and New Technology. Technologically Mediated Innovations in Political Practice in Western Europe*, London: Routledge, pp. 33–53.

Bleicken, J. (1994) *Die athenische Demokratie*, Paderborn: Ferdinand Schöningh.

Budge, I. (1996) *The New Challenge of Direct Democracy*, Cambridge: Polity Press.

Cohen, J. (1989) "Deliberation and Democratic Legitimacy," in A. Hamlin and P. Petit (eds) *The Good Polity*, Oxford: Blackwell, pp. 17–34.

Cohen, J. and Sabel, C. (1997) "Directly-Deliberative Polyarchy," *European Law Journal*, 3: 313–342.

Cooke, M. (2000) "Five Arguments for Deliberative Democracy," *Political Studies*, 48: 947–969.

Dahl, R.A. (1989) *Democracy and its Critics*, New Haven, CT: Yale University Press.

—— (1971) *Polyarchy. Participation and Opposition*, New Haven, CT and London: Yale University Press.

van Deth, J. (2000) "Interesting but Irrelevant: Social Capital and the Saliency of Politics in Western Europe," *European Journal of Political Research*, 37: 115–147.

van Dijk, J. (2000) "Models of Democracy and Concepts of Communications," in K.L

Hacker and J. van Dijk (eds) *Digital Democracy. Issues of Theory and Practice*, London: Sage, pp. 30–53.
Downs, A. (1957) *An Economic Theory of Democracy*, New York: Harper.
Eder, W. (1998) "Aristocrats and the Coming of Athenian Democracy," in I. Morris and K.A. Raaflaub (eds) *Democracy 2500? Question and Challenges*, Archeological Institute of America, Colloquia and Conference Papers No. 2, Dubuque, IA: Kendall/Hunt, pp. 105–140.
Euripides (1970) *Hiketiden*, edited by Dietrich Ebener, Berlin: Akademie-Verlag.
Fishkin, J.S. (1995) *The Voice of the People. Public Opinion and Democracy*, New Haven, CT: Yale University Press.
—— (1991) *Democracy and Deliberation. New Directions for Democratic Reform*, New Haven, CT: Yale University Press.
Fuchs, D. (2000a) "Demokratie und Beteiligung in der modernen Gesellschaft: einige demokratietheoretische Überlegungen," in O. Niedermayer and B. Westle (eds) *Demokratie und Partizipation. Festschrift für Max Kaase*, Wiesbaden: Westdeutscher Verlag, pp. 250–280.
—— (2000b) "Demos und Nation in der Europäischen Union," in H.-D. Klingemann. and F. Neidhardt (eds) *Die Zukunft der Demokratie. Herausforderungen im Zeitalter der Globalisierung*, Berlin: edition sigma, pp. 215–236.
—— (1998) "Kriterien demokratischer Performanz in Liberalen Demokratien," in M.Th. Greven (ed.) *Demokratie – eine Kultur des Westens?*, Opladen: Leske & Budrich, pp. 151–179.
Galston, W.A. (1999) "(How) Does the Internet Affect Community?," in E.C. Kamarck and J.S. Nye, Jr. (eds) *Democracy.Com. Governance in a Networked World*, Hollis, NH: Hollis Publishing, pp. 45–62.
Gerhards, J. and Neidhardt, F. (1991) "Strukturen und Funktionen moderner Öffentlichkeit. Fragestellung und Ansätze," in S. Müller-Doohm and K. Neumann-Braun (eds) *Öffentlichkeit, Kultur, Massenkommunikation. Beiträge zur Medien- und Kommunikationssoziologie*, Oldenburg: Bibliotheks- und Informationssystem der Universität Oldenburg, pp. 31–89.
Grossman, L.K. (1995) *The Electronic Republic. Reshaping Democracy in the Information Age*, New York: Viking.
Habermas, J. (1992) *Faktizität und Geltung. Beiträge zur Diskurstheorie des Rechts und des demokratischen Rechtsstaats*, Frankfurt am Main: Suhrkamp.
Hacker, K.L. and van Dijk, J. (eds) (2000) *Digital Democracy. Issues of Theory and Practice*, London: Sage.
Hansen, M.H. (1991) *The Athenian Democracy in the Age of Demosthenes. Structure, Principles and Ideology*, Oxford: Blackwell.
Held, D. (1996) *Models of Democracy*, 2nd edn, Cambridge: Polity Press/Blackwell Publishers Ltd.
Hoff, J., Horrocks, I. and Tops, P. (eds) (2000) *Democratic Governance and New Technology. Technologically Mediated Innovations in Political Practice in Western Europe*, London: Routledge.
Kaase, M. (2002) "Elektronische Demokratie: Wird endlich ein Traum wahr?," in D. Fuchs, E. Roller and B. Wessels (eds) *Bürger und Demokratie in Ost und West*, Wiesbaden: Westdeutscher Verlag, pp. 260–283.
Kamps, K. (ed.) (1999) *Elektronische Demokratie? Perspektiven politischer Partizipation*, Opladen: Westdeutscher Verlag.
Kirchgässner, G., Feld, L.P. and Savioz, M.R. (1999) *Die direkte Demokratie. Modern,*

Erfolgreich, Entwicklungs- und Exportfähig, Basel: Helbing und Lichtenhahn/Verlag Franz Vahlen.

Meier, C. (1993) *Athen. Ein Neubeginn der Weltgeschichte*, Berlin: Siedler.

Negroponte, N. (1995) *Total Digital: Die Welt zwischen 0 und 1 oder die Zukunft der Kommunikation*, München: Bertelsmann.

Poster, M. (1995) *The Second Media Age*, Cambridge: Polity Press.

Raaflaub, K.A. (1998) "Power in the Hands of the People: Foundations of Athenian Democracy," in I. Morris and K.A. Raaflaub (eds) *Democracy 2500? Questions and Challenges*, Archeological Institute of America, Colloquia and Conference Papers No. 2, Dubuque, Iowa: Kendall/Hunt Publishing Company, pp. 31–66.

Ravetz, J. (1998) "The Internet, Virtual Reality and Real Reality," in B.D. Loader (ed.) *Cyberspace Divide. Equality, Agency and Policy in the Information Age*, London: Routledge, pp. 113–122.

Rawls, J. (1993) *Political Liberalism*, New York: Columbia University Press.

Rosenfield, I. (1998) "Internet – Die körperlose Psyche," in C. Leggewie and C. Maar (eds) *Internet und Politik*, Köln: Bollmann Verlag, pp. 381–388.

Sartori, G. (1987) *The Theory of Democracy Revisited*, 2 Vols, Chatham, NJ: Chatham House Publishers.

Slaton, D.C. (1992) *Televote. Expanding Citizen Participation in the Quantum Age*, New York: Praeger.

Smith, A.D. (1991) *National Identity*, London: Penguin.

Turkle, S. (1995) *Live on the Screen. Identity in the Age of the Internet*, New York: Simon & Schuster.

Verba, S., Schlozman, K.L. and Brady, H.E. (1995) *Voice and Equality. Civic Voluntarism in American Politics*, Cambridge, MA: Harvard University Press.

Welwei, K.-W. (1999) *Das klassische Athen. Demokratie und Machtpolitik im 5. und 4. Jahrhundert*, Darmstadt: Primus-Verlag.

Wilhelm, A.G. (2000) *Democracy in the Digital Age. Challenges to Political Life in Cyberspace*, London: Routledge.

Zittel, T. (2001) "Elektronische Demokratie. Planskizze für eine Demokratie des 21. Jahrhunderts?," *Neue Politische Literatur*, 46: 433–470.

Part II

Democratic reform and political responsiveness

3 Political participation in party primaries

Increase in quantity, decrease in quality?

Gideon Rahat and Reuven Y. Hazan

Introduction: participatory democracy and party primaries

Candidate and leadership selection methods are the intra-party, institutional mechanism by which parties select their candidates and leaders for the general elections. Candidate selection methods can be distinguished according to several dimensions (Ranney 1981; Gallagher and Marsh 1988; Rahat and Hazan 2001). This study focuses on the party selectorate – the body that selects the party leader and/or its candidates. Parties' selectorates are classified according to their level of inclusiveness. At one extreme, the selectorate consists of the entire electorate of the nation, i.e. all citizens who are eligible to participate in the general elections. At the other extreme, the selectorate – or rather the selector – is a single party leader. Between these poles we can find various alternatives, from a relatively inclusive body of party members through selected party agencies and up to a small, exclusive nominating committee that is composed of just a few leaders. In party primaries, the focus of our research, party members' votes decide the leadership contest, the party's candidate in a single-member district, or the ranking of candidates in the party list for the general elections.

In Israel, like in many other democracies, candidate selection methods are becoming more inclusive (Bille 2001; Scarrow *et al.* 2000). If in the past most party selectorates were party agencies – standing agencies like national or local executives and congresses, or special nomination or selection committees – today more and more parties give rank and file members the right to influence effectively candidate and leadership selection. This general trend makes the analysis of the Israeli case – particularly the adoption of a highly inclusive method of party primaries – relevant for other democracies that are moving in a similar direction.

Although there is much debate on the extent of the decline in party membership and its interpretation, its occurrence, indicated by both absolute and relative measurements, is a clear empirical finding (Scarrow 2000; Mair and van Biezen 2001). In light of this phenomenon, one of the ways that citizens are brought back in by political elites is through increasing their role inside parties (Scarrow 1999). In the arena of leadership and candidate selection, this is expressed by giving rank and file party members the right to decide, in effect, both the leadership and the composition of the parliamentary party before the general elections. While this phenomenon is recognized in the research literature, its political consequences – the behavioral patterns of the newly recruited party members, i.e. the actual impact of democratizing candidate selection methods on individual political participation – are still in need of systematic evaluation.

The first section of this chapter provides empirical evidence from the Israeli case of the political consequences of adopting party primaries for both the quantity and the quality of political participation. Using various indicators, we argue that party primaries somewhat succeeded in stemming the decline in the number of members, yet created incentives that decreased the quality of party membership. The subsequent section presents comparative evidence from research on intra-party participation in other countries, and shows that the experience of other countries is similar to the Israeli case. The third section provides a theoretical discussion of the phenomenon of democratizing candidate selection. The conclusion delineates an improved institutional participatory design for candidate selection methods that is better suited to fostering qualitative participation.

Party primaries and their impact on the quantity and the quality of political participation: the Israeli experience

In the pre-state years, and in the first decades after independence, the classic mass party with its mass membership was a central feature of the Israeli political system. With the adoption of state financing for parties, the growth of the state as a major non-party supplier of services and the depillarization of major parts of society, the value of membership for both members and parties changed (Arian 1998; Galnoor 1982). In the 1970s and 1980s, most parties transferred candidate selection from small nomination committees to the parties' wider and more representative institutions. This was one step towards opening up participation, followed later, in the 1990s, by the larger parties further opening up with the adoption of inclusive party primaries. From this perspective, it can be claimed that as the mass party declined, candidate selection methods opened up.

In 1992, Labor adopted party primaries as its method of selecting its leader and its list of candidates. Immediately after the 1992 elections, Likud (Israel's second major party) followed Labor's reformist spirit and adopted party primaries. Prior to the 1999 elections, Likud returned the selection of its candidate list to the central committee, while Labor again selected its list candidates using party primaries. Both parties continue to use party primaries to select their party chairpersons (who are also their candidates for prime minister). The adoption of party primaries can also be interpreted as an attempt by the large parties to compensate for their inability to reform the malaise of the electoral system. That is, through the addition of a personal element to an extremely party-centered system, party primaries served as a bypass for the unchanged closed-list system (Rahat and Hazan 2005).

Israeli politics in 1992–2003 thus supplies five cases of candidate selection through inclusive selectorates (party primaries) in the two largest parties, four in Labor (1992, 1996, 1999 and 2003), and one in Likud (1996).[1] In addition, there were eight cases of leadership selection by all party members, four in Labor (1992, 1997, 2001 and 2002), and four in Likud (1993, twice in 1999 [before and after the elections] and 2002).

It is indeed a dramatic increase in political participation when a selectorate ranging from 1269 (Labor's Central Committee delegates in 1988) to 3153 (Likud's Central Committee in 1992) is replaced by one ranging from 110,988 (Labor's membership in 2002) to 305,000 (Likud's members in 2002) (Table 3.1). This was the essence of the adoption of party primaries. In this sense, political participation increased dramatically. Since the Israeli electoral system is a closed-list system, which gives no influence to the voters over the composition of the party lists, nor a chance to ratify their leadership passively, the party primaries could provide an important new venue for increased participation.

Being a party member involved signing a form that declared an affiliation with the party and no affiliation with other parties, and paying an annual fee of about $25 (lower rates were granted to students, pensioners and the unemployed). In order to participate in the party primaries, membership registration had to be completed before a determined date, typically a few weeks before the primaries took place.

The average ratio of dues-paying members, who were eligible to participate in the party primaries, to Labor and Likud voters stood at 1:4.2. In our thirteen cases of party primaries, between one-third and one-sixth of the Labor or Likud voters, i.e. the potential population of party members, if one assumes that a party member is necessarily a party voter, chose to register. Of these, an average 58 percent turned out to vote in the primaries, which means that on average approximately one in 7.4 party voters took an active part in the candidate selection process. These figures indicate the creation of a new arena of partisan political participation in Israeli politics.

The question that immediately arises is whether party primaries brought citizens back into politics. The only available longitudinal data on general party membership (1969–2003) is based on pre-election opinion polls (Arian 1998: 161, and data supplied by Arian on 1999 and 2003). While the validity of such data is questionable (Mair and van Biezen 2001: 6), it is useful for identifying general trends. A gradual but consistent decline in party membership is evident, from about 18 percent of the respondents claiming to be party members in 1969 down to 8 percent in 1984 and 1988. Since 1992, however, the trend has changed, with about 9 percent in 1992 and about 10 percent in 1996 claiming to be party members. The adoption of party primaries in Labor in 1992, and in Likud (and two smaller parties) prior to the 1996 elections, explains the change in the trends. However, the results for 1999 and 2003, in which less than 5 percent and about 7 percent of respondents respectively claimed to be party members, testify that primaries brought about only a provisional recovery.

Our data substantiate this finding (Figure 3.1). Yet we look only at the two main parties, and do so separately. Labor's adoption of primaries in 1992 did not

Table 3.1 Number of party members, participants in party primaries, party voters, and their ratios in Labor and Likud, 1992–2002

Party	*Year*	*Selected*	*Party members (no.)*	*Turnout in primary (no.)*	*Turnout in election (no.)*	*Ratio of members to voters*	*Ratio of participants to voters*
Labor	1992	Chair	151,697	106,347 (70.1%)	906,810	1:6.0	1:8.5
Labor	1992	List	164,163	118,197 (72.0%)	906,810	1:5.5	1:7.7
Labor	1996	List	261,169	194,788 (74.6%)	818,741	1:3.1	1:4.2
Labor	1997	Chair	164,387	114,144 (69.2%)	818,741[a]	1:5.0	1:7.2
Labor	1999	List	163,044	101,087 (62.0%)	670,484	1:4.1	1:6.6
Labor	2001	Chair	117,214	71,957 (61.4%)	670,484[a]	1:5.7	1:9.3
Labor	2002	Chair	110,988	66,256 (59.7%)	455,183	1:4.1	1:6.9
Labor	2003	List	110,988	58,783 (53.0%)	455,183	1:4.1	1:7.7
Likud	1993	Chair	216,000	145,000 (67.1%)	651,229[a]	1:3.0	1:4.5
Likud	1996	List	178,852	91,907 (51.4%)	767,401	1:4.3	1:8.3
Likud	1999	Chair	168,127	52,696 (31.3%)	468,103	1:2.8	1:8.9
Likud	1999	Chair	143,871	50,000 (34.8%)	468,103[a]	1:3.3	1:9.4
Likud	2002	Chair	305,000	140,918 (46.2%)	925,279	1:3.0	1:6.6

Source: Data from the political parties and newspapers.

Note
a Number of voters in the previous general election, since the selection of chair took place after a defeat in the election.

result in an increase in membership, but instead the opposite. In 1996, we do see an increase, but this was due to an extended registration campaign in the atmosphere following the assassination of Prime Minister Yitzhak Rabin. In 1999 and 2003, when Labor continued to use primaries both for its leadership and its candidate selection, its membership declined to an all time low. Likud's story is somewhat similar. In 1996, when Likud first used primaries for selecting its candidates, its membership did not increase. In 1999, it no longer selected its candidates by primaries, yet its membership did not decline. In 2003, with only leadership selection open to the party members, Likud's membership dramatically increased – due to the virulent contest between Prime Minister Ariel Sharon and his challenger, Benjamin Netanyahu. In short, although the adoption and subsequent elimination of party primaries can be expected to have a direct impact on the quantity of party members, the empirical data either support this only at the early stages, or do not provide supporting evidence at all.

We now look beyond the numbers, to analyze the question of the quality of membership and its meaning. Duverger's (1954: 90–116) taxonomy of degrees of participation in political parties (Figure 3.2) sets reasonable expectations from party members. It is built from concentric circles of increasing affiliation and participation. The widest circle is that of electors – citizens who merely vote for a given party. The next is that of supporters – electors who also acknowledge that they favor a particular party and may engage in some party activity. The third circle is the party members – who are at minimum supporters who are formally registered with the party, and a minority of whom actually takes an active part in party activities (Selle and Sväsand 1991; Heidar 1994). Finally, we find the innermost circle of militants or activists – members of the party who see to

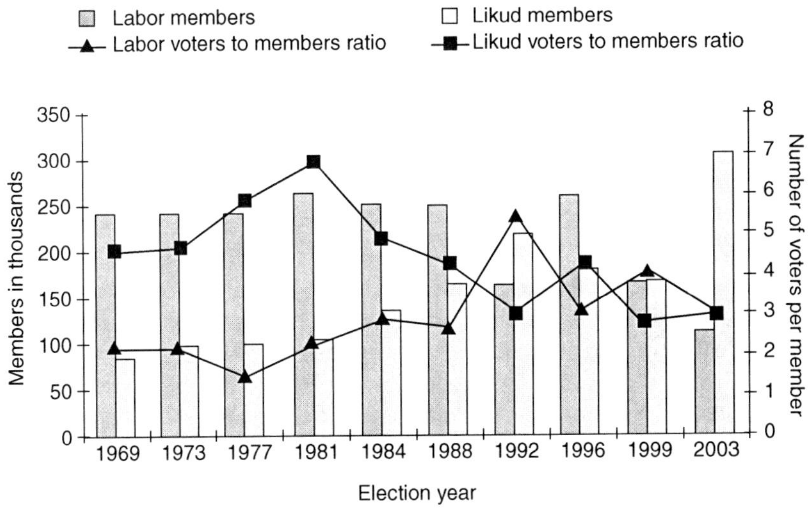

Figure 3.1 Number of members and ratio of voters to members in Labor and Likud, 1969–2003.[2]

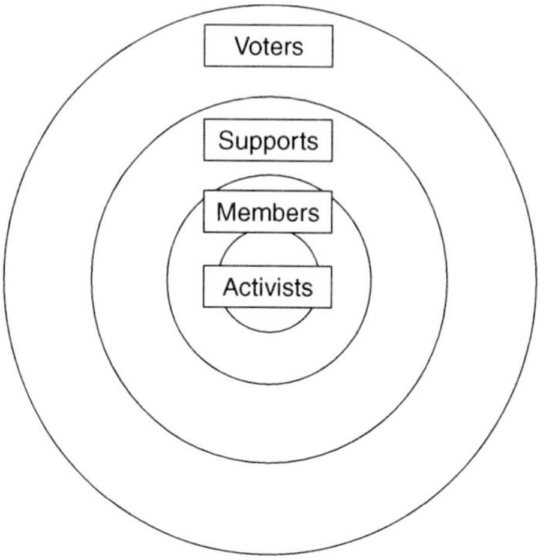

Figure 3.2 Degrees of participation in political parties (source: elaborated from Duverger (1954: 90–91)).

its organization, operation, propaganda, etc. Following Duverger's taxonomy, and that of other scholars (Seyd and Whiteley 1995), party members are expected at minimum – even when parties intentionally lower the barriers for entrance in order to recruit "supporters" (Scarrow 1994) – to be loyal voters for the party and to be affiliated and engaged with it for more than a short period.

As the following discussion demonstrates, many party members did not fulfill even the minimal requirements of being party voters and supporters. In addition, the majority of members in the 1990s did not forge any long-term affiliation with the party, but rather registered with the sole purpose of taking part in the primaries. About one-half of these dues-paying, empowered members did not even bother to collect the "merchandise" that they had paid for in advance, and did not participate in the primaries.

Double registration

An indication of the problematic nature and quality of party membership is the phenomenon of *double registration*, the simultaneous enrolment of citizens in more than one party, which stands not only against the rules of the parties' constitutions, but is also against the Parties Law in Israel. This phenomenon was apparent already in 1993, when a Likud spokesperson estimated that about one-quarter of its members who had the right to select the Likud's leader in its first ever party primaries were members of other parties as well (Yedioth Aharonoth 1993). The recognition of this problem led the Knesset, Israel's parliament, to pass legislation that authorized the Party Registrar to collect membership data from all parties and to cross-reference it. The 1996 figures revealed that 8 percent of Labor members and 12 percent of Likud members were also members of another party (Party Registrar 1996). The Parties Law and the 1996 cross-referencing still did not put an end to this phenomenon. In 2002, Labor still found that 4 percent of its members were also registered in Likud.

This phenomenon does not result from the adoption of primaries per se, since it was also evident in parties that did not conduct primaries. However, it provides an indication that the quality of membership did not improve, even though one might have hoped that the now empowered party members would claim an affiliation with only one party.

Opportunistic membership

It appears that many citizens registered with a party in order to select a particular candidate, without intending to vote for this candidate's party in the general elections (Weiss 1997). A preliminary examination of the 1996 Knesset election results uncovered 13 towns in which the number of Labor members was larger than the actual number of voters (Rahat and Sher-Hadar 1999). In the Likud 1999 leadership primaries there were ten villages and towns where the number of members exceeded the number of voters. A shared characteristic of most of these towns, low socio-economic standing, indicates that the news stories concerning patron–client methods in the registration campaigns were evidently grounded in reality. The evidence for opportunistic membership can also be seen in a poll published before the 2002 leadership contest in the Labor Party, which showed that fully one-quarter of Labor members would not vote for the party in the general elections if their particular candidate for the party leadership did not win (Ha'aretz 2002).

Instant membership

Instability is another sign of the problematic quality of membership, as it indicates that people join the party, or are recruited, yet do not stay affiliated after the primaries are over. A measure of this is the difference between the number of party members during the primaries, and the number of members when party primaries did not take place. Registration campaigns prior to the primaries led to an increase of between 59 and 332 percent in the number of party members. When there were no primaries on the horizon, the number of members dramatically decreased back to its former levels (Table 3.2). It would therefore appear that most of the members either joined the parties, or were recruited, with the sole intention of participating in the primaries, and not in order to create a significant link between themselves and the party.

Uninformed and self-denied membership

It is questionable whether party members know that by registering to take part in the party's internal contest they become its members. A survey prior to the 1996

Table 3.2 Membership at the beginning and at the end of registration campaigns in Labor and Likud, 1991–2002

Party	*Year*	*Members at the beginning (no.)*	*Members at the end (no.)*	*Growth rate from beginning (%)*	*Decline rate till next beginning (%)*
Labor	1991–1992	80,000	164,163	105	−51
	1995–1996	80,000	261,169	226	−73
	2001–2002	70,000	110,998	59	
Likud	1992–1993	50,000	216,000	332	−58
	1995–1996	90,000	178,852	99	−44
	2001–2002	100,000	305,000	205	

Source: Data from the political parties and newspapers.

elections (Arian and Amir 1997) found a relative gap of almost 50 percent between those who declared that they were party members (9 percent) and those who declared that they participated in the party primaries (13 percent). Together with the gap between the number of those who claimed to be members of parties and those who actually were, this statistic implies that many of those who registered to participate in the candidate selection process lacked any awareness of being enlisted as party members (Rahat and Sher-Hadar 1999), or preferred not to admit their membership due to the negative reputation the parties possessed (Arian and Amir 1997). This indicates the problematic nature of the relationship between the parties and their newly empowered members.

A gap between attitudes towards primaries and actual behavior

Taking into account Duverger's (1954) taxonomy (Figure 3.2), together with the fact that many registered members joined, or were recruited, only for the sake of the primaries, we would expect the members' participation rate in the party primaries to be somewhere between the level of participation in candidate selection by central committees (activists) and participation in the general elections (voters). That is, party members should be less motivated than party activists, but more than the average citizen. However, the average rate of participation for all 13 cases of party primaries is 58 percent, which is lower than in the central committees (92 percent), but also lower than the average turnout in the general elections for the Knesset (76 percent for 1992–2003).

Table 3.1 shows that there are differences in the rate of participation between the parties and also for the same party at different times. It is tempting to argue that such political variables as competitiveness, the party's being in government (Carty and Blake 1999) or the party's public support affect the rate of member participation. Yet, it appears that the best predictor for participation rates is the relative spread of voting stations. This explains the higher levels in Labor compared with Likud; and the decrease in participation in Labor over the years correlates to the adoption of a more frugal policy concerning the spread of polling stations. The fact that this "technicality" is the best predictor for participation stands in contrast to the rate of participation in party congresses, which take place in one location yet manage to draw more than 90 percent of the participants. In the general elections, polling stations are widespread and election day is a holiday, which makes voting a relatively easy task. Yet, when one remembers that most new members paid for the right to participate in the party primaries, participation seems quite low. This seems to indicate not only that these recruited members are instant members, but that they are also passive members.

The strategic few and the passive many

All interested players – the candidates, the activists and the parties – put an emphasis on the quantitative side of the registration campaign rather than the qualitative. They interpreted numbers as political power and sought to reap the immediate rewards: candidates and activists vis-à-vis each other, concentrating on the forthcoming intra-party struggle; the party vis-à-vis other parties, especially prior to the general elections. The fact that almost one-half of the members did not bother to participate in the primaries, together with the widespread incidence of uninformed and self-denied membership, indicated that most members were not strategic actors who decided to take advantage of the opportunity that party primaries granted them. On the contrary, the new party members played the game as relatively passive participants. Phenomena such as double registration, opportunistic and instant membership, and the gap between attitudes and behavior were the result of the interactions between a few interested strategic actors – such as interest group leaders, vote contractors and the competing candidates – and a largely passive and uninterested mass. Consequently, most of the party members did not join a party on their own initiative, but rather were mobilized by these few strategic actors.

When party membership recruitment is largely directed by political entrepreneurs, instead of being an outgrowth of grassroots efforts, the passive many will outnumber the strategic few. The two main parties did not make a serious effort to control registration, and focused rather on recruiting more members than the other party – what Scarrow (1994: 46) calls to "improve membership statistics" – as a demonstration of their public "credibility."

Democratizing candidate selection: comparative evidence on participation

Massive registration of party members prior to intra-party selection (party congresses, conventions, etc.), with little regard for the quality of those recruited, is not new. Incentives to do so were evident even in the days of the classic mass party. Duverger (1954) noticed that local branches tried to inflate membership numbers in order to enhance their representation in the ruling party institutions, while Michels (1962) presented evidence of unstable membership.

The new element when it came to party primaries was empowerment. One would expect these newly empowered members to become more affiliated with the party that gave them more privileges – privileges that were once exclusive to smaller circles of elites – and to be more active than in the past. In short, members were expected to move closer to the circle of party activists, in terms of attitudes and behavior. Yet, the comparative evidence elaborated below shows that while basic democratic instincts make people supportive of enhanced intra-party democracy, this is not enough to convince most of them actually to join a party. Of those who do join, about half fail to participate in the selection process. Moreover, most of the new party members vanish as soon as the party primaries are over.

Israel's experience with trying to meet the challenge of declining party membership by empowering party members is quite common. Britain (Webb 2002), Germany (Scarrow 2002), France (Knapp 2002), the Scandinavian countries (Sundberg 2002) and Ireland (Murphy and Farrell 2002) all provide examples of parties that are expanding and empowering their selectorates, yet here too these efforts have failed to enlarge the number of members significantly.

Unlike their European counterparts, Canadian parties have succeeded in attracting new members, and reversing the downward trend in party membership, through registration campaigns for the party leadership and the selection of candidates (Carty 2002). However, Israel's experience with instant membership is well-known by the Canadian parties as well. Carty and Blake (1999) show that the drive for registration prior to leadership selection greatly increases the number of party members. In the four events they analyzed, membership grew by between 176 and 365 percent. Moreover, they claim that, "It is a reminder that much of the (formal) membership growth may be relatively artificial, the product of the determined efforts of candidates' leadership campaigns to sign-up new members. In some cases these leadership campaign members soon melt away" (Carty and Blake 1999: 221). National membership in the Progressive Conservative Party increased by 500 percent – from 18,000 to 90,000 – in advance of the leadership selection contest in 1999, and then fell back to 18,000 (Carty 2002). The Alliance Party's registration campaign prior to its leadership selection in 2000 led to an increase in party membership from 68,000 to 123,000. A year later, the number declined again to 68,000 (Malloy 2003). If membership turnover rates of about 50 percent over a four-year period were described as "extensive" (Selle and Sväsand 1991: 463–464), then the Israeli and Canadian turnover rates can be described as hyper-extensive.

The Canadian case also illustrates the gap between the participatory ideal and the behavior of most party members. Young and Cross (2002) show that party members had positive attitudes about the new participatory devices, and called for further reforms in this direction. Their actual behavior, though, is quite different. The rate of participation in Canadian party primaries for leadership selection ranges from 24 to 75 percent (Cross 1996), leading Carty and Blake (1999: 221) to argue that, "Modest turnout rates among members for a leadership vote suggest many members of Canadian parties have only the most minimal commitment to their party." Malloy (2003) claims that the new members not only lack long-term commitment, they also do not contribute to an increase in other partisan activities.

Research on participation and activism in German parties in the 1960s found that party members did not use the participation mechanisms that were available to them (Gunlicks 1970). Nevertheless, in the 1980s and 1990s, the veteran German parties adopted additional participatory devices, including member participation in candidate and leadership selection, as a reaction to declining membership and electoral losses and in response to demands for more direct political participation. While instant membership seems not to be the case in Germany, rates of participation were similar to the Israeli and Canadian cases: between 34 and 57 percent (Scarrow 1999). The German Green Party institutionalized a series of organizing principles inspired by grassroots participatory notions, but still failed to attract large numbers of party activists. In addition, Poguntke (1992) argues that those people who could be expected to be active in party participatory democracy are loyal to specific policies and not to a party organization. They can be mobilized for the promotion of specific goals, but not for continuous partisan activity.

The comparative evidence thus points to what was identified in the Israeli case: citizens perceive party democratization positively yet fail to behave according to those ideals. There is a gap between the perception of enhanced intra-party political participation and the reality that the potential benefactors of this new circle of participatory democracy fail to seize this opportunity.

Participation in candidate selection: a theoretical discussion

A major problem in the normative discussion of intra-party democracy is the parallel that is made between parties and the state (Hands 1971). This problem is illustrated, at one end, by Michels's (1962) conclusion that democracy in general is unachievable, based on his study of the German Social Democratic Party. At the other end are the proponents of participatory democracy, who call for parallel features of state democracy in the intra-party arena.

First, there is no parallel in terms of participation. A state is a non-voluntary, compulsory organization. As such, in order to be called a democracy, it must supply its citizens with the conditions for political participation, for being electors and for being elected. Parties, however, are voluntary associations. As such, they may set their own rules, and whoever is unhappy with these rules has the choice of "voice" or "exit" (Hirschman 1970) to another party, or can establish a new party.

Second, these voluntary associations, which are weaker than the state, enhance other democratic dimensions that are not addressed by the state. Especially important is the democratic value of representation. That is, it is particularly in those electoral systems where parties have a greater say in parliamentary composition vis-à-vis the wider public – closed-list systems and multi-member districts – that women's representation is highest (Darcy *et al.* 1994). The creation of a relatively balanced list may therefore mean limiting the impact of intra-party participatory democracy (Hazan and Rahat 2000). This may also be the case regarding the creation of higher levels of competition in order to offset incumbency (Hazan 2002: 115). By the same token, intra-party political participation should strive for some balance between personal responsiveness, on the one hand, and party cohesion, on the other, in order to achieve what Shugart (2001) called "electoral efficiency" – the translation of the will of a majority of voters into policies.

Third, in terms of participation, parties, as voluntary associations, have not only the right (which the state lacks) but also the imperative to sustain themselves as arenas for voluntary participation. In order to do so, they must have the ability to use selective incentives in order to encourage higher, more sincere levels of activism that extend beyond the selection event itself. Tan (1998) found an inverse relationship between party membership size and intra-party participatory democracy. This seems to be enhanced by the adoption of party primaries, and by its related by-product, mass registration on the eve of intra-party elections. Yet, as this chapter has shown, the incentives for registration in party primaries can be damaging for the party. Registration of this kind is not of the faithful party supporters, but rather in support of the personal aspirations of the candidates. Enhanced and equivalent political participation in candidate selection thus damages the differential structure of rewards in parties – the privileges of long-time loyal activists are equal to those of new, temporary and unfaithful registrants.

These developments are in accordance with the model of the cartel party (Katz and Mair 1995). According to this approach, the parties penetrate the state and form a cross-party cartel. The intra-party relationships postulated to exist inside the parties forming the cartel assume and require a considerable degree of elite autonomy. The cartel model suggests that one possible strategy used by the party leaders in order to achieve this necessary autonomy is to empower the ordinary party members. An increase in the nominal power of the base of the party will come at the expense of the power of the middle-level activists who are the ones who might be able to coordinate an effective challenge to the autonomy of the party leaders. By increasing the participation of the party members, power shifts both up and down, at the expense of the middle.

Thus, the cartel party model leads the party leaders to adopt a democratization strategy that will give them greater leverage and will dilute the influence of the ideologically motivated and organizationally entrenched activists. The leaders will now face a less informed, unstable and atomistic crowd of party members. The rationale behind this is that the less involved party members are more likely to be swayed by such factors as name recognition, and hence are more likely to take cues from the highly visible party leadership. As Mair (1997: 149) explains, "the 'ordinary' members, who are at once more docile and more likely to endorse the policies (and candidates) proposed by the party leadership and by the party in public office."

Von Beyme (1996: 147) calls the parties in the post-modern era "omnibus parties" where "people enter the vehicle, are carried for a while and drop out when they do not see any reason to go further. The relationship to the party among the members is as instrumental as for the leaders." This seems to be the case enhanced by party primaries. Kitschelt (1988: 130) encapsulated the major points of our argument when he claimed that, "The very emphasis on individualist, participatory norms and ideologies is likely to create unexpected perverse effects in the parties' behavior, such as a lack of activists' commitment to party work, high turnover, and the rise of informal party elites." Candidate selection becomes a personal enterprise rather than a partisan matter, an enterprise of instant members recruited by individual politicians, and not one of drawing new active members.

Conclusion: an improved institutional participatory design

Various solutions can be suggested to the problems of membership quality that stem from the adoption of party primaries. The first is to adopt the logic of "If you can't beat them, join them," implying a further opening of the parties, which would enable non-partisans to participate in party events, such as policy decisions and candidate selection (Poguntke 1992). In this case, increased participation is seen as an end in itself, with no aspirations for enhancing the power of parties as collective associations. As Dalton (1996) states, we may have less participation per event, but wider participatory events. This direction points toward the Americanization of politics – parties become empty vessels, mediators of candidates and interest groups, rather than associations with a substance of their own.

Another solution (Teorell 1999) might be to reject the participatory democracy model as too demanding (and maybe too naïve), leaving no room for the choice not to participate. Instead, parties should adopt the model of deliberative democracy, a model that does not reject representative government yet suggests adding aspects that the "competitive model" lacks, and that go beyond the electoral process. Leaders and members would be linked by a deliberative poll: a statistically representative sample of supporters would deliberate with the party leaders on policy issues, and a statistically representative sample of members would deliberate candidate selection. This recommendation seems to solve the problems of size and free-riding, yet is prone to many ensuing problems. The bias of group thinking and the problem of legitimizing the poll in the eyes of most citizens, who never learned the basic rules of statistical probability, are just two such problems.

Our suggestion is to enable the various circles of participation in the party to take part in intra-party politics – that is, meaningful participation should be granted to rank and file members – but to maintain a structure of intra-party selective incentives at the same time. Regarding candidate and leadership selection, this could be achieved as long as parties involve several party agencies in the process, granting the more exclusive circles the ability to screen candidates but giving members the right to decide between a few viable options. This is the current tendency in the British parties. While it may not save them from a decline in the number of members, it seems to be the optimal balance between wider participation and the needs of the party as a voluntary association.

In summation, one should ask whether positive intentions concerning participatory democracy can lead to the demise of meaningful, qualitative participation before going too far with the opening up of candidate selection.

Notes

1 Two smaller parties also gave their members a role in candidate selection prior to the 1996 elections, but they are not included in this analysis (see Hazan 1997).

2 Number of party members is based on data available from political parties and newspapers from the closest year to the general election. For Labor, 1969–1984, we calculated the number of voters based on 85 percent of the votes that the joint Alignment list won in the elections. This reflects the ratio of list positions between Labor and Mapam – the components of the joint lists. For Likud, until 1992, we calculated the number of members based on data from Herut (Schwartz 1990) – the main component of the Likud alliance – plus rough estimation based on a 3:2 ratio representing the number of members from other components of Likud.

References

Arian, A. (1998) *The Second Republic: Politics in Israel*, Chatham, NJ: Chatham House.

Arian, A. and Amir, R. (1997) *The Next Elections in Israel: How Should We Vote?*, Jerusalem: Israel Democracy Institute. [Hebrew]

Beyme, K. von (1996) "Party Leadership and Change in Party Systems: Towards a Post-modern Party State?," *Government and Opposition*, 31: 135–159.

Bille, L. (2001) "Democratising a Democratic Procedure: Myth or Reality? Candidate Selection in Western European Parties 1960–90," *Party Politics*, 7: 363–380.

Carty, K.R. (2002) "Canada's Nineteenth-Century: Cadre Parties at the Millennium," in P. Webb, D.M. Farrell and I. Holliday (eds) *Political Parties in Advanced Industrial Democracies*, Oxford: Oxford University Press, pp. 345–378.

Carty, K.R. and Blake, D.E. (1999) "The Adoption of Membership Votes for Choosing Party Leaders," *Party Politics*, 5: 211–224.

Cross, W. (1996) "Direct Election of Provincial Leadership in Canada," *Canadian Journal of Political Science*, 29: 295–315.

Dalton, R. (1996) *Citizen Politics*, Chatham, NJ: Chatham House.

Darcy, R., Welch, S. and Clark, J. (1994) *Women, Elections, and Representation*, Lincoln, NE: Nebraska University Press.

Duverger, M. (1954) *Political Parties: Their Organization and Activity in the Modern State*, London: Methuen.

Gallagher, M. and Marsh, M. (eds) (1988) *Candidate Selection in Comparative Perspective: The Secret Garden of Politics*, London: Sage.

Galnoor, Y. (1982) *Steering the Polity: Communication and Politics in Israel*, Beverly Hills, CA: Sage.

Gunlicks, A.B. (1970) "Intraparty Democracy in Western Germany: A Look at the Local Level," *Comparative Politics*, 2: 229–249.

Hands, G. (1971) "Roberto Michels and the Study of Political Parties," *British Journal of Political Science*, 1: 155–172.

Ha'aretz (2002) "Elections 2003: 'Dialogue' Poll," 15 November: 2.
Hazan, R.Y. (2002) "Candidate Selection," in L. LeDuc, R.G. Niemi and P. Norris (eds) *Comparing Democracies 2: New Challenges in the Study of Elections and Voting*, London: Sage, pp. 108–126.
—— (1997) "The 1996 Intra-Party Elections in Israel: Adopting Party Primaries," *Electoral Studies*, 16: 95–103.
Hazan, R.Y. and Rahat, G. (2000) "Representation, Electoral Reform and Democracy: Theoretical and Empirical Lessons from the 1996 Elections in Israel," *Comparative Political Studies*, 33: 1310–1336.
Heidar, K. (1994) "The Polymorphic Nature of Party Membership," *European Journal of Political Research*, 25: 61–86.
Hirschman, A.O. (1970) *Exit, Voice, and Loyalty: Responses to Decline in Firms, Organizations and States*, Cambridge, MA: Harvard University Press.
Katz, R.S. and Mair, P. (1995) "Changing Models of Party Organization and Party Democracy: The Emergence of the Cartel Party," *Party Politics*, 1: 5–28.
Kitschelt, H. (1988) "Organization and Strategy of Belgian and West German Ecology Parties: A New Dynamic of Party Politics in Western Europe?," *Comparative Politics*, 20: 127–154.
Knapp, A. (2002) "France: Never a Golden Age," in P. Webb, D.M. Farrell and I. Holliday (eds) *Political Parties in Advanced Industrial Democracies*, Oxford: Oxford University Press, pp. 107–150.
Mair, P. (1997) *Party System Change: Approaches and Interpretations*, Oxford: Oxford University Press.
Mair, P. and Biezen, I. van (2001) "Party Membership in Twenty European Democracies 1980–2000," *Party Politics*, 7: 5–21.
Malloy, J. (2003) "High Discipline, Low Cohesion? The Uncertain Patterns of Canadian Parliamentary Party Groups," *Journal of Legislative Studies*, 9: 116–129.
Michels, R. (1962) *Political Parties*, New York, NY: Free Press.
Murphy, R.J. and Farrell, D.M. (2002) "Party Politics in Ireland: Regularizing a Volatile System," in P. Webb, D.M. Farrell and I. Holliday (eds) *Political Parties in Advanced Industrial Democracies*, Oxford: Oxford University Press, pp. 217–247.
Party Registrar (1996) A *Summary of Results Concerning Double Registration*, 13 March.
Poguntke, Th. (1992) "Unconventional Participation in Party Politics: The Experience of the German Greens," *Political Studies*, 60: 239–254.
Rahat, G. and Hazan, R.Y. (2005) "Israel: The Politics of Extreme Proportionality," in M. Gallagher and P. Mitchell (eds) *The Politics of Electoral Systems*, Oxford: Oxford University Press, pp. 333–351.
—— (2001) "Candidate Selection Methods: An Analytical Framework," *Party Politics*, 7: 297–322.
Rahat, G. and Sher-Hadar, Neta (1999) "The 1996 Party Primaries and their Political Consequences," in A. Arian and M. Shamir (eds) *Elections in Israel 1996*, Albany, NY: State University of New York Press, pp. 241–268.
Ranney, A. (1981) "Candidate Selection," in D. Butler, H.R. Penniman and A. Ranney (eds) *Democracy at the Polls: A Comparative Study of Competitive National Elections*, Washington, DC: American Enterprise Institute, pp. 75–106.
Scarrow, S.E. (2002) "Party Decline in the Parties State? The Changing Environment of German Politics," in P. Webb, D.M. Farrell and I. Holliday (eds) *Political Parties in Advanced Industrial Democracies*, Oxford: Oxford University Press, pp. 77–106.

—— (2000) "Parties without Members? Party Organization in a Changing Electoral Environment," in R.J. Dalton and M.P. Wattenberg (eds) *Parties without Partisans*, Oxford: Oxford University Press, pp. 79–101.
—— (1999) "Parties and the Expansion of Direct Democracy: Who Benefits?," *Party Politics*, 5: 341–362.
—— (1994) "The Paradox of Enrolment: Assessing the Costs and Benefits of Party Membership," *European Journal of Political Research*, 25: 41–60.
Scarrow, S.E., Webb, P. and Farrell, D.M. (2000) "From Social Integration to Electoral Contestation: The Changing Distribution of Power within Political Parties," in R.J. Dalton and M.P. Wattenberg (eds) *Parties Without Partisans*, Oxford: Oxford University Press, pp. 129–153.
Schwartz, R. (1990) "From Opposition Party to a Government Party – The Herut Movement," PhD Thesis, Jerusalem: The Hebrew University of Jerusalem. [Hebrew]
Selle, P. and Sväsand, L. (1991) "Membership in Party Organizations and the Problem of Decline in Parties," *Comparative Political Studies*, 23: 459–477.
Seyd, P. and Whiteley, P.F. (1995) "Labour and Conservative Party Members," *Parliamentary Affairs*, 48: 457–471.
Shugart, M.S. (2001) "'Extreme' Electoral Systems and the Appeal of the Mixed-Member Alternative," in M.S. Shugart and M.P. Wattenberg (eds) *Mixed-Member Electoral Systems: The Best of Both Worlds?*, Oxford: Oxford University Press, pp. 25–51.
Sundberg, J. (2002) "The Scandinavian Party Model at the Crossroads," in P. Webb, D.M. Farrell and I. Holliday (eds) *Political Parties in Advanced Industrial Democracies*, Oxford: Oxford University Press, pp. 181–216.
Tan, A.C. (1998) "The Impact of Party Membership Size: A Cross-National Analysis," *Journal of Politics*, 60: 188–198.
Teorell, J. (1999) "A Deliberative Defense of Intra-Party Democracy," *Party Politics*, 5: 363–382.
Webb, P. (2002) "Political Parties in Britain: Secular Decline or Adaptive Resilience?," in P. Webb, D.M. Farrell and I. Holliday (eds) *Political Parties in Advanced Industrial Democracies*, Oxford: Oxford University Press, pp. 16–45.
Weiss, S. (1997) *14,729 Missing Votes*, Tel Aviv: Hakibbutz Hameuchad [Hebrew].
Yedioth Aharonoth (1993) "The Likud Decides," 9 March: 10.
Young, L. and Cross, W. (2002) "The Rise of Plebiscitary Democracy in Canadian Political Parties," *Party Politics*, 8: 673–699.

4 The Scottish Parliament

A new era for participatory democracy?

Peter McLaverty and Sue Morris

Introduction

In this chapter we review what is meant by participative democracy and what has happened in Scotland following the establishment of the Scottish Parliament in 1999. The principles that underpin the workings of the Scottish Parliament include the development of a participative approach and power sharing with the people. The core of the chapter involves an analysis of the achievements and limitations of the Scottish Parliament in promoting participatory democracy. In particular we examine:

- The argument that democracy demands the existence of a strong sense of community among citizens and whether this exists, or can be enhanced, through the workings of the Scottish Parliament.
- The extent to which the Scottish Parliament reflects, or avoids, the potential clash between representative and participatory democracy.
- The willingness of Members of the Scottish Parliament (MSPs) to share power with the wider citizenry.

Our analysis is informed by our research on public engagement with the committees of the Scottish Parliament, using documentary analysis and in-depth interviews with MSPs, committee clerks and representatives of organizations in Scottish civic society. This chapter therefore contributes directly to debates about the relationship between the participation of individuals and institutional design to enhance power sharing with citizens.

We argue that while there is no generally accepted conception of participatory democracy, the concept includes citizens' involvement in direct policy making and policy implementation. It demands more of citizens than voting for representatives who will act on their behalf. Participatory democracy can be seen as promoting direct government by the people, rather than relying on government of the people and for the people. In other words, participatory democracy involves people gaining greater direct control over the areas of society that have a major impact on their lives.

The Scottish Parliament is not sovereign and has limited formal powers because the devolution settlement reserved certain key policy areas to decision making within the UK (Westminster) Parliament. The UK and other Western democracies are increasingly transferring power from the nation (sovereign) state to regional and global institutions. This context raises the question of whether the limited power of the Scottish Parliament constrains the development of participatory democracy.

The meaning and practice of democracy

Democracy and participation

Positions taken by modern writers on the relative value of representation and participation to democracy differ along a spectrum. At one end of the spectrum are those, such as John Burnheim (1985), who support strong participation and at the other are those, such as Joseph Schumpeter (1976), who support strong representation. In between these positions are those who tend towards the participative end of the spectrum but argue that representation is unavoidable, such as Philip Green (1985), and those who support a representative system but want representatives to be more accountable and (or) for representatives to reflect more accurately the composition of the society, such as Beetham *et al.* (2002).

In the 1980s, Burnheim (1985) argued that we should move away from the idea of "catch all" representatives as the basis of democracy. Returning to the conception of democracy practiced in Ancient Athens, he calls for a system where those who were most affected by a particular policy area would control that area (Burnheim 1985: 5–9, 107–110). He supports the use of random selection, or statistical sampling, in appointment to positions and the rotation of posts (Burnheim 1985: 9, 106–124). Burnheim wants to see an end to the state, and government as we have known it in recent liberal democracies. His model of governance is a highly decentralized one, where power rests within local communities. However, he also argues that his proposals are suitable for all political levels, from the local through to what we would now term the "global" (Burnheim 1987). As well as supporting random selection for public duties, Burnheim argues for a type of "functional democracy." His position is that individuals cannot be experts in all areas and are more interested in some matters than others (Burnheim 1985: 5–9, 107–110). Burnheim argues that we should make a virtue of this, rather than trying to find ways around it. He therefore supports the creation of "functional groups." In Burnheim's model, however, unlike in Ancient Athens, there is no compulsion on people to participate in the functional groups. Instead, participation is completely voluntary (Burnheim 1985: 110–113, 118–120).

Pateman (1970) traces her commitment to participatory democracy to the work of writers such as Rousseau, J.S. Mill and G.D.H. Cole. She argues for democracy to be extended beyond the formal political sphere and supports the development of industrial democracy. Unlike Burnheim, she does not deny elected representatives a role in democracy. But like him, she supports the promotion of functional democracy. Pateman's support for participatory democracy is based on what Geraint Parry (1972: 19–26) has called developmental reasons: political participation helps people to develop their capacities and to become more complete.

It is argued that there are two features which are common to both the Athenian model of democracy and the liberal democratic model, and which, indeed, may be *the* core features of any system that can be called democratic: political equality among the group members; and popular control or sovereignty (see Arblaster 2001; Beetham 1999: 4–5). Jane Mansbridge (1983), while tending towards the participatory approach, argues that where members of a group (or a sub-group of a larger group) share the same opinions and the same outlook, there is no need for political equality as any member of the group can represent all the members. For Mansbridge, direct individual participation is necessary only where people's opinions and outlooks differ. Hence, she supports representation in certain circumstances but for different reasons from those commonly used to support liberal democracy.

Democracy, participation and representation

The relationship within democracy between participation and representation is considered by Philip Green. A key argument for the necessity of the move from a participatory to a representative form of democracy is that participation relies on a small number of citizens. Green (1985: 176, 184–188) accepts the point about the importance of size. But he argues that representation is the primary democratic concept for other reasons as well, and that the relationship between participation and representation is not one that is antagonistic (Green 1985: 181–182). He argues that even after decisions have been made by the members of a group in what he terms "town meeting democracy," representatives are needed to take the decisions forward (Green 1985: 176–177): participatory forms of democracy necessarily involve representation. The important point for Green is that the ideal of democracy is one in which all members of the group participate in deciding what should be done and representatives take the decisions forward. Green (1985: 183) argues that in complex, large societies, bargaining between representatives of different groups should be the basis of democratic working. This he argues will also be the norm between members of a group. In this argument, the important concern is how the representative relates to the represented.

For Beetham *et al.* (2002: 209) participation can enhance representation, rather than be an alternative to it. However, their position is different from Green's. They argue that participation by citizens, not only in formal politics, but also in civil society, can help to keep representatives and government accountable between elections. They accept that there may be problems associated with some forms of participation, which can give influence to groups who are not representative of the wider population and can favor the already well organized and articulate.

Robert Dahl (1989) has argued that with the establishment of nation-states, the Athenian form of democracy became impracticable: representative democracy became the only sustainable form. He calls the move to representative democracy the "second democratic transformation" (Dahl 1989: 213) and argues that modern representative democracy and participatory democracy, as it existed in Ancient Athens, are radically different conceptions. For Dahl, citizens are only able to participate in the governing of the polis in a limited and largely indirect way.

Towards participatory democracy in Scotland?

There are, therefore, differences between writers about what should be the relationship between representation and participation in a democratic form of government. How does the spectrum of positions relate to the principles behind the operation of the Scottish Parliament? This section provides information on the establishment of the Parliament, its underpinning principles and its operation in the first term.

The positive result of the 1997 referendum on a Scottish Parliament was the culmination of a long struggle for devolution in Scotland. There was a strong feeling at the time that the new Scottish Parliament offered an opportunity for a fresh approach to parliamentary affairs and that the Scottish Parliament should not reflect practice at Westminster. Devolution policy was progressed in a political climate of low turnout for democratic elections in the UK, which became an increasing concern for politicians in late twentieth century Britain and has remained so in the twenty-first century. The strength of feeling evident in Scotland in the growing insistence on devolved Scottish government, and in the subsequent referendum result, suggest a strong political culture among the people of Scotland. Moreover, the increased citizen participation intrinsic in operating a devolved Parliament suggests at least implicit support in Scotland for a participatory approach to politics.

Political culture is a very difficult concept to define. Research has been carried out in Britain to try to define whether there are strong or weak political cultures in the different constituent parts of the nation-state. Brown *et al.* (1999: 75–91) argue that there is a distinctive political culture in Scotland, supported by the findings of research carried out as part of the Scottish Election Survey 1997. It seems that elite political discourse directly shapes popular opinion. Survey research shows that Scots do regard themselves as Scottish, rather than British (Brown *et al.* 1998: 208–223; Brown *et al.*, 1999). This is perhaps not surprising given that Scotland has retained its distinct legal, education and banking systems since the union with England in 1707, and had administrative devolution throughout the twentieth century before gaining political devolution in 1999. It would be rash to draw too many conclusions from the survey findings but they do suggest that a sense of political community does exist in Scotland and that it pre-dated the formation of the Scottish Parliament. If a sense of community is important for a strong democracy, as some writers argue, then the existence of shared identity in Scotland should make it easier to promote citizen participation in the Scottish Parliament. This issue is considered further below in the section on the reaction of the Scottish people, where we produce survey data on people's attitudes to the Scottish Parliament.

Principles underpinning the Scottish Parliament

The CSG (Consultative Steering Group) was set up by The Scottish Office after the positive outcome to the referendum on devolution in Scotland. The CSG was chaired by Henry McLeish, then Scottish Office Minister for Devolution. Its remit was to bring together views on and consider the operational needs and working methods of the Scottish Parliament, as well as to develop proposals for the Parliament's procedural rules and Standing Orders. The CSG first met in January 1998 and its report was published in December 1998 (Consultative Steering Group on the Scottish Parliament 1999).

The CSG drew on the Government's White Paper (*Scotland's Parliament*) and the work of the Scottish Constitutional Convention in considering their remit. The CSG in its work took the general system of representation found in UK government as its starting point. To some extent, the inclusion of a proportional representation element in the electoral system for Members of the Scottish Parliament goes some way towards enhancing participation, in that political representation is extended to those parties that are unlikely to win any seats in a first past the post system. The CSG, however, wanted to go further than this in its promotion of increasing citizen involvement in the workings of the Scottish Parliament, as well as greater opportunity for citizens to make their views known to the Members of the Scottish Parliament (MSPs) and the Parliament's officials. While the CSG report does not explicitly address the relative value of, or the relationship between, representative and participative approaches, the conception of parliamentary democracy implicit in the CSG's final report can probably be placed near the center, along with writers, such as Beetham *et al.* who see participative techniques as enhancing the traditional system of political representation.

The Consultative Steering Group (1999: 3) developed key principles that both informed their work and provide benchmarks to assess the Parliament's success in achieving participative democracy: power sharing between the people, the Parliament and the Scottish Executive, accountability to the people, accessibility, openness, responsiveness and a participative approach to all stages of the legislative process, promoting equal opportunities for all.

The CSG report also made specific proposals for mechanisms to ensure operation of the four principles in practice (Consultative Steering Group on the Scottish Parliament 1999: 144–145). These are discussed in more detail later in this section. Generally, however, the Group envisaged wide participation but argued that no single model for consultation, participation and involvement would be appropriate in every case. They also noted that effort was required from both the parliament and the people with whom it interacts to achieve participative democracy.

The CSG proposals can be seen in two broad overarching categories: information provision and education; and gathering views from those outwith the parliament and government. In particular, the CSG accorded great importance to the proposed Scottish Parliament Information Centre and Education Service in information provision and education and to the proposed parliamentary committees in gathering views and expertise from across Scotland. Implicit in this approach, however, is the lack of direct democracy, in which citizens are actually taking, rather than informing, policy decisions.

How well the Scottish Parliament was working in its first term was investigated by the Procedures Committee. The committee inquiry was announced in April 2001 with the remit to consider: "Whether the key CSG principles as endorsed by the Parliament – sharing power, accountability, accessibility and equal opportunities – are being implemented in the Parliament, to what extent and with what success" (Scottish Parliament Procedures Committee 2003a). Findings from survey and focus group work commissioned from Market and Opinion Research International (MORI) suggest that members themselves think the parliament is open and accessible (Scottish Parliament Procedures Committee 2003b); staff also thinks this is the case but that the parliament could do still better. People who have had no contact, however, disagree and in their view the parliament is not open and accessible. Members of the public who have experienced some contact with the parliament and particularly those who have given evidence to committees are generally positive about their experiences.

In the remainder of this section, we look at the operation of the parliament from the perspective of participative democracy, using research we conducted for the Scottish Parliament as the basis of our analysis.

Access to parliament for members of the public

Plenary sessions of the parliament are held in public. Committees generally meet in public, but can decide to hold meetings or parts of meetings in private. Some capacity for private committee meetings was proposed by the CSG on the grounds of necessity, for example to discuss agendas and agree reports. Members of the public are able to obtain free tickets to attend parliamentary business, enabling public access to plenary meetings in the chamber, committee meetings at the parliament in Edinburgh and where they are held throughout Scotland. In 2001, 12 committee meetings were held outside Edinburgh: these ranged from Aberdeen to Dumfries. The parliament has also held Open Days for the general public, when visitors can access the parts of parliament usually reserved for MSPs and staff. Meetings of the Scottish Parliament Corporate Body (SPCB), the Business Bureau and the committee conveners' group are always held in private, although SPCB minutes are available on the parliament's website.

As well as proposing strong information and education systems between the parliament and the people, the CSG proposed power sharing between the executive, parliament and the people. Civic participation, in this context, involves promoting the active involvement and participation of people in the political decision-making process, through specific events designed to elicit views on topics of interest to parliamentary committees. The target groups for civic participation events are often those that are not generally involved in the policy process or in the work of the committees. For example, children and young people have been a target group as have people running small businesses. Committees have also invited those from traditionally socially excluded groups to give evidence. Civic participation events would include, for example, engaging specific groups, representative samples of the population, or local communities in discussion of the potential impact of proposed legislation or to help inform a committee's views on policy-relevant topics.

Among our interviewees there was a widespread feeling that the parliament had made little process in advancing power sharing. There was also the feeling, which was expressed by MSPs, clerks and representatives of organizations, that power sharing was probably impossible. Moreover, respondents also said that power sharing was not really desirable, as MSPs should make final policy decisions.

The Scottish Parliament committee system

The CSG envisaged an important role for parliamentary committees in relation to both power sharing and openness and accessibility. As proposed by the CSG, there are both mandatory committees and subject committees in the Scottish Parliament. In the first term of parliament, subject committees have been introduced to reflect Scottish Executive Departments. Despite these committees' power to introduce bills, they have mainly operated to consider the executive's legislative proposals in their policy areas and to scrutinize the work of the departments most relevant to them. Mandatory committees include a European Committee and an Equal Opportunities Committee, despite these matters being reserved to Westminster. The CSG thinking behind this is that there should be specific Scottish Parliament contributions to policy making on European issues, and a role for the parliament in monitoring and encouraging equality of opportunity in the approach to representative and participative democracy in Scotland.

Mandatory and subject committees draw on various external sources to inform their considerations. This may take the form of information and research briefings prepared by Parliament researchers or via commissioned research, oral and written evidence and responses to specific consultations, informal meetings with members of the public, visits by committee members to organizations, and specially designed participation events. This type of dialogue encourages people to reflect on their views in presenting them to MSPs, but also encourages MSPs to reflect on the opinions they currently hold.

Arguably the most innovative aspect of the Scottish Parliament committee system is the introduction of the CSG-proposed mandatory Public Petitions Committee as a mechanism to allow members of the public to raise issues with the parliament directly. This has resulted in a committee that is operating to good effect in terms of encouraging people to put their views to the parliament. Anyone can raise a petition, so long as its subject matter is within the scope of the Scottish Parliament. The remit of the Public Petitions Committee (PPC) is to consider and report on whether a public petition is admissible; and if so, what action is to be taken on the petition. The electronic petitioning of parliament is now possible.

Information, advice and support are available to anyone wishing to submit a petition. The procedure and guidance (quick and detailed guides) for submitting petitions are available on the parliament's web pages and have been distributed to Citizens Advice Bureau and the Parliament's Partner Library network. In addition, the committee clerks offer assistance to petitioners in complying with the guidance and the rules on admissibility. Petitioners are actively encouraged to present their petition formally to the committee and the clerks offer them assistance in their preparation.

In deciding whether action should be taken by the parliament the committee may request comments from the Scottish Executive or other bodies with a relevant interest in a petition. It then considers the responses received and makes a judgment on whether further action should be taken by the parliament. Where it is agreed that action is required, the relevant subject committee(s) may be asked to further consider the issues raised. In other cases, the Scottish Executive, local authorities and other public bodies are asked to take action or provide information.

During Parliamentary Year 1999–2000 around 57 percent of petitions considered by the PPC were formally referred to subject committees. By Parliamentary Year 2000–2001 this figure dropped to 17 percent, following the introduction of the PPC's more detailed initial scrutiny of petitions. This reflects an increasingly pro-active approach by the PPC in considering petitions itself, rather than routinely referring them elsewhere in the first instance.

The Public Petitions Committee monitors the progress of petitions referred to other committees or elsewhere to ensure that petitioners ultimately receive a response to the issues they have raised. The committee also ensures that petitioners are kept informed of progress at each stage of the parliament's consideration of their petition. In our interviews, many respondents, not only MSPs and clerks but also representatives of organizations, expressed their enthusiasm for the petitioning system which they said was working very well.

Of course, the Scottish Parliament is not the only sub-central parliament in Europe to operate a petitions system. Many Länder parliaments in Germany have a petitions committee and encourage the public to submit petitions. In Lower Saxony, for example, which does not have a specific petitions committee but sends petitions to the relevant specialist committees for discussion, around 7,000 petitions were presented to the parliament in a five-year period in the 1990s (Lazarowicz and Jones 2004a). As a comparison, in the period between the 7 May 2004 and 6 May 2005 the Scottish Parliament Public Petitions Committee received 110 new petitions (Scottish Parliament Petitions Committee

2005). In the Austrian Länder petitions also play a part in policy making. Legislation can be proposed by public initiative which includes the submission of petitions (Lazarowicz and Jones 2004a). The Scottish Parliament, then, is not unique in encouraging the public to petition the parliament. In British terms, however, the petitions system in Scotland is very unusual and highly innovative.

Innovative practices in the Scottish Parliament

The CSG proposed a number of innovative practices for the Scottish Parliament, including that committees be allowed to co-opt non-MSPs onto committees where relevant experience or expertise was lacking. Arguably, this would have enhanced the representation of minority groups, given that the parliament has no MSPs from minority ethnic groups or who have registered disabilities. The parliament shied away from this approach and no allowance for non-elected committee members was incorporated into Parliament's Standing Orders.

Committees routinely invite wide-ranging responses to consultation and also routinely invite witnesses to appear in person at committee meetings to give evidence on Inquiries, proposed legislation and topical issues. Such meetings are almost always held in public and the verbatim account is given in the Official Report. Case study visits have also been undertaken by committees and these involve sub-groups of committee members going out to meet with those who have particular interest in some aspect of their work. These meetings generally involve officials, employers, workers and other community representatives in a Scottish locality. Unlike evidence taking sessions, such meetings are not held in open forums. The thinking behind these case study visits is that open dialogue between members and those involved in a specific issue is valuable and can provide rich seams of information. The principle of openness is to be modified where there are reasons to believe that ensuring anonymity is the only way to obtain frank accounts. Respondents in our interviews regarded study visits as a good way for MSPs to gain information and ideas from groups and individuals, and to supply information and ideas. The groups visited have included schoolchildren, prisoners and people living in deprived areas who do not engage widely in formal politics.

Less routine activities are also organized by committees and the following examples give some flavor of these:

- In Session 1, the Enterprise and Lifelong Learning Committee held a number of innovative events particularly designed to give consumers a voice. A Lifelong Learning Convention held late in 2002 was intended to facilitate debate on the committee's interim report on lifelong learning by all those with an interest. This input was taken into account by the Committee and fed into the process of producing the final report.
- The Justice 1 Committee commissioned a survey, focus groups and hosted an "Open Space" event to try and obtain a more sophisticated understanding of people's views on alternatives to custody than any one of these methods

would provide on its own. The techniques used in Open Space events are about enabling participants to set the agenda and finish with firm action points.

- The Equal Opportunities Committee had young gypsy travelers as witnesses and provided breakfast during their visit to the Parliament to help in making them welcome and comfortable.

Participation in the Scottish Parliament

It is clear that these Scottish Parliament initiatives go some way towards a participative approach to governance; however, they are based on a framework of representative democracy, albeit one that includes an element of proportional representation in a British electoral system for the first time. These initiatives are more concerned with promoting transparency of Parliamentary operation, access to parliamentary debates and committee meetings, promulgation of information about the parliament, and obtaining external input into the work of the parliament, rather than promoting direct citizen participation in political decision-making.

A number of the mechanisms used by the Scottish Parliament are also used by other sub-national parliaments. For example, in scrutinizing legislation, a number of parliaments in Europe take advice and evidence from outside bodies. In some cases, such as the Brussels-Capital Region, consultative bodies have been established and these can be consulted, and in some cases have to be consulted, when relevant legislation is being considered (Lazarowicz and Jones 2004b). Citizens' initiatives, where parliaments consider proposals submitted by a group of citizens, are used by some parliaments (Lazarowicz and Jones 2004b) but not by the Scottish Parliament (though the Scottish Parliament does make use of public petitions). A number of other mechanisms for engaging with the public are used by various parliaments, such as citizens' juries, local referendums and prior appraisal of legislation by the public, which are not used, or have not yet been used, by the Scottish Parliament (see the chapters in Loughlin 2001). The Scottish Parliament would appear to be adopting a style of governing which, while unusual in the UK context, seems to be more common in parts of continental Europe. David Arter (2004), for example, argues that the Scottish Parliament has strong similarities with the Scandinavian assemblies and particularly the Finnish Parliament. The use of study visits, especially to groups and areas where people are not heavily involved in formal politics, does seem to be a quite innovative development by the Scottish Parliament.

Despite early signs that the Scottish Parliament is taking seriously its remit to create a modern democratic forum, with emphasis on accessibility and participation for the people of Scotland, the parliament has only limited ability to ensure ongoing governance based on power sharing and an inclusive approach. In considering the approach of the Scottish Parliament, and its role in the development of participatory democracy, its wider political context is relevant. The next section considers the parliament's relationships to the UK Parliament at Westminster, to the Scottish Executive and its place within the wider context of increasing political decision-making at a supranational level, and considers the parliament's limitations in establishing a participative approach to democracy in Scotland.

Limitations on participative democracy in Scotland

In an unguarded moment Tony Blair once said that the Scottish Parliament would have no more power than an English Parish Council, by which he meant that the establishment of a Scottish Parliament would not be a major development. It is worthwhile, therefore, considering the powers of the Scottish Parliament and the impact this may have on the ability of the parliament to promote participatory democracy. If the Scottish Parliament has no real powers, does it matter how it operates and why should people bother to participate in the activities of a powerless body?

The devolved settlement

The Scotland Act of 1998 sets out the powers of the Scottish Parliament.[1] The Act is based on devolution of power from the UK Parliament to the Scottish Parliament. Under devolution, decisions on certain policy areas are reserved to the UK Parliament and on which the Scottish Parliament cannot make legislative proposals. Crucially, these are constitutional issues; fiscal and monetary policy, including taxation; foreign affairs; defense and national security; social security; and broadcasting. Outwith these reserved policy areas, and working within the budget set for it by the UK Parliament, the Scottish Parliament is free to decide policy within Scotland, including limited tax varying powers to raise or lower income tax payments by up to 3 percent. The Scottish Parliament has law-making powers and this distinguishes it from the Welsh Assembly, which does not have power to pass primary legislation. Nevertheless, the Scotland Act allows the UK Parliament to retain the right to make laws affecting Scotland.

Among the policy areas which have been devolved are health, education and training (including schools, further and higher education), local government, social work, housing, criminal justice, the environment, and rural affairs, including agriculture, forestry and fisheries. Clearly the devolved policy areas are important for Scottish citizens and play a major part in people's lives. How policies are developed and how services are provided is important both for service users and for the wider community. It would be hard therefore to take seriously an argument that the Scottish Parliament's devolved power is of no significance.

Arguably a more serious point is that under devolution, Scotland is responsible for internal policies on a range of social and economic issues, but that decision-making is undertaken within a tightly bounded framework (of fiscal, foreign and social security policy). This framework does not allow for decisions on means of raising government revenue, relationships with other national and international entities, or redistribution of wealth. The Scottish Socialist Party, the Scottish National Party and the Scottish Greens are committed to independence rather than devolved government for Scotland to ensure control over these key issues to the Scottish people. The other parties represented in the Scottish Parliament remain positive about Scotland's position within the UK nation-state and support Scottish devolution rather than independence.

The Scottish Parliament and the Scottish Executive

It has been argued that the emphasis placed on promoting citizen participation within the Scottish Parliament largely ignores the Scottish Executive, which is the most important branch of Scottish devolved government. James Mitchell (2000: 614) argues that the parliament has importance because it determines membership of the executive, as well as legitimizing the work of the executive. For him, political power rests much more in the executive than it does in the parliament. Thus in terms of the policy cycle of agenda setting and policy initiation and development, through implementation and evaluation of policy initiatives, the approach of the Executive is as key an issue as the parliament's approach to participation. Indeed, the CSG report noted that its four key principles applied to the operation of the executive as much as to the operation of the parliament.

It can be argued that in the new constitutional arrangements for Scotland, the executive has taken seriously its role in involving public participation in its policy initiatives, most notably in the increasing number of consultations on proposed policy reform and exercises undertaken to seek public opinion on legislative proposals. As with the parliament, however, these methods are most evident at the early stages of the policy cycle and involve only input into the decision-making process rather than attempts to establish mechanisms for direct democracy. The practice of ministerial questioning by parliamentary committees as part of the evidence-taking sessions on legislative proposals and as part of committee inquiries may also be seen as increasing the ability of non-executive representatives to participate in government decision-making, but again only indirectly. The traditional mechanism of plenary debates and elected members voting on particular issues, leading to decisions being taken on the basis of parliamentary majorities, remains a core element of the new Scottish politics.

The reaction of the Scottish people

What impact has the Scottish Parliament and its operation had on attitudes in Scotland? The Scottish Social Attitudes Survey 2001 (Bromley and Curtice 2003: 16) found some negative attitudes towards the Scottish Parliament. Only 38 percent of the people they surveyed thought that having a Scottish Parliament gave ordinary people a greater say in the governance of Scotland. This is a large reduction from the 64 percent in 1999 who thought ordinary people had more say in how Scotland was governed, as a result of the Scottish Parliament. However, the survey also found that people do believe that the Scottish Parliament makes decisions in a different way from the Parliament at Westminster. In total, 58.5 percent of the electorate voted in the Scottish Parliament elections in 1999; after the parliament had been running for four years, the turnout at the 2003 election fell to just below 50 percent (Electoral Commission 2003).

Other research carried out for the 2001 Scottish Social Attitudes Survey relates to the discussion above about the role of political culture. The research shows that those who stress their Scottish identity are more likely than those who do not to take a positive attitude on the question of whether the Scottish Parliament has or will improve the Scottish economy and the NHS. However, in respect of the question of whether the Scottish Parliament has improved education, the differences among respondents, in terms of strength of Scottish identity, are small and statistically insignificant. The same is true for responses to the important question of whether the Scottish Parliament has given people more say in how Scotland is governed. For this question positive responses in the categories range from 41 percent for those who regard their identity as more Scottish than British to 34 percent for those whose identity is more British/British not Scottish, with those who regard themselves as Scottish not British recording 36 percent, along with those who are equally Scottish and British (see Rosie and Bond 2003).

Conclusion

The positions taken within academic literature on democracy tend to range along a spectrum of representative and participative democracy, with the strongest contrast between those who argue for undiluted representative, indirect democracy and those who argue that people should govern themselves directly through public participation in political decision-making. A common approach in recent writing is to view representation as the unavoidable basis of modern democracies, but to increase public opportunities to participate in the policy-making process.

The Scottish Parliament was established at the end of the twentieth century, with an explicit set of principles to inform its procedures and its work. These principles reflect key values of power sharing, openness, accessibility, accountability and equality of opportunity. In its first term, the parliament has endorsed these principles and, while relying on the traditional system of political representation in the UK, has taken some steps to modify the representative approach through increasing public participation in its work.

The approach taken to participative democracy by the Scottish Parliament is primarily one of enhancing citizens' ability to elect MSPs who reflect wider representation than before, and to develop mechanisms to overlay the system of representative democracy with enhanced participation in the policy process for members of the public.

The participative approach is based on empowering citizens by maximizing the information they can obtain about the work of the parliament and by encouraging public contributions to policy debates, mainly through mechanisms to encourage contributions of information and views to the parliamentary committees. There is no suggestion that citizens will take part in direct decision-making; rather that the parliament is able to take account of information and views in making decisions itself.

The Public Petitions Committee is the only committee formally and consistently to extend this remit, by inviting petitions on any devolved matter by members of the public. Both groups and individuals are able to petition the parliament in this way. Nevertheless, while citizens are able to set the agenda for PPC considerations, there is no scope for the taking of decisions by the citizenry on the matters raised.

In many ways, the Scottish Parliament shows evidence of working towards open and accessible government. In terms of input to the legislative process, the parliament shows evidence of a great deal of gathering of views from a wide range of interests. Perhaps most importantly, the parliament itself has recognized an increasing need for proactive encouragement of civic participation. A new Participation Services team was formed in autumn 2002 by realigning existing staff services. This suggests endorsement of the view that the Parliament should be proactive in providing opportunities for the people of Scotland to engage with it and its work. In the UK context, this certainly represents a move towards Parliamentary engagement in participative democracy.

There are signs that the Scottish Executive is placing more emphasis on public participation in the policy process, particularly at the initial stages of policy initiation and formulation. Nevertheless, both parliament and executive have responsibility for a limited range of social and economic policies as determined by the UK Parliament at Westminster. The UK remains the sovereign state with Westminster control over key policy areas, including the extent of devolution within the UK.

Ultimately, however, developments in participation are necessarily bounded by the context in which the parliament operates, the resources and time available, the political agenda, and the development of increasingly effective methods and techniques. Arguably the most important element in achieving participatory democracy is public insistence on participative approaches to, and willingness to participate in, the process of governance.

Note

1 For an electronic version see www.opsi.gov.uk/acts/acts1998/19980046.htm (accessed 10 January 2006).

References

Arblaster, A. (2001) *Democracy*, 3rd edn, Buckingham: Open University Press.

Arter, D. (2004) *The Scottish Parliament: A Scandinavian Style Assembly?*, London: Frank Cass.

Beetham, D. (1999) "Defining and Justifying Democracy," in D. Beetham, *Democracy and Human Rights*, Cambridge: Polity Press: 1–29.

Beetham, D., Byrne, I., Ngan, P. and Weir, S. (2002) *Democracy under Blair: A Democratic Audit of the United Kingdom*, London: Politico's.

Bromley, C. and Curtice, J. (2003) "Devolution Scorecard and Prospects," in C. Bromley, J. Curtice, K. Hinds and A. Park (eds) *Devolution – Scottish Answers to Scottish Questions?*, Edinburgh: Edinburgh University Press, pp. 7–29.

Brown, A., McCrone, D. and Patterson, L. (1998) *Politics and Society in Scotland*, 2nd edn, Basingstoke: Macmillan.

Brown, A., McCrone, D., Patterson, L. and Surridge, P. (1999) *The Scottish Electorate*, Basingstoke: Macmillan.

Burnheim, J. (1987) "Democracy, Nation-States and the World System," in D. Held and C. Pollitt (eds) *New Forms of Democracy*, London: Sage, pp. 218–239.

—— (1985) *Is Democracy Possible?*, Cambridge: Polity Press.

Consultative Steering Group on the Scottish Parliament (1999) *Shaping Scotland's Parliament*, London: The Stationery Office (Presented to the Secretary of State December 1998).

Dahl, R. (1989) *Democracy and its Critics*, New Haven, CT: Yale University Press.

Electoral Commission (2003) *Official Report on the Scottish Parliament and Local Government Elections*, Edinburgh: Electoral Commission.

Green, P. (1985) *Retrieving Democracy*, London: Methuen.

Lazarowicz, M. and Jones, A. (2004a) *Parliamentary Practices in Devolved Parliaments*, Edinburgh: Scottish Office. Online. Available at: www.scotland.gov.uk/government/devolution/ppdp-03.asp (accessed 28 October 2004).

—— (2004b) *Parliamentary Practices in Devolved Parliaments*, Edinburgh: Scottish Office. Online. Available at: www.scotland.gov.uk/government/devolution/ppdp-00.asp (accessed 28 October 2004).

Loughlin, J. (ed.) (2001) *Subnational Democracy in the European Union Challenges and Opportunities*, Oxford: Oxford University Press.

Mansbridge, J. (1983) *Beyond Adversary Democracy*, Chicago, IL: University of Chicago Press.

Mitchell, J. (2000) "New Parliament, New Politics in Scotland," *Parliamentary Affairs*, 53: 605–621.

Parry, G. (1972) "The Idea of Participation," in G. Parry (ed.) *Participation in Politics*, Manchester: Manchester University Press, pp. 3–38.

Pateman, C. (1970) *Participation and Democratic Theory*, Cambridge: Cambridge University Press.

Rosie, M. and Bond, R. (2003) "Identity matters: The Personal and Political Significance of feeling Scottish," in C. Bromley *et al. Devolution – Scottish Answers to Scottish Questions?*, Edinburgh: Edinburgh University Press, pp. 116–136.

Schumpeter, J. (1976) *Capitalism, Socialism and Democracy*, London: Allen and Unwin.

Scottish Parliament Petitions Committee (2005) 2nd Report 2005 (Session 2), *Scottish Parliament Paper 358*, Edinburgh: Scottish Parliament.

Scottish Parliament Procedures Committee (2003a) The Founding Principles of the Scottish Parliament: The Application of Access and Participation, Equal Opportunities, Accountability and Power Sharing in the Work of the Parliament, 3rd Report, vols 1 and 3, *Scottish Parliament Paper 818*, Edinburgh: Scottish Parliament.

Scottish Parliament Procedures Committee (2003b) The Founding Principles of the Scottish Parliament: The Application of Access and Participation, Equal Opportunities, Accountability and Power Sharing in the Work of the Parliament, 3rd Report, vol. 3, Appendix F, *Scottish Parliament Paper 818*, Edinburgh: Scottish Parliament, pp. 82–112.

Part III

Democratic reform and direct democracy

5 The effects of direct democracy and city size on political participation

The Swiss case[1]

Simone Baglioni

Introduction

This chapter aims to discuss how personal resources and context are shaping political participation in Switzerland. Political participation is measured here by means of several indicators: first, the degree of involvement in political parties; second, the use of direct democracy; third, the participation in non-conventional but still legal political actions; fourth, the participation in non-conventional and illegal political actions; fifth, general interest towards different levels of politics, and sixth and finally, people's decisions to get politically involved or to engage in civic-organized or informal networks. These forms of political participation can be perceived as the consequence of individual – internal – resources, and environmental – external – constraints and opportunities.

A wealth of research focusing on civic engagement as well as on political conventional and non-conventional participation demonstrates that the choice of becoming an activist depends on the one hand upon some personal characteristics such as the educational level, the professional condition and the income, but also on the person's attitude vis-à-vis the social environment, that is, his/her capability of being open to (and interested in) the rest of the world. On the other hand, these personal features are in turn influenced by the different contexts in which people are embedded: by the specific community they live in (opportunities and problems are dissimilar depending on whether we live in a large city, in a medium town, in a village in a rural area or in a suburb of a metropolitan one); by the type of state they are situated in (being a member of an advocacy group in a dictatorship or in a democracy generate two different patterns of participation) (Birnbaum 1993; Gamson and Meyer 1996; Hadenius 2001; Kitschelt 1986; Kriesi 1996; Pateman 1970; Schofer and Fourcade-Gourinchas 2001; Skocpol and Fiorina 1999; Skocpol *et al.* 2000); by the type of democratic system they are citizens of (participatory regimes have been recognized to foster citizens' participation in the public sphere in a more effective way than representative ones) (Baglioni 2004; Kriesi 1995; Wernli 1998).

I will focus my comparative analysis on the impact of different empirical models of democracy existing in Swiss communities on political participation. I will also consider the effect of the size of the community as an intervening variable. Switzerland is particularly useful for a comparative analysis of citizens' involvement because of its federal structure, which, to a certain extent, allows us to study the effects of both a participatory and a more restricted model of direct democracy in one single country.

All cantons in Switzerland provide opportunities for direct decision-making. However, Swiss cantons differ regarding the particular model of direct democracy. In the context of the federal constitution the Swiss cantons are free to decide on a comprehensive model of direct democracy with full access to every tool related to direct decision-making (referenda and constitutional as well as legislative initiatives) and with low barriers in the process of using these tools (i.e. the need for a low number of signatures to use those instruments and the existence of a longer time period in which to collect them). However, Swiss cantons can also choose a more restricted model of direct democracy with a limited number of available tools and with higher barriers in the process of direct decision-making (Kriesi 1995; Kriesi and Wisler 1996; Wernli 1998). We assume that in the former model people are encouraged (and sometimes even "obliged"!)[2] to take part in public life, while in the latter model citizens tend to be less involved. Those cantons closer to the participatory model should also be inhabited by citizens who are more interested in politics and even more conscious about politics (Wernli 1998).

Two cantons have been selected for this comparative analysis representing the two models of democracy: the German-speaking canton of Berne, which is characterized, like most of the other Swiss German areas, by a participatory environment, and the French-speaking canton of Vaud, which is, as are most of the Latin areas, close to a more restricted model of direct democracy. To study the impact of the second contextual element in our analysis, namely size, political participation has been analyzed in eight communities, four per canton, representing a large town (where "large" is in relation to the country, i.e. about 120,000 inhabitants), a middle-sized town, a suburb and a rural village.

The impact of size on political participation is the subject of various theories of democracy: starting with those who cleared the path, Dahl and Tufte (1973), one might expect a more vibrant political participative landscape to be associated with the larger communities than with the smaller and/or the rural ones (even if they discovered that political contacts between leadership and people and the effectiveness of political acts work better in smaller places). Indeed, these two scholars pointed out that the richness and dynamism of civic and political life within a community tend to increase with its size. Their argument follows these lines: the more complex a society becomes, the more complex its social and political fabric will be, and the more its citizens will be involved in public activities thanks to the vast array of opportunities that such a complex society is able to offer them. On the contrary, Oliver (2000) in his study on city size and civic involvement in metropolitan America has discovered that if we control for individual characteristics, attendance to political rallies or participation to local elections as well as contacts with politicians or administrators, they decrease with the growth of the size of the place people live in. Gamm and Putnam (1999), from their side, in a study on the evolution of voluntary associations in the US during the time span of a century (1840–1940) observed that associational life was more vibrant in the smaller cities of the hinterland instead of in the larger ones of the North-East and of the Mid-West. This second group of argument follows from classic social theory stressing the importance of small communities for keeping people bound and interested in dealing with their common destiny as inhabitants of the same community.

The following analysis is based on two hypotheses: the first assumes that political participation as a sum of political interest and behaviors will be more developed in the participatory canton of Berne than in the representative one of Vaud. Moreover, linked to this hypothesis is the presumption that we will find different levels of political involvement as long as we will consider communities of different size. The second hypothesis assumes that individual characteristics matter in ways already pointed out by previous research: people with a high educational level and income will be those showing a more robust political attitude. However, it will also be worth taking into consideration peoples' attitudes towards their social environments, assuming that those more interested in the communities' affairs as well as those with a stronger confidence vis-à-vis the other members of their society will be associated with higher degrees of political participation. Figure 5.1 summarizes these hypotheses.

The data that I present and discuss in this paper come from a survey carried out in the year 2001. The survey covers about one thousand people who are active in some way in an association based in one of the eight communities belonging to one of the two cantons selected.[3] The fact that I will discuss data of the political involvement of people already active does not detract from the significance of the findings provided these persons are active in very different

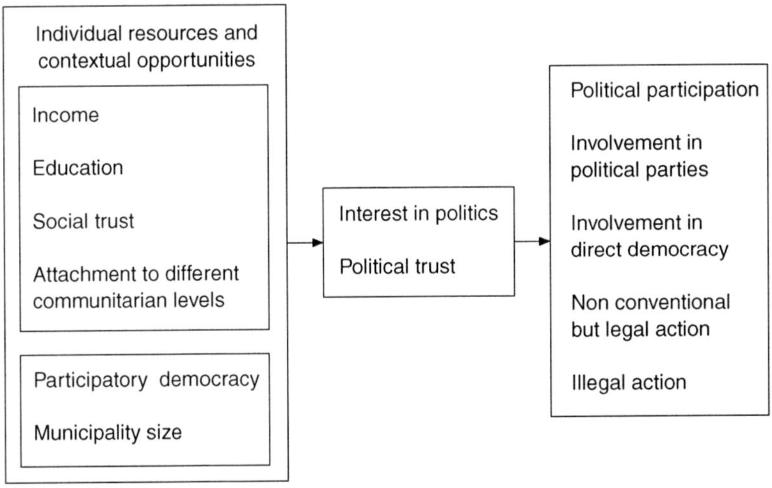

Figure 5.1 A causal diagram of political involvement.

manners and as long as personal and contextual effects on shaping different types of political behavior can be found.

In the following part of the chapter, I first summarize the patterns of political participation in the two cantons and in the different communities. In a second step, I then aim to understand which factors account for the differences eventually found.

Political participation in two Swiss cantons

Tables 5.1 to 5.3 show how interested in politics respondents are. As we can see, activists living in the German canton of Berne score higher in terms of general interest. Their numbers exceed those of their French-speaking homologues, when we look to the "very interested" category for example, by almost 10 points (Table 5.1). These findings confirm previous research (Wernli 1998) and show that, in general, the interest in politics is lower in the less participatory areas of the country. If we distinguish between different areas of interest – between the local and national levels of politics (Table 5.2) as well as the European or international (Table 5.3) levels of politics – the differences between the cantons still remain. Particularly interesting are the results concerning international and European politics. Indeed, the fact that people living in the Berne area are more interested in local politics can be understood, and could even have been foreseen, by taking into account the more developed familiarity they have with instruments of direct democracy, a factor which often brings them closer to their local environments and which also fosters their interest in local politics. The same applies to their interest in national politics, with the additional reason that these respondents live in the canton which hosts the national capital, Berne, where the national political arena is based. However, the results regarding the supranational level of politics are surprising. We should have expected a less developed political interest in the canton of Berne. This is because in the Swiss German-speaking areas the opening of the country to intergovernmental bodies, such as the UN or the EU, has been most controversial and has been perceived in critical ways (Linder 1998). However, quite in contrast to this assumption, people living in those areas seem to be more interested in European questions and international developments than those living in the more "open to the

Table 5.1 In general, how interested in politics are you?

	Swiss German (%)	*Swiss French (%)*
Not interested at all	9.4	9.5
Not very interested	24.8	33.9
Quite interested	38.7	37.9
Very interested	27.0	18.6
	100.0	100.0
	n = 488	*n* = 451

Table 5.2 Interest in local and national politics, by type of canton

	Local politics		*National politics*	
	Swiss German (%)	*Swiss French (%)*	*Swiss German (%)*	*Swiss French (%)*
Not interested at all	6.8	7.1	6.4	7.4
Not very interested	23.4	26.7	20.3	25.9
Quite interested	39.1	39.7	48.2	46.9
Very interested	30.7	26.5	25.2	19.9
	100.0	100.0	100.0	100.0
	n = 488	*n* = 453	*n* = 488	*n* = 448

Table 5.3 Interest in European and international politics, by type of canton

	European politics		*International politics*	
	Swiss German (%)	*Swiss French (%)*	*Swiss German (%)*	*Swiss French (%)*
Not interested at all	8.8	9.5	9.4	10.9
Not very interested	29.7	31.2	29.0	31.6
Quite interested	47.5	47.3	43.5	43.3
Very interested	13.9	11.9	18.1	14.2
	100.0	100.0	100.0	100.0
	n = 488	*n* = 452	*n* = 487	*n* = 450

world" French-speaking regions. The reported findings suggest that institutional differences between the two Swiss cantons affect political interest in all areas and at all levels of politics. These effects seem to be stronger than cultural bias or traditional attitudes.

Interest in politics can also be measured by taking into consideration the frequency at which individuals read about politics in the newspapers, watch political programs on television and look for political news on the Internet. As shown in Table 5.4 the first indicator is the most reliable one as a large portion (almost half) of the respondents use the newspapers to obtain information about politics, while a quarter of them turn to radio for the same purpose and only a small minority claims to use the Internet. However, across all these indicators those interviewed in the German-speaking area are more interested in politics than those in the French canton. Almost 55 percent of the former read about politics in newspapers every day vis-à-vis the 42.2 percent of the latter. A similar pattern can be found with regard to the remaining categories.

As Wernli (1998) has demonstrated in his study on political involvement in Switzerland, participatory institutions also help in strengthening people's political consciousness: in the frame of a direct democracy, citizens are often called

Table 5.4 Interest in politics: different indicators, by type of canton

	Swiss German		*Swiss French*		*n*
	Every day (%)	*Never (%)*	*Every day (%)*	*Never (%)*	
Reading about politics in newspapers	54.9	6.1	42.2	5.3	490/450
Watching political programs on TV	15.5	7.4	14.1	6.4	485/453
Reading, or looking for politics on the Internet	6.7	46.8	5.4	46.6	481/444

to take a position (and a decision) in the public domain. In other words, they are encouraged to collect information about facts upon which they have to express themselves. This process strengthens their public awareness and leads them to value political participation. This assumption also holds true in light of our results. The inhabitants of the canton of Berne feel stronger about the importance of living in a society that fosters political participation compared with those living in the canton of Vaud (see Table 5.5). As shown in Table 5.6, the former also seem to be more certain of their political opinions than their French-speaking counterparts. We could speak of a phenomenon of mutual influence between participatory institutions and the citizenry: the participatory institutions of the Berne region make their inhabitants more conscious of their political role through a continuous and solicited exercise of their political duties and rights, and as a reaction, the citizens of this region care for their participatory system and do not only believe that an active citizenship is good for democracy, but that all societies should encourage such an active involvement. And even more significantly, they are ready to defend their political arguments.

A last glimpse at the differences in political involvement between people living in the two cantons comes from the analysis of different degrees of engagement in the realm of political parties. Respondents from the canton of Berne appear to be more committed to becoming active in political parties than those living in the canton of Vaud. Table 5.7 presents different modalities of being active in a political party (or not being active at all) moving from a position of being a member to a more comprehensive profile of someone who besides being a member also gives to the party his free time, as well as some money and who has friends within it. Notwithstanding the fact that the majority of those interviewed was not involved in any political party, the Swiss German respondents again show a deeper interest in political participation since their scores are higher (apart from the last category) than those recorded by their French-speaking counterparts.

Having considered the effects of the cantonal context on political participation we can now turn to the effect of community size on the level of political participation. Tables 5.8 and 5.9 provide a first overview regarding the results of

Table 5.5 Importance of living in a society which fosters political participation, percentages of respondents considering it very important

	Swiss German	*Swiss French*
%	35.6	32.8
n	485	446

Table 5.6 Would it occur to you to engage in discussions to defend your political opinions?

	Swiss German (%)	*Swiss French (%)*
Yes	71.0	67.7
No	23.9	22.5
No strong opinion	5.1	9.1
n	489	449

Table 5.7 Participation in a political party: different levels of involvement, by canton

	Swiss German (%)	*Swiss French (%)*
Not involved in a political party	58.1	64.7
Member	26.2	24.9
Member and activist	3.8	1.9
Member, activist and donor	2.4	1.7
Member, activist, donor and volunteer	5.6	1.9
Member, activist, donor, volunteer and with friends in the party	4.0	4.7
	100.0	100.0
	n = 503	*n* = 465

this analysis. Table 5.8 demonstrates that interest in politics appears to differ between respondents living in a large city, in a middle-sized city, in a suburb and in a rural village. The highest level of political interest is associated with those interviewed living in the villages (45.2 percent of them declaring to be quite interested in politics and 32.3 percent to be very interested). The table provides an obvious message: with the exception of the suburban environment, interest increases in all cases when the size of the place diminishes. The sum of interested persons equals 60.7 percent for those living in the large city, 66.9 percent for the inhabitants of the middle-size ones and 77.5 percent for the interviewed living in a village. The lowest score of political interest is associated with the inhabitants of suburbs, 47.0 percent. This last figure tells us that the size of the place is just one side of the coin.

Apart from the size, we should also take social and economic structure into account while we consider community as a factor influencing political behavior. The assumption is that a lack of diversity provides a negative stimulus on political behavior because it fosters the emergence of ghettos and suppresses any community involvement regardless of size. Indeed, as has been pointed out by Oliver (2000) in his American study:

> [S]ubdividing populations into smaller political units alone will not be sufficient to stimulate civic involvement because the racial and economic segregation that accompanies such fragmentation will counteract the civic virtues of smaller city size.
>
> (Oliver 2000: 372)

The responses of those living in suburbs could be interpreted in a similar way. These communities turn into marginalized agglomerations in which the positive externalities of being a small municipality are neutralized by being neither a city nor a village and of not having that strong sentiment of being a unique community that pushes people to engage in the public sphere.

A relationship between size and political participation also emerges when we consider involvement in a political party as an indicator for political participation (Table 5.9): those respondents living in the villages are more dedicated to

Table 5.8 Interest in politics, by size of the place where the respondent lives

	Large city (%)	*Middle city (%)*	*Suburb (%)*	*Village (%)*
Not interested at all	10.4	7.5	4.4	9.7
Not very interested	28.8	25.6	48.5	12.9
Quite interested	37.9	42.5	29.4	45.2
Very interested	22.8	24.4	17.6	32.3
	100.0	100.0	100.0	100.0
	n = 680	*n* = 160	*n* = 68	*n* = 31

Table 5.9 Participation in a political party: different levels of involvement, by size of the place where the respondent lives

	Large city (%)	*Middle city (%)*	*Suburb (%)*	*Village (%)*
Not involved in a political party	62.1	55.8	71.8	46.9
Member	25.3	28.5	19.7	31.3
Member and activist	2.9	3.0	2.8	3.1
Member, activist and donor	1.9	3.0	1.4	3.1
Member, activist, donor and volunteer	4.0	4.8	1.4	15.6
Member, activist, donor, volunteer and with friends in the party	3.9	4.8	2.8	–
	100.0	100.0	100.0	100.0
	n = 700	*n* = 165	*n* = 71	*n* = 32

this type of political activity. This holds true regarding the most basic form of involvement in party politics, namely becoming a party member (31.3 percent). However, this also holds true regarding more comprehensive types of involvements such as actively support a party as a volunteer and/or as a donor. Again, the suburb we studied represents the type of municipality where citizens are least inclined to be active in political parties. Two-thirds of the respondents living in this type of municipality claim to be not involved at all in this kind of activity. Compared with this, less than half of those living in a village are not involved at all in party politics. The negative externalities of living in such a place also affect political participation in its most active forms.

The bivariate analysis presented in this first part of the chapter stresses the importance of contextual factors in shaping political behavior. We were able to demonstrate that the level of political participation differs with different models of direct democracy as well as different sizes of the community people live in. However, this bivariate analysis only provides a first and very simple sketch of a far more complex picture. Two main questions remain open to further inquiry: first, political behavior is not only determined by institutional or external factors, but also by individual characteristics. Any comprehensive analysis of political behavior has to take this factor into account; second, any comprehensive explanatory model of political participation has to determine the relative weight of each of these factors. The following multivariate analysis aims to provide at least some preliminary answers to these two areas of concern.

Models of direct democracy and political participation in context

Several researchers stressed that there is no single motive to explain entirely why a person decides to engage in specific political or civic activities. As humans are complex entities living in sophisticated social environments, it is plausible to assume that political behavior is affected by a combination of factors.

Starting with general interest in politics as an indicator, we see in Table 5.10 that several personal characteristics positively influence respective individual attitudes. First, those who have a higher level of education and dispose of a certain income, usually the elders, are more interested in politics than others. But this does not tell the whole story. What also seems to be important is the person's endowment in terms of social trust and openness to the rest of society: those more trustworthy as well as those who are attached to their municipality and to the world are capable of a stronger interest in politics than those lacking these qualities. Trust towards others is important not only in explaining civic engagement or voluntarism in the public sphere, but it seems to be a crucial prerequisite for political mobilization too. From our results we can assume that it is the trust in others and the attachment to ones community, both the local and the global one, that provide people with an incentive to expand their interest in what is going on in the political realm.

Table 5.10 The effects of individual resources and contextual opportunities on general interest in politics[a]

	General interest in politics	
	Beta	*Sig.*
Gender	−0.03	0.340
Age	0.10	0.009
Education	**0.17**	**0.000**
Income	0.12	0.001
Social trust	**0.11**	**0.002**
Left–right self-placement	−0.10	0.011
Community size	−0.03	0.330
Canton	**−0.11**	**0.001**
Attachment to the community	0.10	0.019
Attachment to canton	−0.02	0.626
Attachment to Switzerland	−0.06	0.196
Attachment to the entire world	0.10	0.006
Adjusted R^2	0.14	
n	707	

Notes
a The figures represent standardized (Beta) coefficients using linear regression models.
Gender: male (1), female (2).
Age: years.
Education: 14-point scale based on respondent's highest level of education from no education at all (0) to university (14).
Income: 15-point scale based on respondent's monthly income from 0–500 (1) Swiss francs to 15.000 or more (15).
Social trust: "Generally speaking, would you say that most people can be trusted (10), or that you can't be too careful in dealing with people (0)?."
Left–right self-placement: ten-point scale (0) Left, (10) Right.
Canton: Berne (1), Vaud (2).
Community size: four-point scale based on respondent community, from village (1) to big city (4).
Attachment to community: ten-point scale.
Attachment to the canton: ten-point scale.
Attachment to Switzerland: ten-point scale.
Attachment to the entire world: ten-point scale.
General interest in politics: four-point scale, not interested at all (1), not very interested (2), quite interested (3), very interested (4).

However, as it has been pointed out by Newton and Norris (2000), political variables have to be taken into account as a factor explaining political participation: and Switzerland is no exception in this sense. The respondent's self-placement on the left–right scale appears to be an important indicator of someone's political consciousness and the data show that the more the interviewee placed himself or herself on the left, the more his/her interest in politics grew.

Table 5.10 also shows the importance of the institutional context: indeed, the variable concerning the canton is statistically significant and meaningful. The more participatory structure of the canton of Berne results to be a condition encouraging political interest, as anticipated by the bivariate analysis. On the contrary, city size appears as a non-relevant dimension, and even controlling for other characteristics the meaning of this contextual measurement still remains statistically non-significant.

We can now move on in our attempt to understand the multiple roots of political participation by taking another indicator into account: the involvement in political parties. Table 5.11 presents the results of a linear regression similar to that we have already performed above. However, this time the table also contains new predictors. It includes a variable that measures general interest in politics itself as well as a variable that measures the respondent's confidence in certain political institutions. We altered the model for two reasons: first, because we assume that the people who are most interested in politics will tend to be more involved in political parties than those who are less interested, and second,

Table 5.11 The effects of individual resources and contextual opportunities on involvement in political parties[a]

	Involvement in political parties	
	Beta	*Sig.*
Gender	0.04	0.289
Age	0.02	0.552
Education	0.05	0.126
Income	0.02	0.639
Social trust	−0.04	0.300
Left–right self-placement	**−0.08**	**0.028**
Community size	−0.06	0.056
Canton	−0.01	0.884
Trust in the cabinet	−0.04	0.574
Trust in the national parliament	−0.17	0.023
Trust in the municipal board	0.11	0.032
Trust in political parties	**0.18**	**0.000**
Attachment to community	0.07	0.104
Attachment to canton	−0.10	0.033
Attachment to Switzerland	0.06	0.222
Attachment to the entire world	−0.03	0.402
General interest in politics	**0.39**	**0.000**
Adjusted R^2	0.24	
n	688	

Notes

a The figures represent standardized (Beta) coefficients using linear regression models. For a descriptive of predictors see previous table.

Trust in the cabinet: "How much do you trust the Cabinet ?" (0) No trust at all, (10) Very high trust.

Trust in the national parliament: "How much do you trust the National Parliament?" (0) No trust at all, (10) Very high trust.

Trust in the municipal board: "How much do you trust the Municipal Board ?" (0) No trust at all, (10) Very high trust.

Trust in political parties: "How much do you trust Political Parties ?" (0) No trust at all, (10) Very high trust.

Involvement in political parties: whether respondent was a member, an activist, a donor, a volunteer, had friends in or nothing in common with a political party. Scale ranged from 0 to 6.

because confidence in political institutions, especially in political parties, might turn out to be important to convince a person that it is worthy to engage himself into politics. The coefficients of the table tell that these assumptions were correct: general interest in politics emerges from the analysis as the strongest predictor and trust in political parties appears as well as a good explanatory variable. Other forms of public confidence are also relevant; for instance, trust in municipal boards is positively correlated with this form of political engagement.

In order to explore the Swiss case further, we included other forms of political participation into our analysis such as involvement in direct democracy, participation in non-conventional but legal action and, finally, participation in non-conventional and illegal action. The first column of Table 5.12 illustrates the results of the multivariate analysis.

Three factors appear to be crucial in shaping the use of direct democracy: the self-placement position on the left–right scale, which scores as the most relevant factor together with the respondent's general interest in politics, both followed by the degree of involvement in political parties. Those who report themselves furthest to the left, those whose general interest in politics is more developed and those who are already engaged in politics through a political party are the ones who are more likely to get involved in direct democracy. Moreover, as it could have been guessed, direct democracy experience is negatively correlated with trust in governmental institutions, at either local or national level (however, statistical significance for these last predictors is weak).

People tend to exercise their right to direct decision-making as long as they don't trust the traditional (i.e. representative) way of taking political decisions. The role of social and economic factors, as well as the role of the institutional framework is resumed, as we have seen from Table 5.10, by the strength of the predictor "general interest in politics" which depends on individual education and income but also on the respondent's canton of residence. Summarizing these findings, we can argue that direct democracy involvement will increase with the educational level of the person as well as with his/her income. In the same way, we may assume that people living in the canton of Berne, thanks to its participatory model of democracy, will be more open to direct democracy use. These characteristics will foster the creation of an attitude of interest and trust towards the social environment that will translate into a high interest in politics and into a greater disposition towards engagement in political parties.

Participation in non-conventional but legal political action is also positively correlated to the respondent's self-placement on the left–right scale (with those on the furthest left more open to non-conventional political engagement), general interest in politics and involvement in political parties. This last result is particularly interesting: in fact, from a theoretical perspective one might have expected a different result, with those less involved with parties as the more willing to participate on a non-conventional basis. But our results contradict this assumption. It seems plausible further to argue that if a person becomes interested in politics, he/she will tend to participate using the full range of participative tools, since any form of involvement does not exclude the possibility of

Table 5.12 The effects of individual resources and contextual opportunities on political participation[a]

Predictors	*Direct democracy*		*Non-conventional pol. action (legal)*		*Non conventional pol. action (illegal)*	
	Beta	*Sig.*	*Beta*	*Sig.*	*Beta*	*Sig.*
Gender	0.07	0.040	0.01	0.915	−0.08	0.027
Age	0.04	0.235	−0.03	0.448	−0.11	0.005
Education	0.05	0.147	−0.01	0.870	−0.04	0.287
Income	−0.07	0.052	0.03	0.444	−0.07	0.069
Social trust	0.01	0.951	−0.05	0.206	−0.04	0.300
Left–right self-placement	**−0.24**	**0.000**	**−0.29**	**0.000**	**−0.11**	**0.005**
Size of community	−0.03	0.332	−0.01	0.765	−0.04	0.251
Canton	0.04	0.255	−0.02	0.501	0.05	0.197
Trust in the cabinet	−0.13	0.055	−0.02	0.776	−0.18	0.006
Trust in the parliament	0.15	0.067	−0.03	0.741	−0.02	0.844
Trust in the municipal board	−0.13	0.020	−0.03	0.560	0.09	0.111
Trust in political parties	−0.01	0.768	−0.09	0.056	0.01	0.862
Attachment to community	0.05	0.261	0.06	0.185	0.04	0.395
Attachment to canton	−0.01	0.816	−0.03	0.507	−0.06	0.208
Attachment to Switzerland	0.05	0.271	0.01	0.865	−0.17	0.001
Attachment to the entire world	0.03	0.475	0.07	0.047	0.17	0.000
General interest in politics	**0.24**	**0.000**	**0.25**	**0.000**	**0.17**	**0.000**
Involvement in political parties	**0.13**	**0.001**	**0.12**	**0.001**	**0.06**	**0.110**
Adjusted R^2	0.20		0.24		0.19	
n	688		688		674	

Notes

a The figures represent standardized (Beta) coefficients using linear regression models. For a descriptive of predictors see previous table.

Direct democracy: whether respondent experienced in the last 12 months any of a range of 3 activities linked to direct democracy such as signing an initiative or a referendum, signing a petition, collecting signatures. Scale ranged from 0 to 3.

Non-conventional but legal political actions: whether respondent experienced any of a range of 3 activities such as demonstration, strike or boycott in the last 12 months. Scale ranged from 0 to 3.

Non-conventional and illegal political actions: whether respondent experienced any political illegal action in the last 12 months.

participating through another one: direct democracy participation does not exclude the possibility of also being active in a political party; on the contrary, the latter will foster the former type of participation, and involvement in political parties does not exclude in turn the option of being active through boycott.

Participation in illegal political actions is the last type of activity we wish to examine. The third column of Table 5.12 suggests that beside those predictors that have been important in the previous categories, and that remain to be important here (such as the self-placement on the left–right scale and the general interest in politics), other factors shape people's attitudes regarding the possibility to behave in a non-legal way. Distrust in the national government and the attachment to the world community (antithetically to the attachment to the country which is negatively correlated to this form of participation) are most important here. These last predictors are of some interest because they fit well in the situation we can imagine when we think of illegal political action: usually these acts of dissent are carried out by social movements or by civil society organizations or groups whose main goal is to protest against (or to fight against, depending on the intensity of the act itself) a decision or attitude of a governmental actor. This governmental actor can be a local actor but also a global one (for example, the new global movement, mobilized on global issues and against supranational governmental bodies), and very often claims are made in the name of collectivities or individuals based far from the country where the events take place, which might explain the negative correlation between this form of participation and attachment to Switzerland.

Concluding remarks

This analysis demonstrates the important role of individual resources and contextual opportunities in shaping citizens' political behavior in Switzerland. The stock of factors triggering a person to become interested in politics is wide-ranging. The social and economic background of the respondents is significant, as is their attitude towards the environment in which they are located, expressed by their trust in others and by their degree of attachment to the community they live in. This interplays with their self-placement on the left–right scale. Political participation strongly depends on the interest a person has in politics and on his/her confidence in political institutions. The higher the interest, the more the person will be convinced of the importance of getting involved in a political party, of using instruments of direct democracy, of engaging in non-conventional but legal actions and even in illegal ones. On the contrary, the relation between political trust and political involvement is not always positive: the higher the trust in political parties the more people will be willing to participate in a party's activities. However, the lower the trust in representative institutions such as the cabinet or the municipal board, the higher the possibility for a person to engage in direct democracy or in non-conventional, legal and illegal political actions. But political interest and political trust are not the only factors to explain political involvement. What matters is also the type of community where people live and the type of democratic system.

Regarding the type of community, the results are in line with the findings in the literature on this topic. The bivariate analysis shows differences in patterns of participation between persons living in a large city or in a village (with the smaller communities as the ones where interviewees tend to participate more) and the multivariate analysis presents insignificant results about it. Perhaps the size counts, but what counts more is the socio-economic composition of the community, that is, size alone does not tell a lot about citizens' participation, it has to be accompanied by the consideration of social and economic variables.

As pointed out by recent studies on civic and political engagement in the US (Oliver 1999, 2000), the positive externalities that a small community could produce with respect to citizens' involvement can be easily neutralized if the small community is in reality a sort of ghetto with a population which is economically and socially very homogeneous. This is supported by our analysis, which demonstrates that those respondents who live in a suburban environment are least involved in politics.

Regarding the type of direct democracy, the participatory model appears to be more successful than the more restrictive model in fostering citizens' engagement in the political sphere. Indeed, the participatory system provides a stimulus to citizens to participate actively in the public life and this, in turn, stimulates peoples' interest in politics. Participatory democracy also means a politically more conscious citizenry: an easier access to participatory instruments as well as the frequency in which they are called to express themselves in the public sphere together with stronger political interest makes people living in participatory societies aware of the important role they have to play to make democracy work.

In sum, the adoption of a contextual approach, including both individual and environmental aspects, revealed itself as a useful strategy in the understanding of some of the mechanisms underlying political participation.

Notes

1 This chapter illustrates a small portion of extensive research concerning civic engagement and political participation in Switzerland. The study belongs to the CID project and it has been funded by the Swiss National Fund for Scientific Research (grant n. 1214–057261.99) and supported by the European Science Foundation. I am grateful to Hans-Peter Kriesi, who has directed my research, for his constant support and for his thoughtful supervision. I would like to thank also the participants of the ECPR workshop "Bringing citizens back in: participatory democracy and political participation," Edinburgh, 28 March–2 April 2003 for their comments on a previous version of this paper. Of course, responsibility for what is written is mine.

2 I refer here to the situation in the canton Schaffouse where voting is compulsory and those not fulfilling their duty are fined.

3 The survey belongs to the CID (Citizenship, Involvement and Democracy) project and the same questionnaire is used to interview activists in the whole network of countries involved in the project. The first part of the research was dedicated to studying associational landscapes in several local communities. The data on activists whose political participation I present here derive from the associations found in that previous phase.

References

Baglioni, S. (2004) *Société civile et capital social en Suisse*, Paris: L'Harmattan.
Birnbaum, P. (1993) "Mouvements Sociaux et types d'Etats: Vers une approche comparative," in F. Chazel (ed.) *Action collective et mouvements sociaux*, Paris: PUF, pp. 163–175.
Dahl, R. and Tufte, E.R. (1973) *Size and Democracy*, Stanford, CA: Stanford University Press.
Gamm, G. and Putnam, R.D. (1999) "The Growth of Voluntary Associations in America 1840–1940," *Journal of Interdisciplinary History*, 29: 511–557.
Gamson, W. and Meyer, D. (1996) "The Framing of Political Opportunity," in D. McAdam, J. McCarthy and N.Z. Mayer (eds) *Opportunities, Mobilizing Structures and Framing: Comparative Applications of Contemporary Movement Theory*, Cambridge: Cambridge University Press, pp. 275–290.
Hadenius, A. (2001) *Institutions and Democratic Citizenship*, Oxford: Oxford University Press.
Kitschelt, H. (1986) "Political Opportunity Structures and Political Protest: Anti-Nuclear Movements in Four Democracies," *British Journal of Political Science*, 16: 57–85.
Kriesi, H. (1996) "The Organizational Structure of New Social Movements in Relation to Their Political Context," in D. McAdam, J. McCarthy and N.Z. Mayer (eds) *Opportunities, Mobilizing Structures and Framing: Comparative Applications of Contemporary Movement Theory*, Cambridge: Cambridge University Press, pp. 158–184.
—— (1995) *Le système politique suisse*, Paris: Economica.
Kriesi, H. and Wisler, D. (1996) "Social Movements and Direct Democracy in Switzerland," *European Journal of Political Research*, 30: 19–40.
Linder, W. (1998) *Swiss Democracy. Possible Solutions to Conflict in Multicultural Societies*, London: Macmillan.
Newton, K. and Norris, P. (2000) "Confidence in Public Institutions: Faith, Culture or Performance?," in S.J. Pharr and R.D. Putnam (eds) *Disaffected Democracies. What's Troubling the Trilateral Countries?*, Princeton, NJ: Princeton University Press, pp. 52–73.
Oliver, E.J. (2000) "City Size and Civic Involvement in Metropolitan America," *American Political Science Review*, 94: 361–393.
—— (1999) "The Effects of Metropolitan Economic Segregation on Local Civic Involvement," *American Journal of Political Science*, 43: 186–212.
Pateman, C. (1970) *Participation and Democratic Theory*, Cambridge: Cambridge University Press.
Schofer, E. and Fourcade-Gourinchas, M. (2001) "The Structural Contexts of Civic Engagement: Voluntary Association Membership in Comparative Perspective," *American Sociological Review*, 66: 806–828.
Skocpol, Th. and Fiorina, M. (eds) (1999) *Civic Engagement in American Democracy*, Washington, DC: Brookings Institution Press.
Skocpol, Th., Ganz, M. and Munson, Z. (2000) "A Nation of Organizers: The Institutional Origins of Civic Voluntarism in the United States," *American Political Science Review*, 94: 527–546.
Wernli, B. (1998) *Contraintes institutionnelles, influences contextuelles et participation aux élections fédérales en Suisse*, Thèse de Doctorat, Département de Science Politique, Université de Genève.

6 Direct democracy and political participation from a cross-national perspective

Silvano Moeckli

Introduction

In recent decades, there has been a worldwide increase in the number of referendums (LeDuc 2003: 21). However, it would be premature to envisage this development as a move towards a more participatory democracy or as an increase in the quality of democracy in general. In most states where referendums were submitted to a vote on a national level, they were initiated by the political majority on issues and at a time politically opportune for that majority. The referendum thus served as a plebiscite (Moeckli 2003).

It is important to distinguish between two main types of procedures involving direct democracy: *direct democracy by plebiscite* and *direct democracy by minority action.*[1] Strictly speaking, direct democracy refers only to the latter situation, where a minority of qualified voters or members of parliament can bring an issue before the electorate against the will of the political majority. This is what I call *minority direct democracy*. A further precondition is that putting an issue to referendum does not face excessively high hurdles. Only with low hurdles can direct democracy evolve into a routine procedure; where barriers are high, direct democracy remains an exceptional recourse. If a political majority holds a referendum on an issue that it could decide on its own, this constitutes a plebiscitary direct democracy.

On the basis of the strict standard stated above, only a few political systems worldwide qualify as minority direct democracies. Only Switzerland, Liechtenstein and about half the member states of the United States occupy the highest rung of this ladder, while Italy, Denmark and a few new democracies in Central and Eastern Europe qualify for the next-highest rung.[2]

If we examine the level of political participation in minority direct democracies, it becomes immediately apparent that participation is lowest where the opportunities for participation are greatest – in Switzerland and in the member states of the US. Do we have to conclude due to this observation that direct democracy is not conducive to greater participation, but, on the contrary, encourages abstention from political engagement? My argument is that this would be an oversimplified view of the matter. It is the contention of this analysis that, on balance, direct democracy has had a positive impact on the electorate's involvement in political decisions and on the political system's responsiveness to the electorate. Voter turnout for specific referendums does not accurately gauge this impact. With respect to Switzerland and the US in particular, we must also keep in mind how frequently voters are asked to cast a ballot and how many issues are decided at the ballot box at all governmental levels. Furthermore we must take into account the anticipatory effects of direct democracy institutions as well as their side effects within the entire political decision-making process.

Structure and methodology

This analysis is structured in the following way: I will start out with hypotheses regarding the relationship between the form of government and political participation. I will then test these hypotheses in light of global data on voter participation. In a next step I will study in detail participation in referendums and elections in states with minority direct democracy and with plebiscitary direct democracy. I will also enter into a short discussion on the relationship between authoritarian political systems and political participation.

An interim finding is that more opportunities for participation do not lead to greater actual participation in the stage of decision-making. This finding calls for an explanation. I will elucidate the effects of minority direct democracy with the help of a model of the political decision-making process. I will investigate how the design of direct democracy affects political participation in the various stages of the political decision-making process (functions of direct democracy). I will also shed some light on the longer-range ramifications of direct democracy on the structure of the political system and demonstrate that the lower level of participation characterizing minority direct democracy at the decision-making stage is counterbalanced by a greater involvement of the electorate in the total decision-making process and by the political decision-makers' greater responsiveness to the electorate. Another signpost of greater voter involvement is the frequency with which voters are called to the ballot box and asked to decide specific issues at all governmental levels.

My approach will be empirical as well as theoretical. The only explanatory variable that is easily quantifiable is voter participation. It is easily demonstrated – from an examination of specific votes cast at the national level – that direct democracy does not lead to a higher participation in referendums and elections. In fact, the opposite is true. In the context of this study, on the other hand, we can give only theoretical support to the contention that, on balance, electoral participation and responsiveness to voter preferences are higher under minority direct democracy.

Participation in referendums and elections in a comparative perspective

Hypotheses

Under ideal-typical conditions we would expect that an increase in participation opportunities would induce a concomitant rise in electoral participation and that this participation would remain at a consistently high level as long as these opportunities remain available to citizens. We would anticipate that where the rights of direct democracy are added to the right to vote for officeholders, voter participation would be enhanced. Conversely, we would expect a somewhat lower participation in authoritarian systems, inasmuch as the results of (unfree) elections and referendums hardly impinge on the position and decisions of the ruling class. In Table 6.1 we use arrows to formulate these expectations as hypotheses and to demonstrate the results of testing these hypotheses with empirical data.

The conclusion of Table 6.1 is that empirical evidence does not confirm the hypotheses stated in it. Participation is not linked to the quality of democracy in free states. In free states and in states with minority direct democracy, voter participation declined in the last decades, while it rose in partially free and in unfree states.

According to data from the International Institute for Democracy and Electoral Assistance (IDEA),[3] voter participation – as defined by the ratio between voters and registered voters – remained within the 75 to 80 percent range

Table 6.1 Regime type and electoral participation: hypotheses and empirical findings

	Hypotheses		*Empirical findings*[a]
	Electoral participation (cross-section)	*Trend (longitudinal section)*	
All states	↑	→	↑[b]/↓[c]
Free states	→	→/↑	↓[d]/↑[e]
Partly free states	→	→/↑	↑[d]
Not free states	↓	↓	↑
States with minority direct democracy	↑	→/↑	↓

Notes

a See databank by the International Institute for Democracy and Electoral Assistance (IDEA). Here electoral participation is defined as the ratio of voters to the "voting age population," that is, the resident foreign population is included. In my data I use "persons eligible to vote" as a standard, unless otherwise specified.

b Until 1989.

c After 1989.

d 1970–1997.

e Under exceptional circumstances.

between 1945 and 1980 worldwide. Since then, voter participation has gradually declined to barely 70 percent.

Between 1945 and 1970, voter participation in 36 established democracies stayed consistently above 80 percent, but since that time it has declined to 72 percent. In all other states, participation prior to 1979 was barely above 70 percent but climbed to 80 percent by 1989. It has subsequently declined again to 70 percent. It can be generally stated that voter participation has declined since 1990 worldwide. Two explanatory factors can be cited for this decline. The first is that voter participation in Central and Eastern European states declined after their democratization in 1989. The second factor is the increase in the number of "electoral democracies" from 41 percent in 1988 to 61 percent in 2003 (117 states as an absolute number), partially because developmental aid was made contingent on political democracy.[4] Paradoxically, participation in unfree states has gradually risen from 50 percent in the early 1970s to 65 percent at the end of the 1990s.[5]

Voter participation and ballots cast in nine states with direct democracy, 1970 to 2000

If one assumes that components of direct democracy enhance the quality of democracy by providing additional means to participate, one might be inclined to argue that participation would increase under direct democracy. This assumption will be put to a test in a comparative analysis which covers nine states. I will first examine variations in terms of the percentage of ballots cast over a period of 30 years, the number of times voters went to the polls and the number of referendums submitted. In a second step, these data will be analyzed in terms of voter participation.

California is included in this comparison, even though it does not constitute a sovereign state. However, with 22 million qualified voters, it is the largest political system in terms of population in which various instruments for direct democracy exist.

In the case of Switzerland and California, there seems to be a (negative) relationship between the number of times that votes are cast and voter participation (Table 6.2). It must be kept in mind that both political systems are federally organized, so that the national level is not the only one under consideration, and that voters go to the polls for additional elections and referendums at a lower governmental level. In the November 1988 general election, for instance, qualified voters in Berkeley (California) were asked to decide on 58 ballot items in all. Two years later, the number of items on the ballot had risen to 72 (Moeckli 1996a). In Switzerland, voters on average go to the polls five times a year and each time decide on a multitude of issues at the national, cantonal and community level. Additionally, in 85 percent of the 2,800 communities, annual participation in a citizens' assembly on a community level has to be added. The Swiss went to the polls on 264 occasions between 1848 and 2004, with 514 measures on the ballot. Since 1970, they have gone to the polls 103 times and have had to

Table 6.2 Number of times voters go to the polls (excluding elections for officeholders), number of referendums, and average voter participation from 1970 to 2000 on a national level (or on the state level in the case of California)[a]

State	*No. of times voters go to the polls*	*No. of referendums*	*Average voter participation (%)*
Switzerland	94	264	41.8
California[a]	35	444	43.9
France	4	4	44.1
Italy	13	54	63.8
Denmark	8	8	81.1
Ireland	14	19	51.4
Austria	2	2	73.3
Liechtenstein	33	43	70.0
Australia	6	19	94.3

Source: Moeckli (1994: 146), updated.

Note

a In California, referendums are always timed to coincide with elections. The level of participation in referendums is thus the same as the level of participation in elections.

decide on 295 measures (57 percent of the total since 1848). Direct democracy has increased markedly in intensity in the last few decades.[6]

Participation in the four French referendums varied strongly, depending on the issues at stake.[7] Average voter participation is remarkably high in Italy – considering that Italians went to the polls 54 times. However, it must be kept in mind here that an abrogative referendum can be approved only if at least 50 percent of qualified voters cast their ballots. This quorum was not attained in the voting on 21 May 2000 (29.4 percent).[8] Average participation was also high in the eight referendums in Denmark. Six of these referendums dealt with the issue of its relationship with the European Community, subsequently the European Union.[9] Ireland provides for an automatic referendum for constitutional changes; the fact that participation is only average indicates that it is viewed as a routine procedure. With only two referendums held in Austria between 1970 and 1990, the evidence is insufficient for any conclusions. The 1994 referendum on membership in the European Union resulted in a very high participation (82.4 percent). Liechtenstein is a special case, in that it has several direct democracy privileges, like Switzerland, but their scope is limited by ducal prerogatives. The duchy is divided into two political camps, and election campaigns are therefore often quite adversarial. In addition, voting is compulsory, although non-compliance is no longer subject to sanctions. High voter participation in constitutional referendums in Australia is explained by the fact that compulsory voting is enforced.

On specific occasions, very controversial initiatives may increase voter participation. This remains to be an exception in California – as in the case of Proposition 13 in 1978 – because the simultaneously held presidential and congressional elections usually guarantee a stable and relatively high level of participation. In Switzerland, voter participation was especially high in 1922 in the context of an initiative on a one-time capital levy (86.3 percent participation), in the 1974 initiative to limit admission of foreigners (70.3 percent), the 1989 initiative about eliminating the Swiss army (68.6 percent), and the 6 December 1992 referendum on the European Economic Area Agreement (78.3 percent).

Participation in elections and referendums in states with minority direct democracy and in states with plebiscitary direct democracy, 1970 to 2000

From an ideal-typical point of view, participation in elections and referendums should be higher in minority direct democracies than in states with a plebiscitary direct democracy. The facts do not support this assumption.

According to a country-rating by the Initiative and Referendum Institute Europe (IRI) (Kaufmann and Waters 2004), the European countries with the most extensive direct democracy tools are Switzerland, Liechtenstein, Italy, Slovenia, Lithuania, Ireland,[10] Denmark and Latvia. Table 6.3 includes only those states with a longer tradition of direct democracy. Political structures and procedures in states where minority instruments are of recent vintage have not yet been able to adapt sufficiently to them. It is therefore premature to evaluate them. This is particularly true of the new democracies in Central and Eastern Europe, which in some cases have introduced minority instruments (Slovenia, Slovakia, Lithuania, Latvia, Hungary). In all six states under consideration the average participation in parliamentary elections is higher than the participation in referendums. In Italy, Ireland and Liechtenstein, the difference amounts to 20 percent.

Table 6.3 Average participation in the election of officeholders and in referendums 1970–2000 on the national level (or on the state level in the case of California)

State	*Average electoral participation (%)*	*No. of ballot items*	*Average participation in balloting (%)*
Switzerland	48.2	264	41.8
California[a]	51.4	444	43.9
Italy	88.9	54	63.8
Denmark[b]	86.8	8	81.1
Ireland	72.3	19	51.4
Liechtenstein	91.7	43	70.0

Notes

a Electoral participation = years with presidential elections; participation in balloting = years without presidential elections.

b Denmark has a minority direct democracy tool in the form of a parliamentary legislative referendum. It takes only one-third of the parliament to request a referendum. Although this right has been invoked only four times, it probably had a considerable anticipatory effect on the decision process (Svensson 1996).

Table 6.4 Average participation in parliamentary elections and participation in referendums in states with plebiscitary direct democracy, 1970–2000

State	*Average electoral participation (%)*	*No of ballot items*	*Average participation in balloting (%)*
France	72.2	4	44.1
Finland	73.6	1	70.4
Norway	80.9	2	84.1
Sweden[a]	88.5	2	79.4
Austria[a]	88.7	2	73.3

Note

a Austria has a minority instrument consisting of a parliamentary referendum (one-third of the members of the Nationalrat or the Bundesrat) for partial revisions of the constitution, but it has never been invoked so far. The same is true of Sweden.

With the exception of Norway, participation in parliamentary elections is higher in all five states with plebiscitary direct democracy compared with participation in referendums (Table 6.4). The difference in participation is not as high as in states with minority direct democracy – with the exception of France. It must be noted, however, that in all the states under consideration there were very few referendums.

No clear picture emerges from a comparative analysis of participation in elections and participation in referendums in minority direct democracies and plebiscitary direct democracies. Participation tends to be higher when the number of occasions for going to the polls is less frequent, but Italy and Liechtenstein confirm that participation in referendums can be high even when polling is frequent. France on the other hand illustrates the fact that participation in referendums can be low even if voters do not go to the polls frequently, as long as the referendums are not on very controversial issues.

Comparative analysis of Switzerland and California

Switzerland stands alone in category 1 in the IRI's country-rating as "The Radical Democrats." No sovereign state in Europe or elsewhere in the world – with the exception of the mini-state of Liechtenstein – is comparable with Switzerland in the comprehensive and long-standing use of direct democracy tools as well as in the frequency of their application. However, several member states of the United States of America, which surpass Switzerland in population and territory, are level with Switzerland with respect to direct democracy (Cronin 1989; Glaser 1997). Although these states are admittedly only parts of a larger sovereign federal state, a comparison with the American states is more meaningful than a comparison with sovereign states whose direct democracy is far less developed quantitatively and qualitatively than Switzerland's. For this reason, I will compare Switzerland and California regarding participation in elections and referendums over time (Figure 6.1).

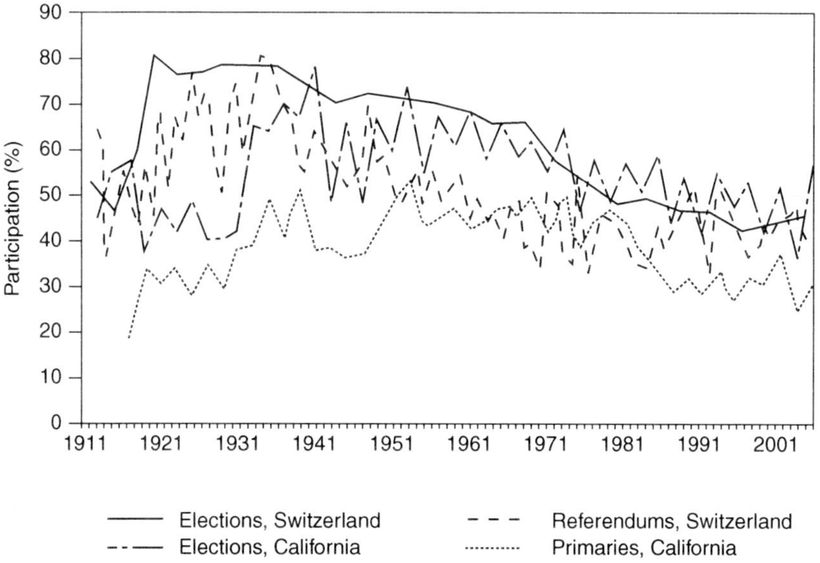

Figure 6.1 Participation in elections and in referendums in Switzerland and California, 1911–2004.

In Switzerland, there is a striking jump in the degree of electoral participation in 1919 at the time of the introduction of the proportional election system. Participation rose by 20 percent compared with 1917 and by as much as 34 percent compared with 1914. As a consequence, between 1919 and 1990, participation in elections was on average higher than participation in referendums. In the past ten years, the two are showing signs of convergence. There is an analogous trend when we go back in history, namely declining participation after the 1930s and stabilization at a 40 to 50 percent level since the 1980s. The reason participation in referendums fluctuated more sharply than participation in elections lies in the greater frequency with which citizens go to the polls to vote in referendums. There is less fluctuation in participation in referendums between 1950 and 1970 compared with other periods, but nevertheless the gradual decline reflected the trend of the preceding 20 years. There is a strong correlation of 0.72 between participation in elections and in referendums.

Turning to California, it is noticeable that there is lower participation in primary elections as well as in elections and referendums that do not coincide with presidential elections. There is a correlation of 0.6 between participation in main and primary elections. As is the case in Switzerland, there has been a downward trend in participation since the mid-twentieth century and stabilization at a lower level since the 1980s.

A comparative analysis of Switzerland and California indicates a sharp increase in electoral participation in the early part of the twentieth century. In

Switzerland this is due to the introduction of proportional voting. In both political systems, voting remained at a high level until the end of the 1930s. Since then we observe a downward trend and a process of convergence towards similar absolute levels of electoral participation. For this reason there is a strong correlation (0.67) between Swiss electoral participation and participation in the general elections in California.

A comparison between Switzerland and California regarding participation in referendums reveals startling similarities.[11] Until the end of the 1930s participation increased in both systems, with Switzerland at a higher level than California. The 1930s were a time when political conflict in both systems was intense. Between 1940 and 1970 we observe a gradual decline in both systems and a process of convergence towards about the same absolute level. Since 1970 participation has stabilized at a low level, with upward and downward spurts. The low-level participation after 1970 may also be related to the growing intensity of direct democracy, that is, the strong increase in the number of times when voters went to the polls.

Participation as an indicator for political pressure

According to Arend Lijphart, voter participation is an excellent indicator of democratic quality (Lijphart 1999; see also Vanhanen 1997: 36). His comparison between 36 states shows that electoral participation is 7.5 percent higher in consensus democracies than in majoritarian democracies.

Lijphart's argument clearly does not apply to elections and referendums in authoritarian systems. In these cases, high participation does not demonstrate the exercise of popular sovereignty and the control of the power of the state. This is because in authoritarian states citizens do not participate in voluntary and autonomous ways, free from state interference; what it does indicate is the pressure from above to participate and the fear of sanctions if one fails to do so. History gives all too many examples of plebiscites and elections controlled by the government, with nearly 100 percent participation or approval.[12]

Voter participation is also within established democracies a questionable indicator for the quality of democracy. Dahrendorf (1975: 77) voices his skepticism with the following statement: "Contrary to the naïve expectation that high political participation is a 'healthy' sign of consolidated and politically reliable (or even democratic) conditions, research shows that it is symptomatic of either political disturbances or of political coercion." As far as Switzerland is concerned, it has been said half-jokingly that participation in referendums either below 10 percent or above 90 percent is a sign of danger. If Switzerland had a 90 percent participation, that might well signal a political crisis.

Interim results

No unambiguous conclusions can be drawn from the data about participation in elections and in referendums in various states and over various periods of time.

It is not possible to divide up states into different categories regarding the level of participation, nor do simple categorizations offer any useful explanations. It would seem that participation in referendums cannot be explained by a few variables and simple causal connections. Moreover, participation in elections and referendums is insufficient by itself as an indicator of the electorate's engagement in the political decision-making process.

> International IDEA has always understood voter turnout to be just one dimension of political participation. It has emphasized that no linear relationship exists between voter turnout and democratic development. It is true that turnout is simply one indicator of political participation – which is indeed a very complex term – and not always the most suitable one.
>
> (Pintor and Gratschew 2002: 14)

A conclusion based on the available empirical data can be stated as follows: more direct democracy does not increase the level of participation; a more comprehensive system of direct democracy actually leads to a decline in participation, as demonstrated by the Californian and Swiss cases. A comparison between the American states provides additional support for this argument. In 34 states in the northern part of the US with and without voter initiatives, average voter participation was the same between 1960 and 1980: 63 percent in years with presidential elections and 46 percent in the off-years. This observation leads to the conclusion that "no evidence exists for the claim that initiatives will increase turnout over time" (Magleby 1984: 97f.).

In short, the data on participation alone cannot provide an adequate foundation for evaluating political participation and the effects of direct democracy. Rather than focus exclusively on the decision-making phase that takes place during elections and referendums, one must consider all aspects of political activity, all occasions for voting, all ballots cast, the entire decision-making process, as well as the effects of direct democracy on the structure of the political system. For this reason I shall refer to a model to elucidate the dynamic aspect of direct democracy.

Participation and responsiveness in the process of decision-making

Participation without minority direct democracy tools

In the following model (Figure 6.2), I make a distinction between five stages of the political decision-making process: input, throughput, output, outcome and feedback. What opportunities for participation exist in a purely representative democracy with the right to vote in elections only for citizens without affiliation to any political party? In terms of input, participation consists of determining the composition of the parliament at fixed intervals and, indirectly, the formation of the government. In some states, it might also be possible to vote directly for the

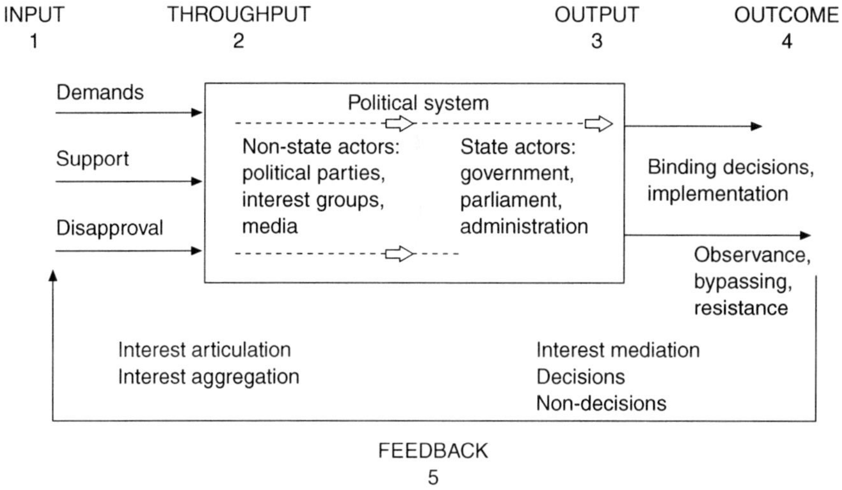

Figure 6.2 Model of the political process without direct democracy.

country's head of state. In federally organized states, there are additional elections at a lower governmental level. In the throughput stage, which is characterized by political debate about substantive questions, the ordinary citizen has no say. In stage 3 (the output phase), the political actors will be mindful of the views and attitudes of parts of the electorate – to win the next elections. Those parts of the electorate left out will be left disgruntled. In stage 4 (the outcome) political decisions will be met with different degrees of acceptance among the electorate. The feedback resulting from the effects of the political decisions in the social realm will be reflected in the election outcome and will thereby influence the input.

In cases where the electorate is convinced that the input provided by elections has a pronounced effect on the output and where elections are the only form of institutional participation, voluntary voter turnout will be high. It is involuntarily high when – in authoritarian systems – the electorate fears that lack of participation will lead to sanctions. However, there is no feedback between output and input, and in the process of implementing decisions, massive pressure is usually applied.

In cases where there are plebiscitary direct democracy institutions unconnected with elections it is possible for the electorate to make political decisions in stage 3 (either consultatively or decisively, depending on the constitutional provisions). Substantive debate does not enter into stage 1 (input) and is triggered by political actors only in stage 2. Nevertheless, if a plebiscite decision contradicts the stand taken by the political majority, the legitimacy of the political actors will be undermined.

Participation with minority direct democracy tools

How does the electorate's situation differ in a political system in which minority direct democracy tools are available at all governmental levels (Figure 6.3)? I distinguish between five functions and five dysfunctions that cannot be elucidated here in detail (Moeckli 2001). I shall limit myself to the effects on political participation. In stage 1 (input), qualified voters can inject their demands directly into the political system on several governmental levels. If direct initiatives exist,[13] as it is the case in California, citizens can even submit their concerns directly to the electorate as a ballot measure, circumventing non-governmental and political actors altogether.

In the case of referendums, qualified voters can decide on issues after parliament has taken action. Whenever parliament takes up proposals concerning the constitution or legislation, it must always consider whether these proposals would have the support of a majority of qualified voters. This has two consequences for political participation: first, parliamentary elections and hence participating in them becomes less important[14] because qualified voters can, if necessary, repudiate parliamentary decisions; second, political actors are under greater pressure to take minority demands into account, if they wish to increase the likelihood of sustaining their decision in a possible referendum. In the long run, this leads to a consensus-oriented decision-making process. If political decisions have a broad-based support, they will generate less intensive conflict, and this in turn will lead to lower participation. A further factor in this is the intensity of direct democracy. As a result of the frequency of consultations and

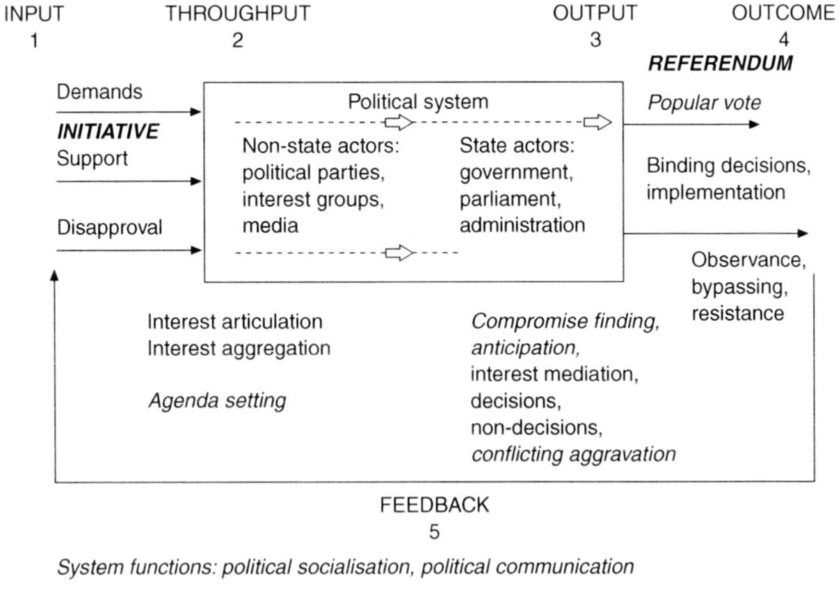

Figure 6.3 Model of the political process with minority direct democracy.

the larger number of items on the ballot, voters tend to make more selective use of their rights.

Alois Riklin and Roland Kley have investigated the burden imposed on qualified voters in the city of St. Gallen (Switzerland) compared with that of qualified voters in Strasbourg (France), Konstanz (Germany) and Bregenz (Austria) (Riklin and Kley 1981: 31). If all the votes cast in elections and referendums between 1956 and 1979 are added up, qualified voters cast their vote at the polls 38 times in Strasbourg, 32 times in Konstanz and 24 times in Bregenz during these 23 years. In St. Gallen, however, a qualified voter was expected to make 503 ballot decisions. Between 1945 and 1979, qualified voters were consulted 229 times in St. Gallen and called upon to cast their ballots in 711 elections and referendums. They thus had to go to the polls an average of 6.5 times a year. Since 1979, the number of decisions to be made in Switzerland at all governmental levels has become even greater. Riklin and Kley claim that there is an inverse relationship between the intensity of direct democracy and the level of participation: "When there is little direct democracy (few voting decisions to be made per year), voter turnout tends to be high, when direct democracy is intensive, voter turnout tends to be low" (Riklin and Kley 1981: 79f.).

Tools for minority direct democracy have functions in the decision-making process that go beyond the function of legitimizing governmental policies. They serve to educate and socialize the electorate, they stimulate political actors to look ahead not only to the next election but to the next referendum and they multiply the points of contact between the electorate and the elected officials.

There is no reason to assume that well-organized interest groups and the special interests they represent are the major beneficiaries of low average voter participation in Switzerland and in US states. Interest groups are eager to voice their concerns, but they are not particularly eager to increase the overall input into the political system. The major political interest groups are not among the most ardent proponents of direct democracy. The reason is that their core aims may well be endangered by intervention by opposition groups via direct democracy. The successful initiatives in California to raise tobacco taxes and to reduce insurance on motor vehicles are a case in point.

For small opposition groups, grassroot public interest groups and individual political actors, the initiative is an optimal tool to articulate their concerns to the public and the government. The Swiss experiences with direct democracy offer perfect examples in this respect: on 8 February 2004, an initiative to keep extremely dangerous criminals locked up won a surprising victory. Two affected women launched this initiative all on their own. Powerful interest groups usually have no need for direct democracy, as they can exert influence through many other channels. It is true that in Switzerland direct democracy encourages cooperative structures by giving an impetus to negotiated settlements. However, cooperative forms of organization arose not so much as a result of direct democracy as through mechanisms for coping with a war economy during both world wars. At the same time, direct democracy also serves as an instrument for oppositional groups to break down these cooperative structures.

Low overall voter participation and selective participation of large parts of the electorate do not necessarily strengthen the hand of a short-range interest-based policy. For one thing, the direct democracy process moves slowly, so that temporary political moods cannot be rapidly converted into election outcomes. In Switzerland, moreover, selective participants are those who can be mobilized to go to the polls over and above the regular voters which account for approximately 30 percent. Their behavior at the polls is far less predictable than that of regular voters who are likely to be well-informed and loyal to their party. On 16 May 2004, a tax package of the federal government with tax relief of 2.7 billion euros was rejected by a two-third majority because many selective participants were under the impression that this tax relief would benefit only a small minority and that the cantons would later have to pay the bill.

The effects of minority direct democracy mentioned above – consensus-oriented decisions along with lower levels of participation – have surfaced most clearly in Switzerland. Figure 6.4 highlights how direct democracy has forced all the elements in the political system to work together and the extent to which, over time, repudiation of parliamentary proposals has declined.

A high level of participation among all relevant political forces in the negotiation stage within the political system is incompatible with high electoral participation in the decision-making stage: you can't have it both ways. Interest groups that are able to voice their concerns within the framework of an inclusive political process have little incentive to mobilize their supporters for referendums. When the outcome of this process is furthermore almost a foregone conclusion, conflicts will be correspondingly low-key. Insofar as participation in the total decision-making process is most inclusive, it is likely to be lower in the decision stage. Under these conditions, low voter participation is not an indicator of low political participation; in fact the opposite is true.

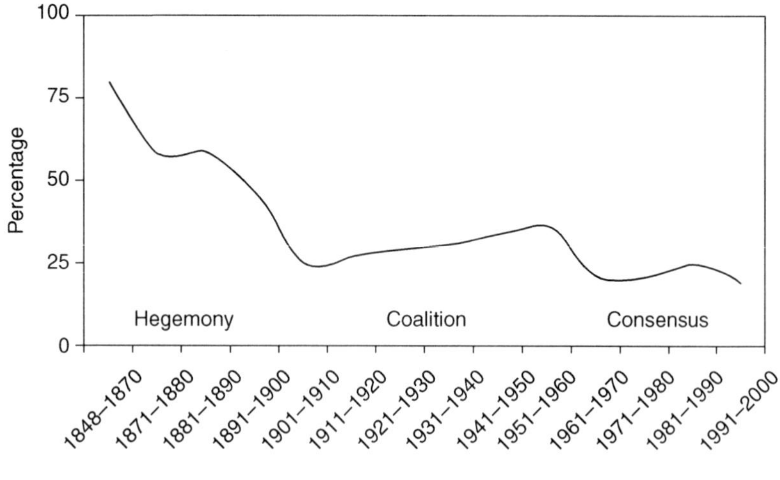

Figure 6.4 Repudiation of parliamentary proposals by Swiss voters, 1848–2000.

In California the political decision process is not characterized by the same consensual pattern as it is in Switzerland because of differences in institutional design and social prerequisites. Most important, the political party system in California is essentially a two-party system, while in Switzerland it is highly fragmented on the basis of linguistic and religious cleavages. The pressure to reach a consensus is high in California as well for various reasons: the government is elected directly by the people; it cannot be brought down by the legislature; constitutional changes enacted by the legislature require a two-third majority and direct democracy strengthens the awareness regarding minority demands. While direct democracy also represents a danger for these very minorities, constitutional review is a strong corrective to this danger.

In line with this model, lower participation in single referendums and elections – compared with elections in purely representative democracies – must be evaluated in light of the larger number of options for qualified voters in a minority direct democracy, the frequency of voting, the large numbers of ballot decisions, the greater responsiveness in the political sphere, and the tendency towards consensus-oriented decisions. A new American study concludes that in US states with direct democracy, politicians respond more rapidly to changes in public opinion and do so, in fact, in anticipation of potential interventions via direct democracy (Matsusaka 2004).

Conclusion

International and longitudinal comparisons show that the relationships between political regimes and political participation are anything but clear-cut. The degree of political participation is influenced not only by the design of political institution but by distinct politico-cultural variables. Even in Switzerland political participation differs in different parts of the country and in different cantons. In plebiscitary direct democracies, participation in elections and referendums is higher than in minority direct democracies. However, one cannot conclude anything about the quality of democracies on the basis of the level of participation.[15]

It is easy enough to prove empirically that (greater) direct democracy does not lead to greater electoral participation. On the contrary: when coupled with frequent elections and ballot decisions, minority direct democracy turns into a routine procedure and encourages a tendency toward lower voter turnout. Only in isolated cases does minority direct democracy increase institutional political participation when prior attempts at reaching a compromise solution about controversial issues have failed.

The model sketched above makes a theoretical argument that supports a positive relationship between direct democracy and participation. It argues that under direct democracy the participation of qualified voters in the decision-making process is improved as a whole, both in terms of participation and in terms of consultation, and that the responsiveness of decision makers is greater than in a purely representative democracy. It is no accident that neither the US nor Switzerland has any direct financing for political parties, that pay for Swiss members of parliament is moderate by international standards, and that many US states have rigorous disclosure rules. Direct democracy makes it very difficult for politicians to dip cavalierly into public funds. Men and women who go to the polls are more inclined to be guided by the common good than are professional politicians. This is not because they are intrinsically more high-minded but quite simply because they have less at stake, and therefore their actions are less costly to them (von Arnim 2001: 373f.).

Minority direct democracy broadens the input stream into the political system and during the preparatory phase of the decision-making process exerts pressure to reach a broad consensus and to involve a large number of actors. As a result, conflict is less intense in the decision-making phase, and this lesser degree of intensity in turn reduces participation in elections and referendums. The pressure toward consensus is increased on the output side by the veto possibilities offered to minorities. Minority direct democracy increases political participation in scope, plebiscitary direct democracy increases it at any given point in time.

Direct democracy can revitalize political activity in two ways: it provides political actors outside the established political institutions with new tools for participation and it compels political elites to be more attentive to voter preferences; political elites can no longer limit themselves to worrying about winning the next elections but must envisage winning a possible referendum. The decision makers must show much more concern for their "base," thereby increasing participation outside the institutional channels of elections and referendums.

Notes

1 See the elaboration of these concepts in S. Moeckli (1996b: pp. 10, 16).
2 See categorization in Initiative & Referendum Institute Europe (2004: 36).
3 International Institute for Democracy and Electoral Assistance (IDEA), Voter Turnout: A Global Survey, www.idea.int/vt/index.cfm (accessed 10 January 2006).
4 Freedomhouse, Freedom in the World 2004, www.freedomhouse.org (accessed 10 January 2006). However, in the 2004 report only 88 states were categorized as "free," which means that 29 states with free and fair elections were designated as only part-free. In 1988, 69 states were electoral democracies, but only 58 states were designated as "free." The number of "part-free" electoral democracies thus increased by 18 in the period between 1988 and 2003. According to Freedomhouse, both free and part-free states are included among the "electoral democracies." Diamond (1997: 7f.), on the other hand, defines "formal" or "electoral" democracies as political systems in which the most important legislative and executive offices are filled by means of regular, competitive elections. However, there remain military or political "power reserves" on which election results exert no influence; there is hardly any horizontal division of power among officeholders; the power of the executive is only partially limited by the rule of law; basic rights and minority rights are not consistently guaranteed; there is access to the media, but no pluralistic media system.
5 Participation is defined here as the ratio of voters to the population of voting age.
6 The increase in the number of referendums on the national level in the last decades is largely attributable to the increase in ballot measures in Switzerland.
7 In the referendum of 24 September 2000 on abbreviating the national president's term of office, participation was 30.2 percent, but in the 23 April 1972 referendum on the

expansion of the European Communities, it was 60.7 percent. In two referendums where there was broad political consensus on the issues, participation was below 40 percent.

8 Anyone who wants no change in the status quo can urge his supporters to stay home. In the referendum of 7 October 2001 and of 16 June 2003, the requisite participation quorum was not attained either.

9 In 41 referendums about "Europe" in Europe between 1972 and 2003 participation was 67 percent. See Initiative & Referendum Institute Europe, *Initiative & Referendum Monitor 2004/2005*.

10 Ireland has no minority instruments, but it is included in our analysis because of its compulsory constitutional referendum, which has no participation and approval quorum.

11 In California, referendums are always timed to coincide with elections. The level of participation in referendums is thus the same as the level of participation in elections.

12 For the 29 November 1987 referendum in Poland, participation was 67.3 percent. In 1984 participation in elections to the National Council and to the Sejm still had the customary participation of 99 percent. This change implies that by 1987 Poles had lost their fear of abstaining from an election or referendum because of greater political openness. In the 15 October 2002 referendum, Iraq's head of state Saddam Hussein got himself re-elected for an additional seven-year term. The next morning, news had already spread that, according to official figures, he had gathered all 11,445,638 votes, or 100 percent of the votes.

13 In Switzerland there exists only an indirect initiative, which is initially addressed to the parliament, which then takes a stand on it. The parliament may work out a counterproposal which it submits to the electorate along with the initiative.

14 Parliamentary elections are also less important when a president is directly elected by the people. Thus in the US in "off years" (without simultaneous presidential elections) participation in congressional elections is about one-third lower than in years with presidential elections. Elections to the European Parliament also have a lower turnout than national parliamentary elections.

15 "Other dimensions of political participation are less amenable to quantification, therefore presenting substantial difficulties for cross-national or regional comparisons. Whether voter turnout in countries or regions is high or low, whether there are changes in one direction or another, whether these differ by country or by region or by old and new democracies is interesting data per se, but it does not reveal much about the state of democracy in the countries that are being compared. In other words, one can hardly extrapolate from higher or lower electoral participation to other characteristics of these democracies. In synchronic comparisons of countries, the limitations are immediately evident when consolidated democracies with relatively low voter turnout are compared to new democracies with relatively high voter turnout. Historical data of voter turnout for one country or region over time is a more meaningful basis for drawing conclusions or comparisons" (Pintor and Gratschew 2002: 14f.).

References

Cronin, Th.E. (1989) *Direct Democracy. The Politics of Initiative, Referendum, and Recall*, Cambridge, MA: Harvard University Press.

Dahrendorf, R. (1975) "Aktive und passive Öffentlichkeit," in F. Grube and G. Richter (eds) *Demokratietheorien*, Hamburg: Hoffmann und Campe, pp. 76–80.

Diamond, L.J. (1997) *Consolidating the Third Wave Democracies*, Baltimore, MD: Johns Hopkins University Press.

Glaser, U. (1997) *Direkte Demokratie als politisches Routineverfahren. Volksabstimmungen in den USA und in Kalifornien*, Erlangen: Palm & Enke.

Initiative & Referendum Institute Europe (IRI) (2004), *Initiative & Referendum Monitor 2004/2005*, Amsterdam.

Kaufmann, B. and Waters, D.M. (2004) *Direct Democracy in Europe. A Comprehensive Reference Guide to the Initiative and Referendum Process in Europe*, Durham, NC: Carolina Academic Press.

LeDuc, L. (2003) *The Politics of Direct Democracy. Referendums in Global Perspective*, Peterborough: Broadview Press.

Lijphart, A. (1999) *Patterns of Democracy. Government Forms and Performance in Thirty-six countries*, New Haven, CT: Yale University Press.

Magleby, D.B. (1984) *Direct Legislation. Voting on Ballot Propositions in the United States*, Baltimore, MD: Johns Hopkins University Press.

Matsusaka, J.G. (2004) *For the Many or the Few. The Initiative, Public Policy, and American Democracy*, Chicago, IL: University of Chicago Press.

Moeckli, S. (2003) "Sachabstimmungen machen noch keine direkte Demokratie," in K. Schmitt (ed.) *Herausforderungen der repräsentativen Demokratie*, Baden-Baden: Nomos Verlagsgesellschaft, pp. 101–119.

—— (2001) "Grösse und Beschaffenheit politischer Einheiten als Voraussetzung für die Funktionsfähigkeit der direkten Demokratie – Funktionen und Dysfunktionen," in Thüringer Landtag (ed.) *Demokratie lebendig gestalten. Ettersburger Gespräche*, Erfurt, pp. 57–78.

—— (1996a) "Direkte Demokratie in den USA," in P. Häberle (ed.) *Jahrbuch des Öffentlichen Rechts der Gegenwart, Neue Folge*, Tübingen: J.C.B. Mohr & Paul Siebeck, pp. 565–581.

—— (1996b) *Instruments of Direct Democracy in the Member States of the Council of Europe*, Strasbourg: Council of Europe Publishing.

—— (1994) *Direkte Demokratie. Ein internationaler Vergleich*, Bern: Haupt.

Pintor, R.L. and Gratschew, M. (eds) (2002) *Voter Turnout: A Global Survey*, Stockholm: International Institute for Democracy and Electoral Assistance IDEA.

Riklin, A. and Kley, R. (1981) *Stimmabstinenz und direkte Demokratie. Ursachen, Bewertungen, Konsequenzen.* Daten zur direkten Demokratie in der Schweiz, im Kanton St. Gallen, im Bezirk St. Gallen und in der Stadt St. Gallen, sowie in weiteren 19 Ländern, St. Galler Studien zur Politikwissenschaft, vol. 9, Bern: Haupt.

Svensson, P. (1996) "Denmark: the Referendum as Minority Protection," in M. Gallagher and P. Vincenzo Uleri (eds) *The Referendum Experience in Europe*, London: Macmillan, pp. 33–51.

Vanhanen, T. (1997) *Prospects of Democracy. A Study of 172 Countries*, London: Routledge.

von Arnim, H.H. (2001) *Das System. Die Machenschaften der Macht*, München: Droemer.

Part IV

Democratic reform and civil society

7 Explaining low participation rates

Collective action and the "concerned unmobilized"[1]

Grant Jordan and William A. Maloney

Olson's non-participation assumptions

Citizen-based collective action in voluntary associations is generally perceived as critical to the health of democracy. Such activity is seen as enriching the voting version of democracy. The commonplace assumption is that the less the extent of citizen involvement (political and social), the greater the democratic failure: more is definitely more attractive. As Oliver (1993: 273) states, before the work of Olson inaction was explained, "in terms of individual 'apathy' (which was, of course, indicated by the failure to act) or by some sort of communal deficit [. . .] which prevented people from acting on their interests." Strangely political science has absorbed the argument of Olson, but still tends to see low participation as the consequence of some sort of pathological personal apathy.

Olson's thesis was a reaction to the traditional Truman-type (1951) argument that when a political, social or economic problem impinged significantly on the life of a citizen, he instinctively acts collectively on the basis of that shared interest. Olson's (1965) counterargument was that: mobilization was not a natural or spontaneous process; not all potential groups would materialize; and membership would be less than Truman envisaged. In short, Olson proposed that large numbers of sympathetic and predisposed citizens free-ride groups whose ends they share. He assumed non-participation to be the natural tendency – participation was to be explained. Thus Olson's Collective Action Paradox suggests that participation occurs under specific conditions – otherwise rational individuals will not be active. Hardin (1995) notes:

> Each of us has an interest in *not* contributing a personal share to, say, a political campaign, because each of us will benefit from all others' contributions while our own contribution may cost us more than it is worth to us alone. Hence, each of us has incentive to be a free-rider [emphasis added].
>
> (Hardin 1995: 50–51)

Thus prospective members – of a group seeking collective goods – will, in this perspective, assess the organization's capacity to secure such generally available goods. If the group is perceived as likely to be successful, then why "pay" (i.e. contribute to group costs) when the benefits will be available without contribution? And if the group will not succeed, why waste support? Famously Olson (1971) proposed:

> If members of a large group rationally seek to maximize their personal welfare, they will *not* act to advance their common or group objectives unless there is *coercion* to force them to do so, or some *separate incentive* distinct from the achievement of the common or group interest, is offered to the members of the group individually [emphasis added].
>
> (Olson 1971: 2)

"Rational" individuals, in the Olsonian approach free-ride because collective goods/rewards alone are insufficient to induce activity. Rational participators are special cases, either forced to do so (e.g. compulsory membership as in union "closed shops") or attracted by (excludable) incentives only available to those in membership.

As is well documented just as Olson's volume was appearing, his identification of a mobilization problem was apparently being contradicted by empirical developments. There was an explosion of the types of organizations Olson claimed were the hardest to mobilize – i.e. membership-based groups seeking public goods and without obvious selective, material inducements to offer. Not only did the number of groups suggest that Olson had over-emphasized the difficulties of mobilization, many surveys found that members[2] joined to secure collective ends per se.

However, Hardin (1982, 1995, 2003) and others do not accept that group proliferation, and even large group membership numbers, deliver the "knock-out" blow to Olson's thesis – given that the "n" mobilized might still be a relatively low percentage of potential joiners:

> When the number of members of a group that would benefit from collective action is small enough, we might expect cooperation that results from extensive interaction, mutual monitoring, and even commitments to each other that trump or block narrowly self-interested actions. But when the group is very large, free-riding is often clearly in the interest of most and perhaps all members.
>
> (Hardin 2003)[3]

Though it is widely assumed that the proliferation of groups disconcerted Olson, this is not the case. He was able to treat them as a minor exception to his thesis. Olson's theory was not that groups could not attract members without selective incentives; it was that the proportion involved would be low because participation was irrational. Olson (1971: 76) in fact does not extensively discuss his case in the free-riding term per se though the sense is strongly implicit.[4] Oliver (1993: 272) argues that he provides a "mathematical proof" coupled with "a persuasive verbal description of the 'free rider' problem." This chapter tries to make distinctions within the practice of free-riding. This is not considered by Olson. He assumed that non-participation was uniformly based on a strategy to secure collective goods with minimal personal investment.

Both Hardin (1982: 106) and Olson (1965: 61) saw the numbers joining public interest groups without coercion or selective incentives as exceptional and accounted for by irrationality, or moral or psychological motives such as altruism or guilt. Olson says social science makes the unjustified assumption that groups act in their self-interest because individuals do:

> There is paradoxically the logical possibility that groups composed of either altruistic individuals or irrational individuals may sometimes act in their common or group interests. But [. . .] *this logical possibility is usually of no practical importance* [emphasis added].
>
> (Olson 1965: 2)

Olson conceded that some membership would sustain some public interest groups, but his assumption was that such behavior would be exceptional and groups would be under-resourced in comparison with the public support they could reflect. The environmental area is a good test, hence why we selected it as the core of the empirical analysis in this chapter. Johnson (1995: 1) noted that a US poll in 1992 found 67 percent of the public agreeing that: "Protecting the environment is so important that requirements and standards cannot be too high, and continuing improvements must be made regardless of costs." From this he estimated that at least 120 million Americans were pro-environmental – yet at the very most 15 million were in membership of relevant groups. The poll and calculations would have to be very wrong to suggest there is not a large pool of (potential) environment supporters that US environmental organizations have failed to mobilize.

In the surveys reported here, from an initial sample of 20,000 UK citizens with a 50 percent response rate (i.e. 10,000 cases) approximately 21 percent (2,137) exhibited strong support for the environment (what we term the "concerned" – see below for further details). However, only 7 percent (i.e. a third of the "concerned") were members of an environmental organization: only one-third of the predisposed were members of relevant groups. Olson's (1965) and Hardin's (1982) interpretation would be that the difference between the "concerned and active" and the "concerned and not active" is largely, if not wholly, accounted for by free-riding. In fact, Olson (1982) specifically cited the environment as an example of sub-optimal mobilization due to the lack of material incentives:

> almost everyone is interested in a wholesome environment, and poll results suggest that in the United States [. . .] There are tens of millions of citizens who think more ought to be done to protect the environment [. . .] Despite this, and despite subsidized postal rates for non profit organizations and

> reductions in the cost of direct mail solicitation due to computers, relatively few people pay dues each year to environmental organizations [. . .] There are surely more than 50 million Americans who value a wholesome environment, but in a typical year probably fewer than one in a hundred pays dues to any organization whose main activity is lobbying for a better environment.
>
> (Olson 1982: 34–35)

Readers of this chapter[5] in draft pointed out that there is an important leap here that assumes that those who share the concern about the environment with members of environmental groups also agree with the goals of the environmental organizations. In fact this turns out to be pretty close to our conclusion! However, Olson and his cohort make the even looser assumption that those who in some general way support a cause and do not join are free-riding. The (more realistic) test set out in this chapter only assumes that those with a strong concern are potential free-riders – and then assesses if the explanation for non-participation is free-riding or something else. By confining the comparison to the "strongly concerned" our data is designed to look at an area where conscious free-riding might be a reason for non-mobilization (as opposed to comparative lack of commitment). Accordingly, the central issues addressed are:

- Does all (or even a substantial proportion) of non-participation by the "concerned non-mobilized" stem from deliberated, economically rational free-riding?
- To what extent should non-participation be sensibly equated with free-riding?

Finally, it should be noted that the environmental example was selected for several additional reasons – apart from Olson's too tempting invitation. First, generally environmental groups seek collective goods that are non-exclusionary with benefits accruing equally to members and non-members alike. Second, typically, (but not always) environmental groups do not offer (significant) material selective incentives (or coerce people) to participate. Third, there are a large and diverse number of well-organized groups that one can join – catering for "general" to "niche-driven" concerns. (Ignorance of opportunities can hardly be a factor). Fourth, many (large-scale) environmental organizations have high-brand recognition, are professionalized recruiting machines, and membership/supportership is relatively easy and comparatively cheap. These factors all reduce entry barriers. The lower the barriers, the "harder" it is for individuals to remain non-members in anything other than a conscious way.

Free-riding: (re) defining the phenomenon

Almost all the challenges to Olson's prediction of under-participation have in practice addressed the wrong population – by focusing on those who participate.

Responding to Tillock and Morrison (1979), Olson (1979) made the point that generalizations about the inactive should not be based on activist studies:

> The problem that it is too late to deal with is the fact that you have an "experiment" with no control group! Out of the tens of millions of Americans who believe the population should not grow [...] you focus on the miniscule minority of 12,000 who *do* belong to ZPG (Zero Population Growth). The relevant group is the group of millions that wants ZPG, not the handful who have proven themselves to be wildly unrepresentative by joining ZPG [...] your sample excludes all the members of the group who make nondeviant choices.
>
> (Olson 1979: 149)

Later in this piece non-group members who have strong pro-environmental views are compared with members who have such views. As noted the test is designed to be as fair as possible to Olson's assumptions. In his letter (above) Olson assumes that there are tens of millions of free riders on the ZPG group because large numbers back zero population growth (the cause), but few are organizational members. Our test focuses more narrowly on those with the strongest support for the relevant cause. Some non-support might simply and reasonably result from lower priority for the goal. Like is compared with like: strongly concerned members with strongly concerned non-members.

There have been few previous studies of non-participants. Walsh and Warland (1983) examined the consequences of the Three Mile Island (TMI) nuclear incident. They sought to explain why some residents who agreed with the "general goals of the citizen protest groups" became politically active, while others – sharing similar views – remained inactive. Despite the very low level of explicit free-riding, Walsh and Warland conclude that:

> high levels of free-riding on both sides of the TMI issue support Olson (1965) vis-à-vis critics who question the magnitude of the free-rider problem (Marwell and Ames 1979, 1980). When only 12 percent of a subgroup defining itself as discontented contributes *any* time or money to an organized political response by fellow citizens, free-riding has to be considered a major problem.
>
> (Walsh and Warland 1983: 778)

This conclusion ignores the fact that these alleged free-riders provide *plausible explanations for their non-participation*. According to Walsh and Warland's data for example, having never heard of the (local) organization (26 percent) was the most important reason advanced. However, these respondents are not deliberate "free-riders" in any conscious (/meaningful) sense. In Olson's argument free-riding is about a choice, but in this use of the term, free-riders simply become everyone not in membership. There is no choice when one is unaware of the options. The following operationalization of the free-rider category by Walsh and Warland reflects this very broad definition of the concept:

> Our *free-rider* category includes citizens other writers would label *adherents* (McCarthy and Zald 1977: 1221), *sympathizers* (Snow *et al.* 1980: 789), or *supporters* (Useem 1980: 360), but it also includes people who agree with the goals of the SMO (social movement organization), but say they have never heard of the protest organization itself [. . .] It seems reasonable, both from a theoretical and from an operational viewpoint, to employ an *objective free-rider* category to refer to all people expressing a preference for a public good being sought by some SMO, regardless of whether they have heard of the SMO or agree with its mode of operating [original emphasis in italics, added emphasis underlined].
>
> (Walsh and Warland 1983: 768)

Unlike the Walsh and Warland piece, this chapter asserts that awareness of the groups available for joining (and agreement with "their" goals and methods) is crucial. To complement the parsimony of Olson's argument, free-riding should be regarded as a specific type of conscious non-membership. Accordingly, a free-rider is someone who is:

- concerned (i.e. values the group goal)
- aware of the group
- believes group activity will produce desirable outcomes
- considers the group(s) in question to be efficient (all these characteristics lead us to label those in the category as "concerned")
- and still refuses to join.

The essence of free-riding is a rational choice to preserve one's own resources rather than contribute to a common pool – even when one supports the collective cause. In considering behavior from a rational perspective, this test is much more realistic than Olson's implicit "everyone not in membership is a free-rider," but of course the definitional realignment alone swiftly reduces the power of Olson's thesis. This definition better fits Olson's argument than the operationalization he used that found ubiquitous free-riding. With our stricter definition, free-riding is much less common than the Walsh and Warland data (above) suggested.

One central purpose of this chapter is therefore to highlight that the Olson/Walsh and Warland/Hardin use of the concept is broader than the Olson argument justifies. Assuming that everyone not participating is free-riding, leads to the discovery of wide-scale free-riding. Operationalizing a more choice-based definition of free-riding does not make the phenomenon disappear – but such a redefinition permits a better understanding of the relative importance of different strands of the "concerned unmobilized."

The empirical evidence below examines why the concerned unmobilized in the environmental area choose non-participation. It focuses specifically on four main areas. First, environmental commitment: i.e. to what extent do both sets of respondents (members and non-members) exhibit pro-environmental attitudes and behaviors? This is important for two reasons: (a) to confirm that respondents are an appropriate test for the central research question; and (b) to see if members and non-members show any commitment differences that might explain their different (non)involvement patterns. Second, it examines the resources (socio-demographics) these respondents possess. Resources are of course a crucial explanatory variable in accounting for political and social participation. Third, previous research has highlighted the importance of the supply-side recruiting methods in contributing to distorted participation. This chapter looks at the possibility of skewed participation as a result of skewed recruitment. Finally, it addresses the question of the rating of group efficacy by potential members – i.e. respondents' views on the effectiveness of environmental organizations and the effectiveness of different types of political involvement (checkbook and active participation). Not supporting a group because one thinks the effort is wasted is not the same as free-riding.

The survey populations: selecting members, non-members and response rates

The survey reported here was conducted after a "piggy back" strategy exploiting an opportunity provided by a large-scale population survey in the UK – *The Citizen Audit* – conducted by Seyd, Whiteley and Pattie (see Pattie *et al.* 2003). The Audit allowed us to identify the "concerned" population who felt strongly about the environment – and whether or not there was associated membership.[6] In line with Olson's strictures above this was primarily a survey of non-members – with members as a control group. *The Citizen Audit* established membership/non-membership and solicited views on the importance of the environment as a topic. (The survey details are reported in note 7).[7]

Preliminary analysis suggested a distinction between non-members who were nonetheless members of other types of group (labeled "environmental non-members") and non-members who had joined no groups whatsoever (labeled "pure non-members"). It was assumed that the "habitual" non-joiners are likely to be closest to Olson's free-rider notion. However, the former are the potentially more interesting (for this study). They are concerned and mobilizable (i.e. members of non-environmental groups) – yet they have not joined any environmental organizations. Accordingly, throughout this chapter the sample is divided into three subsets: Members of environmental organizations ($n = 359$); Environmental Non-members who are members of other organizations ($n = 293$); and Pure Non-members who are not members of any other groups ($n = 96$).

Commitment: confirming the research problem

A basic explanation for the group participation of a minority of concerned respondents could be that non-participants' beliefs are shallower – hence they are less likely to engage in pro-environmental behavior. Sabatier's (1992) commitment theory captures this and concurs with Olson's by-product argument that not all potential members will be in membership. However, it does so, Sabatier argues, for "radically different reasons." It is not because potential members do not receive, or value highly enough, selective incentives. Commitment theory maintains that:

> Expected *collective* benefits arising from a group's political activities thus are critical to political participation [...] [it] expects to find increasing degrees of commitment to collective benefits as one moves from the potential members of a group to its members and then to its leaders [...] most potential members will lack the material or ideological commitment to take the time and expense to join: most people are simply not very interested in, or informed about, policy issues [original emphasis].
>
> (Sabatier 1992: 109–110)

To minimize any "commitment" explanation for non-participation this chapter focuses only on those exhibiting strong pro-environmental views/behavior (it should be borne in mind that within this category the majority are non-members). Thus, a series of "trade-off" questions were used to explore differences, if any, between joiners and non-joiners of relevant groups. Tables 7.1a and 7.1b show that members and non-members share very similar pro-environmental views. For example, all three subgroups are very much against the idea that the economy should get a higher priority than the environment.[8] The percentage figures across all categories are remarkably high. They should be high to reflect the accuracy of the screening processes that lead us to focusing on these respondents. Tables 7.1a and 7.1b confirm these sets of respondents exhibit similarly strong pro-environmental attitudes.

However, it could be argued that pro-environmental attitudes are "cheap." Hence, to what extent do samples engage in pro-environmental behavior – as opposed to expression? Table 7.2 shows ways respondents claim they act, or are likely to act. In terms of willingness to make material sacrifices members, perhaps not unexpectedly, are more willing than non-members. It is worth noting however that in each case the environmental non-members were less enthusiastic than members, but much keener than the pure non-members. "Should not cost me any money" was backed by 50 percent of pure non-members, but 39 percent of environmental non-members and only 2 percent of members. Overall in terms of material sacrifice non-members exhibited less enthusiasm for economically costly options: 59 percent of members were prepared to give up some of their income if it was dedicated to the environment (only 31 of pure and 37 percent of environmental non-members would do likewise). While the differences are not huge they are significant and have a certain face validity. A part of the non-membership decision seems to be about the availability of resources. Olson may not be completely irrelevant!

In terms of activities such as recycling similarities re-emerged – plus 70

Table 7.1a (Pro-)environmental attitudes[a]

Attitudes	*Pure NMs (%)* n = *94*	*Env. NMs (%)* n = *284*	*Members** (%)* n = *348*
Economic development should get a higher priority than the environment	3	3	0
Economic development is important but the environment should be protected at the same time	69	77	82
The environment should get a higher priority than economic development	28	20	18

Table 7.1b (Pro-)environmental attitudes

Attitudes	*Pure NMs (%)* n = *95*	*Env. NMs (%)* n = *284*	*Members* (%)* n = *349*
Industry should be prevented from damaging the countryside, even if this sometimes leads to higher prices	92	98	100
Industry should keep prices down, even if this sometimes damages the countryside	8	2	0

Notes

a The Pearson Chi-square tests were carried out on Tables 7.1a to 7.5 (inclusive) and 7.7. In all cases the tests compared Pure Non-members and Environmental Non-members, and Environmental Non-members and Members. Significance values are indicated in all tables against the Pure Non-members for Pure Non-members and Environmental Non-members comparison, and against the Members for the Environmental Non-members and Members. For each table formatted along the lines of "Strongly agree/agree" versus "Strongly disagree/disagree," or "very likely/likely" versus "not very likely/not at all likely" etc. a two-by-two crosstab of these response options was formed and a Chi-square test carried out.

$^{*}p \leq 0.05$; $^{**}p \leq 0.01$.

Table 7.2 Material sacrifice and action

Material sacrifice	*Pure NMs (%) min.* n = *91*		*Env. NMs (%) min.* n = *286*		*Members (%) min.* n = *343*	
	Agree	*Disagree*	*Agree*	*Disagree*	*Agree*	*Disagree*
I would give part of my income if I were certain that the money would be used to prevent environmental pollution	31	37	37	34	59**	14
I would agree to an increase in taxes if the extra money were to be used to prevent environmental pollution	52	28	58	22	76**	11
The government should reduce environmental pollution but it should not cost me any money	50*	15	39	28	21**	47

Action	*Regularly*			*Never*		
	Pure NMs (%) n = *92*	*Env. NMs (%)* n = *287*	*Members (%)* n = *345*	*Pure NMs (%)* n = *92*	*Env. NMs (%)* n = *287*	*Members (%)* *n* = *345*
Make a special effort to sort glass, tins, plastic and newspapers for recycling?	73	70	90	9	11	2**
Make a special effort to buy organically grown fruits and vegetables?	30	30	43	27	29	19**
Use public transport instead of own vehicle?	42	29	22	25	27	21**

Notes
$^{*}p \leq 0.05$; $^{**}p \leq 0.01$

percent of both non-member categories and 90 percent of members recycle on a regular basis and 30 percent of non-members and over 40 percent of members make a special effort to buy organic produce. However, the significance tests again usefully highlight some important differences. Rather unexpectedly members are significantly less pro-public transport: fewer members (22 percent) than non-members (42 percent pure and 29 percent environmental non-members) are prepared to use public transport on a regular basis rather than rely on their own vehicles. The greater levels of vehicle ownership among members may explain this counterintuitive finding. Only 67 percent of pure ($n = 92$) and 78 percent of environmental non-members ($n = 287$) are owners. The figure for members is 92 percent ($n = 355$). In summary, Tables 7.1a, 7.1b and 7.2 confirm that generally members and non-members think and act "environmentally" and leads us to address the two central points raised above about why only some of the "concerned" are mobilized.

Demographics, resources and the supply-side

As shown in Table 7.3 the demographic differences between members and non-members are striking. There is a major gender divergence, most notably between the pure non-members and the members. The gender ratio among members is 56:44 female: male and the pure non-members is 42:58 (the environmental non-members is 49:51). This echoes the findings of other research (Jelen *et al.* 1994; Jordan and Maloney 1997a; Rüdig *et al.* 1991). Group members tend to be disproportionately female.

There are substantial differences too in the areas of income, educational attainment and occupation. Table 7.3 shows that members are comparatively affluent: 53 percent of members have household incomes over £30,000 per year, the comparable figures for the pure non-members and environmental non-members are 16 percent and 28 percent respectively. Members are also more highly educated: 56 percent hold a university qualification – a figure that is double the environmental non-members (27 percent) and almost three times the pure non-members (19 percent). Finally, members are heavily concentrated in the managerial/professional occupation class: 73 percent compared with 31 percent of pure non-members and 39 percent of environmental non-members.

The differences between members and non-members are generally consistent with Verba *et al.*'s (1995: 468) notion of representational distortion in their work on civic voluntarism. The large differences above between members and the pure non-members could therefore have been predicted and confirm the commonplace finding of skewed participation. However, the members and environmental non-members differences demand explanation. Both sets of respondents exhibited pro-environmental attitudes and have a track record of joining groups – although environmental non-members are not as promiscuous joiners as members whose average number of memberships is 4.3 (the corresponding figure for environmental non-members is 1.6). Nevertheless, it is

Table 7.3 Demographic profiles

Gender	*Pure NMs (%)* n = *89*	*Env. NMs (%)* n = *281*	*Members* (%)* n = *352*
Female	42	49	56
Male	58	51	44
Household income	*Pure** NMs (%)* n = *92*	*Env. NMs (%)* n = *264*	*Members** (%)* n = *341*
Under £192 per week (under £10k)	40	17	7
£192–385 per week (£10–20k)	27	33	21
£385–577 per week (£20–30k)	16	22	20
£577–769 per week (£30–40k)	11	13	17
£769–962 per week (£40–50k)	2	8	11
£962–1,154 per week (£50–60k)	2	3	8
Over £1,154 per week (Over £60)	1	5	17
Highest educational qualification[a]	*Pure NMs (%)* n = *31*	*Env. NMs (%)* n = *119*	*Members** (%)* n = *211*
Non-university	81	73	44
University	19	27	56
Occupation	*Pure** NMs (%)* n = *74*	*Env. NMs (%)* n = *229*	*Members** (%)* n = *305*
Professional or technical work	14	21	52
Manager or administrator	18	18	21
Clerical	11	17	14
Sales	8	10	4
Skilled manual worker	27	18	4
Semi-skilled or unskilled manual worker	23	14	5

Notes

a Educational qualifications were collapsed into two groups. The University-educated group included: Teaching qualifications; University diploma; and University or CNAA first degree.

* $p \leq 0.05$; ** $p \leq 0.01$

important to stress that the environmental non-members are not a sample of non-joiners. So why do these "joiners" not join environmental groups?

The differences between environmental non-members and members fit the pattern of supply-side recruitment (Abramson and Claggett 2001; Bosso 2003; Johnson 1998; Jordan and Maloney 1997a, 1997b) – or what Verba *et al.* (2000) identified as rational prospecting. Many organizations work efficiently (and effectively) at locating and recruiting an attainable membership. Recruitment will be frustrated if the predisposed member cannot afford the subscription. Thus groups deliberately market themselves among those best able to afford support. Members are more affluent and better educated and these qualities are

Table 7.4 Routes into membership of all other (i.e. non-environmental) groups for Non-members, and environmental groups for Members

	Env. NMs (%) n = *194* *All groups*	*Members* (%) n = *346* *Env. groups*
A friend, relative or work colleague gave me an application form	34	12**
I responded to a press advertisement	9	12
I responded to a membership appeal I received through the post	17	28**
I joined after filling in an application form from a leaflet inserted in a magazine	5	13**
I received my membership as a gift	2	12**
I joined at a meeting/conference/event	9	8
I contacted the organization myself	37	31
I joined after looking on the Internet	3	2
Joined at a property or site	n/a	43
Other	17	6

Note
**$p \leq 0.01$

replicated when groups target recruitment. The issue is whether these are the characteristics that lead to membership – or whether the groups search for citizens with such characteristics.

Taking both groups of non-members together only 12 percent of those with household incomes below £20,000 said that they had been asked to join an environmental organization (but refused). The figure for those earning in excess of £20,000 was almost double: 23 percent. A self-reinforcing process of segmented mobilization witnesses groups recruiting on the basis of their existing membership profiles and (for the organizations) reflects an efficient use of organizational resources (see Jordan and Maloney 1997a: 154–155).

Thus the assumption of spontaneous participation – i.e. self-starters along Truman lines (mobilizing on the basis of shared attitudes or concerns) – has been greatly undermined both from the contribution of self-interested, individual rational choice models and supply-side perspectives that emphasize the importance of groups supplying themselves to individuals. The leading position of the Royal Society for the Protection of Birds (RSPB) in the UK and its tenfold increase in membership in the last 30 years (from 98,000 in 1971 to 1.02 million in 2001) reflects the success of regular high-profile press advertising and a professionalized approach to membership recruitment (and retention). Group recruiting efficiency is more relevant to understand the growth than a spontaneous increase in the public affection for birds.

The survey data reported here demonstrates the major success of the two brand leaders in this group market – 71 percent of those in the member category pay dues to the National Trust and 25 percent to the RSPB. The successful "big number" groups are those who recruit proactively. Walker (1991: 49) noted, "The process of political mobilization cannot be fully understood until we realize that mobilizing efforts often come from top down, rather than bottom up." Bosso (1995: 111) similarly notes that the growth in mass membership environmentalism in the US from the 1970s onward, "did not just happen simply because environmental issues became more important. It also was cultivated as part of a conscious effort by many environmental leaders to build member bases[. . .]."

The importance of recruiting strategies received further confirmation when the routes into membership of "other" groups by environmental non-members, and into environmental groups for members are compared. Two profoundly different lists emerged in Table 7.4. For members of organizations other than environmental groups self-starting (37 percent) and social networks of friends, relatives and colleagues (34 percent) were the two most common paths. For environmental group members the comparable figures were 31 and 12 percent. For members of environmental groups the main route to membership was the National Trust option of joining at a site. Partly this is supply-side marketing; partly it is an Olson selective benefit, and partly it is self-selection by the potential member. Those who turn up at sites are particularly "available" for recruitment. But there were other important differences when looking at the membership "trigger." Supply-side features emerged as important for members: 53 percent responded to the group invitation – postal appeal (28 percent), press advertisement (12 percent) and filling-in a leaflet inserted in a magazine (13 percent). The corresponding figure for environmental non-members' paths into "other" groups was 31 percent. In short, environmental non-members appear less open to supply-side recruiting; for them the social network "pull" (34 percent got application form from friend, relative or colleague) was more decisive in their joining decision.

The role of "efficacy" in the non-joining decision

A comparison of reasons advanced for non-membership is generally unrevealing in terms of distinguishing between the types of non-members (Table 7.5). Both subsets opt for the "safe" explanation that they have other priorities, and take care of family and personal matters before worrying about "the state of the world." Pure non-members showed slightly more support for several of the more overtly free-riding options though in absolute terms both sets demonstrated limited support for the propositions that "others will contribute." These engrained non-participators should be the closest to Olson's free-riders. In general however, neither set of non-members pursued free-riding explanations. Circa 20 percent of both groups agreed that environmental organizations did not need members to be effective (see Table 7.6 where 92 percent of members say organizations need members); around 14 percent said that environmental groups had professional staff and did not need support; and only 8 percent of pure and 5 percent of environmental non-members selected the pure Olson option: "I do

Table 7.5 Reasons for non-membership of environmental organizations.

	Pure NMs (%) min. n = *81*		*Env. NMs (%) min.* n = *263*	
	Important	*Unimportant*	*Important*	*Unimportant*
Other priorities more important				
I support the environment but other priorities are more important	58	16	60	20
I take care of my family and myself before I worry about the "state of the world"**	67	6	68	16
Time constraints				
I don't have the time to be active in organizations	50	12	59	14
I don't have time to be active in environmental organizations because I'm too busy in other groups**	10	48	30	41
Cost exceeds expected return (free-riding)				
I think that what I get out of being a member is not worth the time and trouble I would have to put into it	20	32	17	40
I do not need to join because others will contribute	8	50	5	62
Environmental organizations have enough professional staff and do not need my support	13	39	14	42
Environmental organizations do not need members to be effective	22	39	18	48
Never been asked to join				
I have never been asked to join	30	33	32	28
Negative evaluations of activity				
I do not like the confrontational campaigning style of many environmental groups	59	15	51	23
Environmental and conservation organizations can't solve problems like pollution	34	36	31	44
Financial constraints				
I cannot afford the money to be a member	57	23	43	29

Notes
$*p \leq 0.05$; $**p \leq 0.01$

Table 7.6 Reasons for membership of environmental organizations

	Members (%) min. n = *318*	
	Important	*Unimportant*
To show support/contribute		
I wished to make a financial contribution to support an environmental or conservation organization, but I did not have the time to participate more actively	76	7
To show support for the aims and objectives of the environmental or conservation group(s) I joined	87	3
I believe people have a responsibility to contribute to society and this was one of the ways in which I chose to make my contribution	69	10
Environmental and conservation organizations need my contribution if they are to achieve their goals	82	5
Self-regarding explanations (free-riding)		
I wanted to be kept informed about environmental issues	66	10
I was attracted by the benefits of membership (free gifts, magazines, etc.)	21	59
To gain new skills and experience	12	61
Belief in efficacy of collective action		
I believed that I would have more influence as a member of an organization than on my own	80	5
Organizations need active members to be effective	92	1
The more members an organization has the greater influence it will have	88	2
Environmental degradation/threat		
Some important aspects of my life are threatened by environmental degradation	53	20
My deep concern with environmental problems leaves no other alternative than active support for environmental and conservation organizations	39	24

not need to join because others will contribute." Free-riding is simply not a substantial part of the explanation.

However both sets of non-members strongly endorsed other reasons – other priorities, family first, no time – all received over 50 percent support. There is of course the problem of post hoc rationalization, but if the selections are rationalizations the non-members nonetheless select reasons such as "can't afford" that might have even more negative associations than free-riding. It is also interesting that so many (59 and 51 percent) say that they don't like the campaigning style of the groups. Both subgroups share doubts about group efficacy – about one-third of both categories think groups can't solve such problems. Thirty percent of environmental non-members (plausibly) maintain that they are "too busy" in other groups (10 percent of pure non-members still claimed they were too busy in groups to join environmental groups!). Finally, and vitally, there is the issue of "affordability." The relatively less affluent pure non-members highlight this as a significant barrier to their participation (Table 7.3 confirms this group is strikingly less affluent).

Members advanced reasons for participation that other studies have seen as refuting Olson (Table 7.6), i.e. expressions of a strong belief in the efficacy of collective action. In the subset of dimensions relating to the judgment about group efficacy the lowest approval rate is 80 percent. The section relating to a "wish to show support" generates responses nearly as high. Though such findings are conventionally regarded as "anti-Olson," we accept (following Hardin and Olson himself) that what the minority who join believe tells us little about Olson's prediction about the majority who do not join. Self-regarding explanations such as to gain skills were largely ignored (12 percent) (but 21 percent were attracted by "free" gifts).

In a separate question members were asked if there were any circumstances that would lead them to leave the organization (data not presented in this chapter). Members categorically rejected the free-riding thesis. Only 6 percent said they would leave if they thought the organization could achieve its goals without their personal involvement. Forty-five percent maintained that they would get a lot out of membership even if the group failed to accomplish its goals (expressive), whereas 19 percent thought that being a member was rewarding only if the group delivered (purposive). Thus it appears that selective material incentives are not a prime factor in the joining or non-joining decision. (However, it should be stressed that the argument being advanced is not that selective material incentives play no role.)

The relative unpopularity of Olsonian reasons for participation and non-participation might be thought to represent socially acceptable responses. Skepticism that these questions do not tap deep explanations of action should be tempered by noting how seldom the explanations of selective material type (Olson responses) were selected. In addition to this, previous research – on the National Farmers Union Countryside[9] – is instructive. Large numbers of members of the NFU Countryside in the UK had absolutely no qualms whatsoever about saying they joined solely for the selective incentive of cheap insurance. For example, in response to the open question – Why did you join NFU Countryside? (Were there any particularly important reasons or specific events which encouraged you to join?) – 55 percent mentioned insurance services.

Non-members were asked about the likelihood of joining environmental organizations (Table 7.7). Pure non-members said they were less likely to join an organization than environmental non-members, but the differences are relatively small. Few non-members thought that they could be mobilized by simply being asked to join, or if the benefits exceeded the costs. There was also no great support for the idea that opportunities for active participation were a catalyst for membership.

However, the two top factors that would induce (both sets of) non-members to participate were: (a) if some aspect of their life were threatened by environmental

Table 7.7 Likelihood of joining an environmental organization

	Pure NMs (%) min. n = 89		*Env. NMs (%) min. n = 279*	
	Likely	*Not likely*	*Likely*	*Not likely*
If you thought the membership fee would be the only demand the organization would make of you	14	44	21	39
If the organization offered opportunities for active participation	18	45	18	45
If the organization asked you to join	9	51	13	44
If the financial benefits of membership (i.e. free gifts or magazines, reduced entry fees, etc.) were greater than the membership fee	10	56	13	53
If you felt that some important aspects of your life were threatened by environmental degradation	63	17	68	13
If you thought that your membership contributed to environmental improvements**	49	23	66	13
If you had more spare time	44	27	53	21
If nobody else would do it	19	36	17	38

Note
**$p \leq 0.01$.

degradation; and (b) if it was thought that membership contributed to improvements. (Across a wide range of areas members consistently perceived environmental groups to be more effective in environmental protection and advocacy than both groups of non-members.) The first factor suggests the reflective explanation – that environmentalism is a response to the specific – and the latter points towards non-membership being related to skepticism about the effectiveness of groups. Of course relatively negative evaluations of group success could be a post hoc rationalization. However, the combination of evidence suggests that an important part of the explanation of why the concerned unmobilized remain (environmental) non-participants is that they appear to be genuinely less impressed by the groups. This is not free-riding to "let George do it," as Olson would put it, but a suspicion that George is wasting his time.

A comparative assessment of the non-joining decision

Finally, we conducted a multivariate analysis (Table 7.8) and the data squares well with the bivariate analysis presented above (all variables are constructed using additive indices, based on a binary logistic regression and all variables/indices have been standardized). Members are compared with environmental non-members on the assumption that the pure non-members exaggerate further the differences that are in fact striking even in this pairing. While the "habitual" non-joiners are likely to be closest to Olson's free-rider notion, the environmental non-members are more interesting. They are concerned and mobilizable (i.e. have a track record of joining non-environmental groups), yet they have not joined any environmental organization. The strongly concerned members of non-environmental groups are the subset of non-joiners that seem least likely to be free-riders. The multivariate design permits comparison of different dimensions that were identified as accounting for the non-joining behavior. In combination (Model 6) these dimensions discriminate powerfully between joiners and non-joiners.

Attitudinally both sets of respondents compared here are in the strong commitment category (by research design) which naïve pluralism suggested produced (spontaneous) membership. Thus attitudes do not (reassuringly) appear as a dimension leading to difference. However, there are large differences regarding other commitment measures. While members are more likely to act environmentally (e.g. recycle on a regular basis or buy organic food) in Model 1 (commitment) than environmental non-members, this difference evaporates in Model 6 (all-inclusive). However, the significant differences in the preparedness of members and environmental non-members to make material sacrifices in defense of the environment remain strong in both models. Controlling for resource differences (in the all-inclusive model) members are more willing to pay higher (hypothecation) taxes or donate part of their income to fund environmental improvements.

Such basic findings undermine the sweeping assumption by Olson that everyone who is not "in" is a free rider. Here are a set of people who have concerns as strong as members, have joined other groups, but they are very different from environmental members in many regards. As Table 7.2 showed they are less willing than members to make sacrifices and overall less likely to act in pro-environmental ways. Non-participation relates to politically relevant criteria.

Table 7.8[10] also shows the conformity of this piece of participation research with other work. The non-participants are very different in terms of resources. Recruitment also emerges as a strong factor: being asked to join is important. And as demonstrated above, the better resourced are asked more frequently. Environmental non-members' lower mean organizational affiliation rate and their non-involvement in the environmental area may simply reflect a greater "stickiness" in their joining behavior. They may just be generally harder to recruit than members (but clearly not as difficult as the pure non-members). Strikingly 66 percent of environmental non-members said they would consider joining if they thought membership contributed to environmental improvements. The supply-side is crucial – both groups of non-members were much less likely to be invited to join an environmental organization. This has significant democratic implications. Large numbers of participation studies have highlighted the (demand-side) problem of the democratic paradox of the non-involvement of those with fewest resources, i.e. those who stand to gain most from participation

Table 7.8 Explaining membership, standardized coefficients (Members versus Environmental Non-members)

	Commitment Model 1	*Resources Model 2*	*Recruitment Model 3*	*Efficacy Model 4*	*Free-ride Model 5*	*All Model 6*
% correctly classified	63.6	67.9	57.8	67.0	54.5	73.9
R^2 Nagelkerke	0.12	0.20	0.07	0.18	0.01	0.38
Commitment:						
Pro-environmental attitudes	0.01					0.05
Material sacrifice	0.54***					0.39***
Environmental action	0.28***					0.06
Resources:						
Income		0.45***				0.35*
University degree		0.33***				0.30*
Gender: male		−0.15				0.02
Professionals		0.41***				0.31**
Recruitment:						
Been asked to join			0.49***			0.39**
Efficacy:						
Organizational efficacy				0.57***		0.66***
Efficacy of checkbook participation				0.60***		0.54***
Efficacy of active participation				−0.10		−0.35*
Material self-interest					−0.19*	−0.15
Constant	0.22	0.27	0.20	0.11	0.18	0.09
N of cases in analyses	607	588	652	540	629	468

Notes
*$p < 0.05$, **$p < 0.01$, ***$p < 0.001$.

tend to be those who are least involved. However, this study confirms other work that non-involvement also results from a lack of asking. Many of the groups who do the asking, rationally and understandably seek to minimize "their" costs and increase the likelihood that the citizen will respond positively. These organizations are in the business of protest and campaigning, not the enhancement of democracy. This factor should be built into assessments of the quality of democratic systems.

Table 7.8 demonstrates the weakness of a notion of free-riding that assumes that members and potential members were selective benefit driven. This confirms the low rate of selection of overt material self-interest measures in Table 7.5. The fact that resources are not donated by non-members in terms of group subscriptions seems not to relate to the version of material self-interest advanced by Olson. Such an imprecise version elevated "free-riding" to a large-scale phenomenon and significantly increased its importance.

However as is shown in the final column (Model 6) the strongest variable concerns the evaluation of organizational effectiveness. Members and non-members have different attitudes towards the effectiveness of various modes of participation. The active participation options (e.g. being active in a political party, participating in campaigns and public demonstrations, etc.) are not seen as being efficacious by members. They perceive participation by proxy (i.e. donating money or being a member of an interest group) as a more effective means to influence outcomes in the environmental sphere. (Clearly, this is why they are members of environmental groups – after all, many only offer opportunities to contract out of participation, see Maloney 1999). Members join these environmental organizations because they believe they are effective in goal attainment: checkbook participation is a purposive activity. Non-members hold the reverse view perceiving active involvement as more effective. Both efficacy results are rational in the sense that members rate checkbook participation as efficacious and contribute to these groups, and non-members believe them to be less effective and choose not to fund "their" activities. Finally, Table 7.8 shows that while non-members are more likely to endorse material self-interest propositions, the overall impact of this variable is close to nil. The multivariate analysis clearly demonstrates that there are other rational reasons for not joining.

Concluding comment

This chapter rejects the loose definition of free-riding and substitutes a narrower version that emphasizes deliberation and strategic choice. It looked at members concerned about the environment and two subsets of non-members who shared strong pro-environmental concerns. This was a test of free-riding that went to great lengths to find Olsonian-like behavior. It "screened out" free-riding that simply reflected less intensive commitment to the cause. The data in Table 7.8 are therefore striking. It showed that the non-mobilized act consistently within a broad view of rationality. They may have strong environmental concerns – but are less able to invest resources (poorer), less willing to make sacrifices, have fewer of the well-known demographic qualities that generally lead to representational distortion, have been less subject to group recruiting and above all rate the efficacy of the organizations less generously and are less attracted by the check-book participation idea. The reluctance of the pure non-members to join can be directly linked to the greater resource differentials demonstrated in Table 7.3 – a partial justification for their non-participation. It may be harder to persuade this group of the economics of membership. They might like to be able to afford membership, but simply can't (poor riders).

In Table 7.7 pure non-members were significantly less likely than the environmental non-members to join if they thought membership would contribute to environmental improvements. In other dimensions these subgroups were very similar and it may be (with some face validity) that the environmental non-members are more judgmental in terms of group efficacy. They are rather more willing to consider membership – but subject it to an evaluation of efficacy. In conclusion, while free-riding is seen as peculiarly important in the interest group literature, the findings do not encourage much faith in the elegant proposition that low participators are simply being economically rational and "letting George do it." The foregoing analysis confirms the importance of factors such as resources, recruitment and efficacy. However the participatory "instincts" may be different in the heads of these democratic "no shows;" they are choosing not to participate not because they want others to do it for them, but because they are skeptical of such activities and are skeptical of the effect of political action. They are uninvolved because they cannot see the point. In summary, we can – with remarkable certainty – discount the ubiquity of Olsonian free-riding.

Notes

1 This chapter draws on an article by Jordan and Maloney (2006) "'Letting George do it': Accounting for low participation rates," published in the *Journal of Elections, Public Opinion & Parties*, 16 (2): 115–139.
2 While reviewing evidence of what appeals to those in membership, Sabatier (1992: 107) highlights that surveys of members tell us little about the views of non-members.
3 Hardin (2003) asks and answers a question: "'What if everybody failed to take into account the effect of their own vote on the election?' The answer is that roughly half of Americans may well fail to take into account the effect of their own votes on elections, and they vote. The rest ride free." From this standpoint free-riding is simply synonymous with non-participation.
4 Olson stresses the trades' union examples and addresses the concern of unions about "the free-rider."
5 One (helpful) critic said, "I still don't buy that you have to join an organization even if you share the attitudes and even exhibit actions." This chapter agrees. Such a critique applies directly to the generally accepted Olson/Hardin formulation of free-riding.
6 The questionnaire asked: "In the last 12 months have you: been a member of this type of organization (in other words Olson/Hardin formulation of free-riding)

- you have paid a membership fee (if it is required)
- participated in an activity arranged by this type of organization

- donated money as an individual to this type of organization
- done voluntary or unpaid work for this type of organization?"

It also established environmental attitudes. Respondents were asked to indicate their level of agreement with:

- "Protecting the environment is so important that environmental improvements must be made regardless of costs."

Those who strongly agreed/agreed with this statement (the "concerned") were divided into those who were members of environmental organizations and those who reported no contact with these groups.

7 This generated 746 members and 1,391 non-members. Data protection legislation required respondents to express their willingness to be re-contacted. This step led to exclusions: 574 (75 percent) members and 926 (67 percent) "non-members" agreed to participate in our study. This data protection filter may have introduced a bias but the rates of refusal at that stage were broadly similar. Subsequent checking found that 74 respondents, who initially designated themselves as members, now indicated that they had no current or previous relationship with an environmental organization and a further 6 were untraceable, deceased or abroad. It was decided to exclude the "switchers" as we could not reliably classify them. Thus, the effective "*n*" for the member survey fell to 494 and we received 359 usable responses (73 percent response rate). Similar checks on non-members found 132 respondents indicating that they had some form of relationship with an environmental organization and were removed from that population and a further 22 were ineligible. Accordingly the number of potential members fell to 772 and 389 responses were returned (50 percent).

8 Respondents were asked a further series of questions on environmental issues/problems. The vast bulk of members and both sets of non-members exhibited very high levels of "concern." For example, over 85 percent (of members and both groups of non-members) stated that they were concerned about: the disappearance of certain types of plants, animals and habitats throughout the world; local problems (traffic in towns, noise, pollution); and worldwide pollution. On the regulation of industrial pollution over 85 percent of all respondents agreed that "The laws controlling industrial pollution are not strict enough."

9 As the name suggests this organization has an environmental interest in a broad sense, but it is closer to the Olson "ideal type" in terms of a group that attracts members through the provision of material selective incentives (most significantly, competitively priced insurance). In effect, this is a money-generating idea by the NFU to recruit members with small (and largely) recreational farms or even large gardens.

10 The "Resources" and "Recruitment" headings are self-explanatory. Others were constructed as follows: *Commitment*. Pro-environmental attitudes – respondents were asked to assess the balance between: environmental improvement and economic growth; and the prevention of industrial pollution and its impact on prices. Material sacrifice – members and non-members were asked about their willingness to donate part of their income to prevent environmental pollution; tax hypothecation (i.e. to pay higher taxes if the money was used to prevent environmental pollution); and if government should reduce environmental pollution without them having to pay. Environmental action – respondents were asked how often they: recycled glass, tins, plastic and newspapers; made a special effort to buy organically grown fruits and vegetables; and used public transport instead of own vehicle. *Efficacy*. Organizational effectiveness – asked members and non-members how effective they believed that environmental groups were at: protecting the environment at the local, national and international level; raising public awareness of environmental issues; influencing the behavior of ordinary people; influencing government policy and preserving habitats for animals. Efficacy of checkbook participation – respondents were asked how

effective in influencing decisions in society it would be to: donate money to groups/organizations or simply to be a member of an interest group. Efficacy of active participation – members and non-members were asked how effective in influencing decisions it would be to: undertake voluntary work in organizations; be active within a political party; participate in campaigns and public demonstrations; take part in acts of civil disobedience; and attend a meeting or a rally. *Material self-interest* – members were asked if they would be more or less likely to continue to support an environmental organization if it reduced the resources used for core activities (e.g. campaigning, conservation, etc.) to increase the amount of benefits/services available to members. Environmental non-members were asked if they would be more or less likely to join under the same circumstances.

References

Abramson, P. and Claggett, W. (2001) "Recruitment and Political Participation," *Political Research Quarterly*, 4: 905–916.

Bosso, C.J. (2003) "Rethinking the Concept of Membership in Nature Advocacy Organizations," *The Policy Studies Journal*, 31: 397–411.

—— (1995) "The Color of Money: Environmental Groups and the Pathologies of Fund Raising," in A.J. Cigler and B.A. Loomis (eds) *Interest Group Politics*, 4th edn, Washington, DC: Congressional Quarterly Press, pp. 101–130.

Hardin, R. (2003) "The Free Rider Problem," in E.N. Alta (ed.) *The Stanford Encyclopedia of Philosophy* (Summer 2003 Edition), plato.stanford.edu/archives/sum2003/entries/free-rider/ (accessed 16 July 2004).

—— (1995) *One for All: The Logic of Group Conflict*, Princeton, NJ: Princeton University Press.

—— (1982) *Collective Action*, Baltimore, MD: John Hopkins University Press.

Jelen, T.G., Thomas, S. and Wilcox, C. (1994) "The Gender Gap in Comparative Perspective: Gender Differences in Abstract Ideology and Concrete Issues in Western Europe," *European Journal of Political Research*, 25: 171–186.

Johnson, P.E. (1995) "How Environmental Groups Recruit Members: Does the Logic Still Hold Up?," Paper presented at the Annual Meeting of the American Political Science Association, Chicago, IL.

Johnson, E. (1998) "Interest Group Recruiting: Finding Members and Keeping Them," in A.J. Cigler and B.A. Loomis (eds) *Interest Group Politics*, 5th edn, Washington, DC: Congressional Quarterly Press.

Jordan, G. and Maloney, W.A. (1997a) *The Protest Business: Mobilizing Campaigning Groups*, Manchester: Manchester University Press.

—— (1997b) "Manipulating Membership: Supply Side Influences Over Group Size," *British Journal of Political Science*, 27: 549–569.

Maloney, W.A. (1999) "Contracting Out the Participation Function: Social Capital and Checkbook Participation," in J.W. van Deth, M. Maraffi, K. Newton and P. Whiteley (eds) *Social Capital and European Democracy*, London: Routledge, pp. 108–119.

Oliver, P. (1993) "Formal Models of Collective Action," *Annual Review of Sociology*, 19: 271–300.

Olson, M. (1982) *The Rise and Decline of Nations*, New Haven, CT: Yale University Press.

—— (1979) "Epilogue: Letter to Denton Morrison," *Research in Social Movements, Conflicts and Change*, 2: 149–150.

—— (1965, 1971) *The Logic of Collective Action*, Cambridge, MA: Harvard University Press.

Pattie, C., Seyd, P. and Whiteley, P. (2003) "Citizenship and Civic Engagement: Attitudes and Behavior in Britain," *Political Studies*, 51: 443–468.

Rüdig, W., Bennie, L.G. and Franklin, M.N. (1991) *Green Party Members: A Profile*, Glasgow: Delta.

Sabatier, P.A. (1992) "Interest Group Membership and Organization: Multiple Theories," in M. Patrice (ed.) *The Politics of Interest: Interest Groups Transformed*, Boulder, CO: Westview Press, pp. 99–129.

Tillock, H. and Morrison, D.E. (1979) "Group Size and Contributions to Collective Action: An Examination of Olson's Theory Using Data from Zero Population Growth," *Research in Social Movements, Conflicts and Change*, 2: 131–158.

Truman, D.B. (1951) *The Governmental Process: Political Interest and Public Opinion*, New York, NY: Alfred A Knopf.

Verba, S., Schlozman, K.L. and Brady, H.E. (2000) "Rational Action and Political Activity," *Journal of Theoretical Politics*, 12: 243–268.

—— (1995) *Voice and Equality: Civic Voluntarism in American Politics*, Cambridge, MA: Harvard University Press.

Walker, J. (1991) *Mobilizing Interest Groups in America: Patrons, Professions and Social Movements*, Ann Arbor, MI: The University of Michigan Press.

Walsh, E.J. and Warland, R.H. (1983) "Social Movement Involvement in the Wake of a Nuclear Accident: Activists and Free-riders in the TMI Area," *American Sociological Review*, 48: 746–780.

8 Trust and governance

How culture and economics constrain the state[1]

Eric M. Uslaner

Trust in other people is the foundation of social solidarity. Generalized trust, the belief that "most people can be trusted," helps connect us to people who are different from ourselves. Generalized trusters are tolerant of immigrants and minorities and support equal rights for women and gays. Yet, they also believe in a common core of values and hold that ethnic politicians should not represent only their own kind. This trust of strangers promotes the altruistic values that lead people with faith in others to volunteer for good causes and to donate to charity, in each case helping people who are likely different from themselves. Trusting societies have more effective governments, higher growth rates, less corruption and crime, and are more likely to redistribute resources from the rich to the poor (Knack and Keefer 1997; LaPorta *et al.* 1998).

Most contemporary discussions of trust place it as part of the broader notion of social capital (Putnam 1993: 170–173). We tend to assume that wherever there is civic engagement, trust must be either the cause or the effect or both. Putnam (2000: 137) argues: "The causal arrows among civic involvement, reciprocity, honesty, and social trust are as tangled as well-tossed spaghetti" (see also Brehm and Rahn: 1997). I shall argue that trust is important because it has a moral dimension. And this ethical component to trust only matters for forms of engagement that bind us to our larger community.

The roots and consequences of trust are precisely what we would expect of a moral value. Values should be stable over time – and not dependent upon day-to-day experiences. This is precisely what I find for trust. Trust matters for the sorts of things that bond us to others without expectations of reciprocity – giving to charity, volunteering time, tolerance of minorities, and promoting policies that redistribute resources from the rich to the poor. It does not matter for the more mundane forms of civic engagement that have no moral component, including – indeed, especially – membership in voluntary organizations. I rely upon a variety of evidence, much from the United States, since there are more extensive surveys on trust there than elsewhere.

My account of trust as a moral value stands in contrast to the traditional view of trust as based largely upon experience. It also distinguishes between trust in other people and trust in government. There is a large literature that suggests that government can create trust from above: good government performance, strong legal systems, honest government, or specific government policies all have the potential to make people believe that fellow citizens can be trusted. I argue that trust largely emanates from below. We learn it early in life (from our parents) and it is very stable. When trust does change, it is largely in response to the level of economic inequality in society. Trust in other people is largely independent of trust in government – although there are government policies that can shape faith in other people. Where there is a link between trust in other people and the state, it comes through inequality: states can enact policies, especially universalistic social welfare policies that reduce inequality and increase trust. When corruption is perceived to increase inequality, it also leads to less trust.

The cultural and economic bases of trust that I shall put forward constrain the state mightily. Others see the state as in a privileged position to shape trust. I argue instead that the state has little "autonomous" power to shape how people feel about their fellow citizens. Culture and economic inequality are sticky: they do not change easily – and low trust and high inequality reinforce each other to limit the power of political leaders to forge policies that might increase trust.

Varieties of trust

The "standard" account of trust presumes that trust depends on information and experience. Yamigishi and Yamigishi (1994) call it "knowledge-based trust." Offe (1999) states: "Trust in persons results from past experience with concrete persons." The decision to trust another person is essentially strategic. Strategic (or knowledge-based) trust presupposes risk (Seligman 1997: 63). As Dasgupta (1988: 53) argues: "The problem of trust would not arise if we were all hopelessly moral, always doing what we said we would do in the circumstances in which we said we would do it." Trust is a recipe for telling us when we can tell whether other people are trustworthy (Luhmann 1979: 43).

Beyond the strategic view of trust is another perspective. I call it moralistic trust – Mansbridge (1999) favors the term "altruistic trust." Moralistic trust is a moral commandment to treat people as if they were trustworthy. The central idea behind moralistic trust is the belief that most people share your fundamental moral values. They need not share your views on policy issues or even your ideology. When others share our basic premises, we face fewer risks when we seek agreement on collective action problems. Moralistic trust is based upon "some sort of belief in the goodwill of the other" (Seligman 1997: 43; see Yamigishi and Yamigishi 1994: 131).

Strategic and moralistic trust

If the grammar of strategic trust is "A trusts B to do X" (Hardin 1992: 154), the etymology of moralistic trust is simply "A trusts." Strategic trust reflects our expectations about how people will behave. Moralistic trust is a statement about how people should behave. The Golden Rule (which is the foundation of moralistic trust) does not demand that you do unto others as they do unto you. You do unto others as you would have them do unto you. The Eighth Commandment is not "Thou shalt not steal unless somebody takes something from you." Adam Seligman (1997: 47) argues: "Were the trusting act to be dependent (i.e. conditional) upon the play of reciprocity (or rational expectation of such), it would not be an act of trust at all but an act predicated on [one's expectations of how others will behave]."

Strategic trust is not predicated upon uncertainty rather than mistrust (Levi 1997: 3). Moralistic trust puts positive feelings at one pole and negative ones at the other. It would be strange to have a moral code with good juxtaposed against undecided. Moralistic trust is predicated upon a view that the world is a benevolent place (Seligman 1997: 47), that things are going to get better, and that you are the master of your own fate. People who believe that others can be trusted expect that things will get better and that they can make the world better by their own actions (Rosenberg 1956; Lane 1959: 163–166).

A second distinction is the continuum from particularized to generalized trust. Generalized trust is the perception that most people are part of your moral community. Its foundation lies in moralistic trust, but it is not the same thing. Generalized trust is a measure of the scope of our community. Our values (moralistic trust) don't change readily. But the way we interpret them does reflect some experiences from daily life. And this is what distinguishes generalized from moralistic trust: generalized trust goes up and down, though it is basically stable (Uslaner 2002: ch. 3).

The difference between generalized and particularized trust is similar to the distinction Putnam (1993: 93) discusses between "bonding" and "bridging" social capital. We bond with our friends and people like ourselves. People who say that most people can be trusted are generalized trusters. Those who only have faith in their own kind are particularized trusters. When we only have faith in some people, we are most likely to trust people like ourselves. And particularized trusters are likely to join groups composed of people like themselves – and to shy away from activities that involve people they don't see as part of their moral community.

Stolle (1998: 500) argues that the extension of trust from your own group to the larger society occurs through "mechanisms not yet clearly understood." An even more skeptical Rosenblum (1998: 45, 48) calls the purported link "an airy 'liberal expectancy'" that remains "unexplained."

Generalized trusters don't abjure contacts with people like themselves. Much of civic life revolves around contact with people like ourselves. Bowling leagues are composed of people who like to bowl and choral societies are made up of people who like classical music.[2] We are simply unlikely to meet people who are different from ourselves in our civic life. Now, choral societies and birdwatching groups (among others) will hardly destroy trust. They bring lots of joy to their members and don't harm anybody. But they are poor candidates for creating social trust. You don't need trust to form a club. Most people spend minuscule amounts of time in voluntary organizations and even the most committed activists rarely devote more than a few hours a week to group life – hardly enough time to shape, or reshape, an adult's values (Newton 1997: 579).

Measuring trust

The idea of generalized trust is well captured in the survey research question that many of us have relied upon for several decades: "Generally speaking, do you believe that most people can be trusted or can't you be too careful in dealing with people?" The question makes no mention of context (see Hertzberg 1988: 314). The interpersonal trust question that has been so important in much research on social capital does reflect generalized trust. The Pew Center for the People and the Press conducted a survey of metropolitan Philadelphia in 1996 and asked people whether they trusted eight groups of people – and whether they trusted "most people." I performed a factor analysis on these trust questions and found distinct dimensions for trust in strangers (people you meet on the street and people who work where you shop) and for friends and family (your family, your boss, and people at your workplace, your church and your club). The standard interpersonal trust question loaded strongly on the trust in strangers dimension, but not at all with friends and family.

There are two claims about moral arguments that can be tested. First, moral values are stable. We learn to trust others from our parents (Erikson 1968: 103) – not from people in our civic associations when we are adults. If trust does have a moral component, it should not change much over time. And, second, moral values do not depend upon reciprocity. I examined two panel surveys – the 1972–1974–1976 American National Election Study (ANES) and the 1965–1973–1982 Parent–Child Socialization Study conducted by M. Kent Jennings and Richard G. Niemi. In both panels, interpersonal trust was among the most stable survey items.

Across two very turbulent decades (the 1960s and the 1970s), almost two-thirds of young people and more than 70 percent of their parents were consistent trusters or mistrusters. In the ANES panel, interpersonal trust was more stable over time than were abortion attitudes and considerably more consistent than standard measures of political efficacy and ideological self-identification (Uslaner 2002: ch. 3). And trust does not depend upon reciprocity. Trusters are not simply paying back good deeds. People who were helped by others when they were young were no more trusting in a 1996 survey than people who received no such assistance. Trust is also stable over time in the aggregate: the r^2 between generalized trust, as measured in the 1981 and 1990–1995 World Values Surveys between 1980 and the 1990s is 0.81 for the 22 nations included in both waves. Even though the 2001 World Values Survey data on trust often seem anomalous for many countries, the r^2 for trust in the 1990s and 2001 is 0.65.

Trust and optimism

The key basis of generalized trust – and what separates it from both distrust and particularized trust – is a sense of optimism and control.[3] For some people, a lifetime of disappointments and broken promises leads to distrust of others. A history of poverty with little likelihood of any improvement led to social distrust in the Italian village of Montegrano that Edward Banfield (1958: 110) described in the 1950s: "any advantage that may be given to another is necessarily at the expense of one's own family. Therefore, one cannot afford the luxury of charity, which is giving others more than their due, or even justice, which is giving them their due."

Does trust reflect an optimistic world view? In Uslaner (2002: ch. 4) I examine a large number of surveys that ask questions about trust and optimism. No single survey has enough good questions to make the case on its own. But space is at a premium here and I report the findings from two of the analyses. The first model employs data from the 1987 General Social Survey (GSS) in the United States, the second from a 1971 pilot study of Economic Incentives, Values, and Subjective Well-Being conducted by the Survey Research Center in Baltimore and Detroit. The 1987 GSS has some of the best questions on optimism and control. The 1971 Well-Being poll is not quite so representative a survey, but it has the advantage of asking a wide range of questions about both optimism and people's life circumstances – allowing a strong test of the argument that optimism rather than experiences are fundamental to generalized trust.

I estimate both equations using probit analysis. I employ what Rosenstone and Hansen (1993) call the "effect" of an independent variable, the difference in estimated probabilities from the predictor's highest and lowest values, letting the other independent variables take their "natural" values. I describe the full models in Uslaner (2002: 98–102). The effects for measures of optimism and control overwhelm most other predictors in both models. The 1987 GSS has the best measure of long-term optimism, whether life will be better for the next generation. It also contains orientations toward human nature that express optimism (whether pay differences are needed for incentives to work hard and whether people earn advanced degrees for their own satisfaction or for higher pay), as well as other indicators of control over our lives (confidence in science and whether you can get ahead in life without knowing the "right people"). All of these measures are significant predictors of trust and most have effects of 0.10 or greater.

The 1971 Well-Being pilot contains a wealth of questions on both objective and subjective measures of well-being. Subjective measures of optimism matter a lot more than objective ones about economic circumstances. Collectively, the most optimistic person – who wants a fulfilling job, thinks about the future, and believes that she can make it regardless of luck, connections or current economic circumstances – is 36 percent more likely to trust others than the most convinced pessimist. The most prosperous person – with a relatively high family income, who owns his own home, has savings and a pension plan but does not have to make debt payments, whose parents were well-off, and has neither been laid off nor worried about losing his job – is 2 percent less likely to trust others than people who do not fare so well economically. Overall, then, there is strong support for the argument that a sense of optimism and control, rather than life experiences, shapes interpersonal trust. These models give little support to the argument that group membership or informal socializing builds trust.

If civic engagement doesn't lead to trust, might not trust lead to civic engagement (Stolle 1998)? Some forms of civic engagement go beyond the camer-aderie of like-minded folk. They reach out to people who are different – and less fortunate. Giving to charity and volunteering time lead us to reach out to people who are not part of our usual social circles. Both activities call up a sense of generalized (and moralistic) trust. And they also increase people's sense of moral worth, what economists call a "warm glow" from good deeds (Andreoni 1989).

The 1996 American National Election Study (ANES) asked people whether they were involved in 20 different types of voluntary organizations, encompassing religious, political, cultural and professional associations as well as groups addressed to the interests of the young, the old, women, hobbyists and people seeking self-help. The ANES also asked about volunteering and donating to charity as well as talking to neighbors and attending religious services. Overall there are 24 measures of civic engagement. I first estimated a probit model using the 24 indicators of civic engagement and a series of other predictors (see Uslaner 2002: 130–132 for the estimation).

Only two types of involvement have positive coefficients significant at $p<0.05$ or better and three more at $p<0.10$: business, cultural and children's groups, contributions to charity, and attending religious services. Joining an ethnic group makes you less trusting. All other forms of civic engagement – including the political, the religious, volunteering, talking to neighbors, and groups for education, self-help, women, the elderly, hobbyists, fraternal orders, workers and veterans – are moral dead ends.

I then estimated a three-stage least squares model of involvement in business, ethnic, cultural and church groups as well as charitable contributions and volunteering. I report the results for the effects of trust on civic engagement and for civic participation on trust in Table 8.1. Trust has powerful effects on business and cultural group involvement as well as on charitable contributions and volunteering. Trust is the strongest predictor of volunteering, with an impact almost double that of its closest rival, knowing and talking to your neighbors. Beyond church involvement, trust has the greatest effect of any variable on charitable contributions (just beating out family income). Trust matters most on those activities that signify the greatest commitment to your community – donating money and especially giving time. The two organizations where trust has big impacts help build bridges across groups. People make connections in business and professional societies – and these friendships are likely to be particularly important to women and minorities in a world traditionally dominated by white males. Cultural organizations can spread ideas that promote understanding of

Table 8.1 Summary of reciprocal effects of trust and civic engagement: 1996 ANES, three-stage least squares estimates

	Coefficient	*Standard error*	t *ratio*
Effects on trust from:			
Business group involvement	0.076	0.091	0.838
Children's group involvement	−0.155	0.088	−1.763
Ethnic group involvement	−0.088	0.247	−0.354
Cultural group involvement	−0.049	0.168	−0.296
Church group involvement	−0.435****	0.130	−3.358
Charitable contributions	0.669****	0.200	3.342
Volunteering	0.505***	0.163	3.090
Effects of trust on:			
Business group involvement	0.554****	0.117	4.733
Cultural group involvement	0.287****	0.073	3.919
Church group involvement	0.109	0.088	1.232
Children's group involvement	0.056	0.130	0.430
Ethnic group involvement	0.064*	0.048	1.339
Charitable contributions	0.278****	0.072	3.851
Volunteering	0.410****	0.100	4.113

Equation	*RMSE*	*Chi-square*	*N*
Trust	0.590	175.183	998
Business group involvement	0.681	145.672	998
Cultural group involvement	0.409	98.094	998
Church group involvement	0.476	246.222	998
Children's group involvement	0.639	103.058	998
Ethnic group involvement	0.251	28.067	998
Charitable contributions	0.388	236.095	998
Volunteering	0.502	109.390	998

Notes
****$p < 0.0001$; ***$p < 0.01$; **$p < 0.05$; *$p < 0.10$.

other peoples' music, art and drama. Associations based on churches, children and ethnic groups are less likely to build bridges across cultures.

Membership in organizations does not increase trust, no matter what the group is. If you are active in your house of worship, you might form your social circles with people like yourself and develop negative stereotypes of people who don't think as you do. Both giving to charity and donating time create "warm glows," feelings of doing good. Indeed, for both volunteering and especially for giving to charity, the boost in trust from helping others was greater than the impact of trust on acts of beneficence. The impact of volunteering on trust is 20 percent greater than the effect of trust on volunteering. And giving to charity has almost two and a half times the impact on trust that faith in others has on making contributions. But as powerful as giving time and money are, they are not the most important determinants of trust – whereas trust does rank at the top of the factors leading to acts of beneficence.

Trust also has consequences beyond civic engagement. Trusters indeed do reach out to people who are different from themselves. They are more tolerant of gays and lesbians, have more positive views of blacks and immigrants, and are more willing to open markets. Trusters also support policies that remedy the wrongs in our social system – anti-discrimination laws and policies that make it easier for minorities to take their full place in society: military service and adoption for gays, affirmative action for African-Americans (see Uslaner 2002: ch. 7).

Cross-nationally, high degrees of trust lead countries to spend more on redistributing wealth from the rich to the poor. High trusting societies have greater transfer payments, spend more on education, and have larger public sectors more generally (Uslaner 2002: chs 7–8; see LaPorta *et al.* 1998).

Trust and inequality

You can't get to trust just by interacting with people who are different from yourself. We learn trust early in life. Trust does rise and fall – but mainly in response to the economic conditions that provide the foundation for optimism (Uslaner 2002: chs 6, 8). And this dynamic plays out at the aggregate level: how well you are faring economically is not nearly as important as how well the country is doing. When economic inequality is increasing, trust declines. But there is no evidence that trust varies systematically with personal wealth.

Indeed, the level of economic equality is the strongest determinant of trust. There is strong evidence for the linkage in the United States, where we have good time series data on trust and across the American states. There is also powerful evidence cross-sectionally for countries without a legacy of Communism. The Nordic nations – Norway, Sweden, Denmark, and, of course, Finland – have (with The Netherlands) the highest levels of trust of any countries in the World Values Surveys. They also (especially Finland) have the most equitable distributions of income. I show these relationships in Figure 8.1 (see Uslaner 2002: chs 6 and 8 for the data sources and Uslaner and Brown 2005 for the results on the states) for the cross-national comparisons.

Equality promotes trust in two ways. First, a more equitable distribution of income makes people with less more optimistic that they too can share in society's bounty. And optimism is the basis of trust. Second, a more equitable distribution of income creates stronger bonds between different groups in society. When some people have far more than others, neither those at the top nor those at the bottom are likely to consider the other as part of their "moral community." They do not perceive a shared fate with others in society. Hence, they are less likely to trust people who may be different from themselves.

Trust and the state

My view of trust stands in contrast to others who hold that generalized trust is part of the same "trusting" syndrome as confidence in government (Lane 1959: 164) –

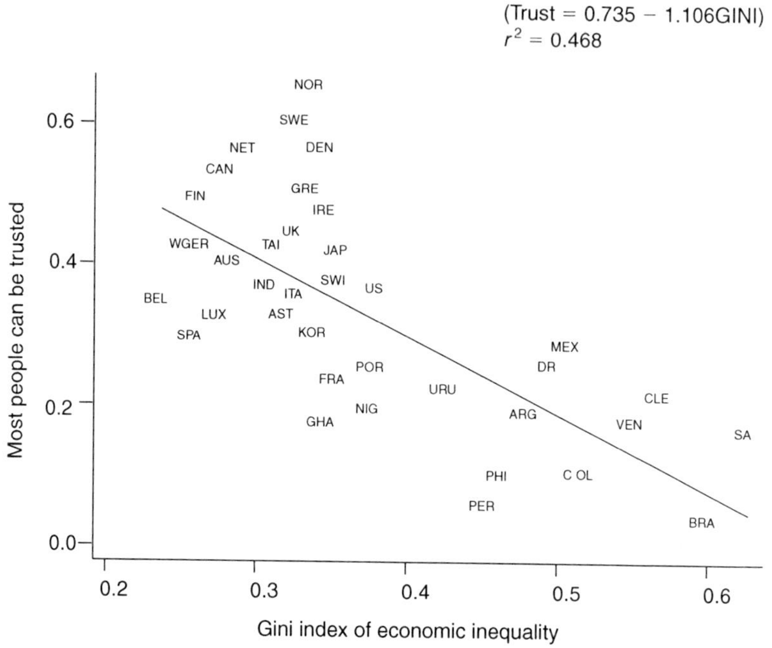

Figure 8.1 Trust and inequality for countries without a communist legacy.

Note
Observations plotted on graph indicate the country of the observation (for example, COL is the observation for Columbia).

or that confidence in government can lead to faith in fellow citizens. By ensuring that people can't get away with cheating each other and flouting the law, the state can create respect for authority. The more experience people have with compliance, the more likely they are to have confidence in others' good will (Brehm and Rahn 1997: 1008; Levi 1997; Offe 1999).

States can build trust in three other ways. First, democracy promotes trust (Brehm and Rahn 1997: 1008). Democratic regimes may be prerequisites for interpersonal trust (Muller and Seligson 1994). Second, strong government performance makes people feel better about government – and ultimately more willing to cooperate with each other (Brehm and Rahn 1997: 1008; Putnam 1993: 180). Third, honesty in government and fairness may promote interpersonal trust. Corrupt governments set bad examples for the types of behavior that will be tolerated from the citizenry. The correlation between societal corruption and interpersonal trust across 52 countries is −0.613. The most corrupt countries have the least trusting citizens. Citizens feel free to flout the legal system, producing firmer crackdowns by authorities and leading to what Putnam (1993: 115) calls "interlocking vicious circles" of corruption and mistrust. Rothstein (2001) elaborates on this linkage:

> if you think [. . .] that these [. . .] institutions [of law and order] do what they are supposed to do in a fair and effective manner, then you also have reason to believe that the chance of people getting away with such treacherous behavior is small. If so, you will believe that that people will have very good reason to refrain from acting in a treacherous manner, and you will therefore believe that "most people can be trusted."
>
> (Rothstein 2001: 491–492)

There is good reason to believe that there is a link between the state and trust. Aggregate analyses show that nations with more trusting populations have more open markets – and "better" government more generally: less corruption, less red tape in bureaucracy, and more efficient judicial systems (Uslaner 2002: chs 7–8; see LaPorta *et al.* 1998). But the bulk of the evidence seems to run from trust to good government rather than the other way around. A trusting citizenry leads to a more caring government – and to a more cooperative culture that promotes efficiency in government.

There is pretty strong evidence that authoritarianism (and especially Communism) leads to lower levels of trust. In countries with no legacy of Communist rule (democracies), the mean proportion of trusters in highly democratic regimes is 0.411, compared with 0.217 in the least democratic countries. Democracies are all over the place in trust, ranging from 0.03 (Brazil) to 0.65 (Norway). Formerly Communist regimes also vary in trust, but only from 0.06 to 0.34. Half of all democracies have more than 34 percent trusters. The standard deviation for democracies is 0.151. It is less than half that value (0.062) for authoritarian states. The formerly communist states of Eastern and Central Europe actually became less trusting as they became more democratic from 1990 to 1995.[4] Democracies make trust possible. They don't necessarily produce it.

Second, strong government performance leads to confidence in government, not faith in other people (Uslaner 2002: ch. 5). The mean tau-b correlation between trust in government and generalized trust in the United States is 0.117 for the ANES question on how much of the time the government in Washington can be trusted to do the right thing (over 13 surveys) and 0.084 for the General Social Survey question on confidence in the executive branch (over 17 surveys) – and the micro-foundations of the two kinds of trust are different (Uslaner 2002: 151–159). There are similar low correlations in other countries (Newton in press). Across 42 nations, there is but a modest correlation ($r = 0.154$) between trust in people and confidence in the legislative branch of government (from World Values Survey data).

It is not surprising that there is no clear link between trust in government and trust in people. Democratic politics is largely confrontational rather than cooperative. Generalized trust is the foundation for cooperation (in solving collective action problems, for example). Political life is all about winning and losing – defeating your opponents in an election and then implementing your policy proposals. Rothstein recognizes this when he points to the courts as the one institution of government that can promote a more cooperative society.

Can we increase trust by creating a stronger legal system? There is strong evidence that countries with higher levels of trust have stronger legal systems and less corruption (LaPorta *et al.* 1998: 335–336; Uslaner 2004a). Coercion can increase compliance with the law. Obeying the law because you fear the wrath of government will not make you more trusting – no matter how equally the heavy hand of the state is applied. It is easy to confuse compliance with voluntary acceptance, to confuse the law-abiding people of Singapore with those of Sweden. Even in high trusting countries such as Sweden, the linkage between confidence in the legal system and the police and trust in people is not very strong (Rothstein 2001).

Courts can save us from rascals only if there are few rascals (see Sitkin and Roth 1993). Law-abiding citizens, not rogue outlaws, create constitutions that work. You may write any type of constitution that you wish, but statutes alone won't create either compliance or trust. Coercion, Gambetta (1988: 220) argues, "falls short of being an adequate alternative to trust [. . .] It introduces an asymmetry which disposes of mutual trust and promotes instead power and resentment."

Any role for the state?

The state is not powerless in producing trust. The state has a powerful tool that it can use to shape the level of trust: shaping public policy. The most important factor shaping trust at the aggregate level, to repeat, is the level of economic inequality. States can reduce inequality through appropriate public policies – most notably universalistic social welfare policies. Means-tested policies may seem politically more profitable in the short run, as parties (especially on the left) seek to reward their electoral coalitions. However, means-tested policies ultimately stigmatize their recipients and create further divisions in a society, leading to lower levels of generalized trust (Rothstein and Uslaner 2005). Policies that reduce inequality have the potential to increase trust.

Legal systems may also have the capacity to shape trust. There is a reciprocal relationship between trust and corruption: the more trust, the less corruption – and the more corruption in a society, the less trust (Uslaner 2004a). In a survey of Romanians in 2003, there is strong support for the arguments that corruption leads to lower levels of generalized trust. But there is no direct connection between the perception that the courts are unfair and generalized trust. Instead, the survey results and aggregate indicators for transition countries more generally trace a clear linkage among corruption and unfair treatment by the courts, on the one hand, and rising levels of economic inequality on the other hand. The linkage from unfair courts and corruption to lower levels of trust depends entirely upon perceptions of growing inequality (Uslaner and Badescu 2004). Romanians are upset by corruption, but not all malfeasance bothers them. Making gift payments to doctors, police officers, teachers, local government officials or bank employees does not make Romanians less trusting. Needing connections to get things done for any of these same actors doesn't lead to less trust either. What matters is having to make "extra" gift payments to courts (Uslaner 2004b).

Government cannot promote trust simply by performing well. Nor does it seem that poor (or even dishonest) government destroys faith in other people. When state wrong-doing exacerbates increasing inequalities, people lose faith that the future will be better than the past and that they are the masters of their own fates. Loss of trust is the natural consequence.

Reprise

The determinants of trust I have discussed fall into three general categories: the cultural, the economic and the experiential. Cultural accounts lead to a pessimistic outlook on increasing trust so that societies can benefit from its blessings (economic growth, better government, more tolerance). If people learn trust early in life from their parents and trust is largely stable, then it seems rather difficult to raise a society's level of trust. Early socialization, especially if children can interact with people of different backgrounds (Uslaner 2002: ch. 6), seems promising. But it is not easy to convince intolerant parents to permit their children to socialize with kids who look very different from their own. Education also builds trust by broadening our perspectives on other cultures – and this seems more promising – but. . .

The "but" is the same qualification that we find for economic policy. Reshaping the distribution of resources in society may seem to be less daunting than reshaping an entire culture. But the level of economic inequality changes slowly and marginally less than trust does. The r^2 for the most commonly used measures of economic inequality (Deininger and Squire 1996) between 1980 and 1990 is not quite as strong as the connection with trust over time, but it is still substantial at 0.676 for a sample of 42 countries. A new inequality database developed by James Galbraith extends measures of inequality further back in time and across more countries.[5] The r^2 between economic inequality in 1963 and economic inequality in 1996 is 0.706 (for 37 countries).

Persistent inequality and low trust combine to produce a "social trap." As Rothstein and I argue (2005): high levels of inequality contribute to lower levels of trust, which lessen the political and societal support for universal welfare programs. Unequal societies find themselves trapped in a continuous cycle of inequality, low trust in others and in government, policies that do little to reduce the gap between the rich and the poor. Demands for radical redistribution, as we see in many of the transition countries, exacerbate social tensions rather than relieving them. There will be no political support for universal programs since the rich benefit from high-level corruption and see the poor as "underserving." The poor see almost all success in the market economy as evidence of dishonest behavior and believe that those who are well off already have taken more than enough from the state. The idea that the better off should also have access to public services and benefits seems awkward. Even if you could generate enough political support to enact universal programs, people may not have enough confidence in government institutions to deliver them fairly and without corruption.

There is little evidence to support the argument that policy change is easier than culture shifts. Had states enacted policies designed to bring education to much larger segments of the society, overall economic inequality should have fallen much more sharply – and there should have been a decrease in educational inequality. World Bank data on educational inequality suggest even greater stickiness than "simple" income inequality: the r^2 between educational inequality in 1960 and 1990 is 0.797 for 53 countries. There is plenty of evidence for a social trap – and for why trust has remained low for many countries.

It would be far easier for the state to mobilize people to join civic groups or simply to socialize in the hope of building trust. The World Bank is much enamored of this approach – establishing bowling leagues in Mali seems a less demanding way of increasing trust (leading to economic growth and ultimately the ability to repay the Bank's loans) than restructuring the country's distribution of wealth. During the Clinton administration, some Americans might recall the proposal to have the police run "midnight basketball" clinics in poor neighborhoods to engage young men and boys who might otherwise wind up in trouble. All of these ideas sound nice – except that it simply doesn't seem that group membership or informal socializing has any capacity to increase trust. And when economic inequality is growing and the demand for good works increases, it is more important than ever to build up bonds across the economic divide. Yet, it is difficult to get people to give what little they have (in money or time) to charitable causes. As inequality has increased in the United States, our social conscience weakens and the rich and the poor become less likely to perceive a common fate: trust has fallen and fewer people seem disposed to give much of themselves (Uslaner 2002: 200–210).

Changing state structures may seem to be easier than changing cultures or the distribution of resources in a society. Yet even here stability reigns. The level of corruption as measured by the Business International Corruption index in 1980–1985 remained largely the same in the Transparency International measure in 2004 ($r^2 = 0.765$ for 39 countries) despite different ways of measuring corruption. The legacy of corruption goes back even further – many centuries by Putnam's (1993) argument about southern Italy. In the United States, there is a moderate negative correlation ($r^2 = 0.284$, $n = 30$) between reporters' perceptions of corruption in the American states in 1999 and the vote for the reformist third-party Presidential candidate Robert LaFollette in 1924 (Uslaner in press).

Were the state autonomous and were the state able to shape trust independent of cultural and economic factors, we might expect greater variations in trust over time and across countries. We see this for trust in government, but faith in other people is not so malleable. Its roots are largely cultural and economic – and that is why states find themselves so weak in shaping how people feel about their fellow citizens.

Notes

1 This paper summarizes the argument in Uslaner (2002). I gratefully acknowledge the support of the Russell Sage Foundation, the General Research Board of the University of Maryland–College Park and the Everett McKinley Dirksen Center for the Study of Congressional Leadership. Most of the data I employ were obtained from the Inter-University Consortium for Political and Social Research, which is absolved from any responsibility for my claims.

2 This result comes from an analysis of the 1993 General Social Survey in the United States, where performing music is best predicted by liking classical music, as well as looking for opportunities to meet others with similar preferences – other predictors are age (young) and income (high).

3 Optimism is the basis of trust, but they are not the same thing. For an extended argument, see Uslaner (2002: ch. 4).

4 These data come from the eight formerly Communist countries surveyed by the World Study in 1990 and the mid-1990s: Belarus, East Germany, Estonia, Latvia, Lithuania, Poland, Russia and Slovenia and the Freedom House freedom scores (see n. 4). The eight formerly Communist countries became 5 percent less trusting, but the average freedom score increased from a "not free" 11 in 1988 to 4.75 in 1998, comparable with India, Chile, the Dominican Republic, the Philippines and Venezuela.

5 The Gakbraith data can be accessed at utip.gov.utexas.edu/web/.

References

Andreoni, J. (1989) "Giving With Impure Altruism: Applications to Charity and Ricardian Ambivalence," *Journal of Political Economy*, 97: 1447–1458.

Banfield, E. (1958) *The Moral Basis of a Backward Society*, New York: Free Press.

Brehm, J. and Rahn, W. (1997) "Individual Level Evidence for the Causes and Consequences of Social Capital," *American Journal of Political Science*, 41: 888–1023.

Dasgupta, P. (1988) "Trust as a Commodity," in D. Gambetta (ed.) *Trust*, Oxford: Blackwell, pp. 49–72.

Deininger, K. and Squire, L. (1996) "A New Data Set: Measuring Economic Income Inequality," *World Bank Economic Review*, 10: 565–592.

Erikson, E. (1968) *Identity: Youth and Crisis*, New York: W.W. Norton.

Gambetta, D. (1988) "Can We Trust Trust?," in D. Gambetta (ed.) *Trust*, Oxford: Blackwell, pp. 213–237.

Hardin, R. (1992) "The Street Level Epistemology of Trust," *Analyse and Kritik*, 14: 152–176.

Hertzberg, L. (1988) "On the Attitude of Trust," *Inquiry*, 31: 307–322.

Knack, S. and Keefer, P. (1997) "Does Social Capital Have An Economic Payoff? A Cross-Country Investigation," *Quarterly Journal of Economics*, 112: 1251–1288.

Lane, R.E. (1959) *Political Life*, New York: Free Press.

LaPorta, R., Lopez-Silanes, F. Schleifer, A. and Vishney, R.W. (1998) "The Quality of Government," unpublished manuscript, Harvard University.

Levi, M. (1997) "A State of Trust," unpublished manuscript, University of Washington.

Luhmann, N. (1979) *Trust and Power*, Chichester: John Wiley and Sons.

Mansbridge, J. (1999) "Altruistic Trust," in M. Warren (ed.) *Democracy and Trust*, New York: Cambridge University Press, pp. 290–309.

Muller, E.N. and Seligson, M.A. (1994) "Civic Culture and Democracy: The Question of Causal Relationships," *American Political Science Review*, 88: 635–652.

Newton, K. (in press) "Trust and Politics," in D. Castiglione, J.W. van Deth, and G. Wolleb (eds) *Handbook of Social Capital*, Oxford: Oxford University Press.

—— (1997) "Social Capital and Democracy," *American Behavioral Scientist*, 40: 575–586.

Offe, C. (1999) "Trust and Knowledge, Rules and Decisions: Exploring a Difficult Conceptual Terrain," in M. Warren (ed.) *Democracy and Trust*, Cambridge: Cambridge University Press, pp. 42–87.

Putnam, R.D. (2000) *Bowling Alone*, New York: Simon and Schuster.

—— (1993) *Making Democracy Work: Civic Traditions in Modern Italy*, Princeton, NJ: Princeton University Press.

Rosenberg, M. (1956) "Misanthropy and Political Ideology," *American Sociological Review*, 21: 690–695.

Rosenblum, N.L. (1998) *Membership and Morals*, Princeton, NJ: Princeton University Press.

Rosenstone, S.J. and Hansen, J.M. (1993) *Mobilization, Participation, and Democracy in America*, New York: Macmillan.

Rothstein, B. (2001) "Trust, Social Dilemmas, and Collective Memories: On the Rise and Decline of the Swedish Model," *Journal of Theoretical Politics*, 12: 477–499.

Rothstein, B. and Uslaner, E.M. (2005) "All for All: Equality and Social Trust," *World Politics*, 58: 41–72.

Seligman, A.B. (1997) *The Problem of Trust*, Princeton, N.J.: Princeton University Press.

Sitkin, S.B. and Roth, N.L. (1993) "Explaining the Limited Effectiveness of Legalistic 'Remedies' for Trust/Distrust," *Organization Science*, 4: 367–392.

Stolle, D. (1998) "Bowling Together, Bowling Alone: The Development of Generalized Trust in Voluntary Associations," *Political Psychology*, 19: 497–526.

Uslaner, E.M. (in press) "The Civil State: Trust, Polarization, and the Quality of State Government," in J. Cohen (ed.) *Public Opinion in State Politics*, Stanford: Stanford University Press.

—— (2004a) "Trust and Corruption," in J. Graf Lambsdorf, M. Taube and M. Schramm (eds) *Corruption and the New Institutional Economics*, London: Routledge, pp. 76–92.

—— (2004b) "Coping and Social Capital: The Informal Sector and the Democratic Transition," Paper presented at the conference on "Unlocking Human Potential: Linking the Formal and Informal Sectors," Helsinki, 17–18 September 2004.

—— (2002) *The Moral Foundations of Trust*, New York: Cambridge University Press.

Uslaner, E.M. and Badescu, G. (2004) "Making the Grade in Transition: Equality, Transparency, Trust, and Fairness," unpublished manuscript, University of Maryland–College Park.

Uslaner, E.M. and Brown, M.M. (2005) "Inequality, Trust, and Civic Engagement," *American Politics Research*, 33: 868–894.

Yamigishi, T. and Yamigishi, M. (1994) "Trust and Commitment in the United States and Japan," *Motivation and Emotion*, 18: 129–166.

9 Workplace democracy

Turning workers into citizens?[1]

Neil Carter

Introduction

The widespread contemporary concern in liberal democracies about declining participation in voting and other political activities has generated considerable interest in a broad range of institutional innovations aimed at encouraging public participation. Yet there has been little discussion of workplace democracy, which is puzzling given that several of the leading proponents of participatory democracy have specifically emphasized the importance of democratizing the workplace. In particular, Carole Pateman (1970) argued that participation in workplace decision-making will spillover into wider society by increasing the probability of participation in politics beyond the workplace. Indeed, Mason (1982: 78) has argued that the similarity between the workplace and government experience in terms of the mode, intensity and quality of participation suggests that the most efficient and effective way of increasing participation in government is to increase participation in the workplace. Thus, in the light of the current search for institutional solutions to the "crisis of participation," the *spillover thesis* merits reassessment.

This chapter provides an evaluation of the spillover thesis, based on a wide-ranging survey of the empirical evidence concerning the relationship between workplace democratization, political efficacy and public participation. The primary focus is on worker co-operatives – organizations owned and controlled by the workforce – where participation might be expected to be most extensive and regular, and therefore to have most impact. The opening sections outline the spillover thesis and assess the empirical evidence for it. The following section provides a detailed examination of the key processes underpinning the educative element of the thesis, focusing on the mode of workplace participation and the subjective experience of participatory mechanisms. The evidence demonstrates that the process of spillover is far more complex and uncertain than its proponents suggest. In particular, there are several factors mediating the impact of workplace participation on political efficacy, which suggests that spillover into wider political participation will be difficult to achieve. The final discussion, building on the work of Greenberg *et al.* (1996), offers a further respecification of the spillover thesis.

The spillover thesis

In *Participation and Democratic Theory* (1970), Pateman outlines a normative case for workplace democracy as a vital means of increasing public participation in the wider polity, which is now widely known as the "spillover thesis." She drew on a rich tradition of classical democratic theorists, notably Rousseau, J.S. Mill and G.D.H. Cole, to attack the elitist theorists, such as Schumpeter and Sartori, for their narrow definition of democracy as competition for office between vote-seeking elites, rather than as involving the active participation of citizens. If her critique of liberal democracy as a very "thin" form of democracy is now familiar, nonetheless Pateman's book was a landmark, opposing the then dominant assumption in political science that the prevailing pattern of low political participation and widespread apathy was normal and, as it was "nobody's fault" (Sartori 1962), should be accepted as given.

Pateman insisted that the existence of liberal democratic institutions at a national level is not sufficient for democracy; instead, a healthy polity needs regular and active participation by all its citizens. For Pateman, participation, apart from being a good thing in itself, also plays a crucial educative role. Following Rousseau and Mill, she argued that individual attitudes and behavior are shaped by the institutions within which they act. So, where individuals actively engage in democratic institutions – debating and deliberating – they are more likely to develop the necessary attitudes, skills and psychological qualities that contribute to individual political efficacy, and which in turn will increase political participation. Thus the act of participation is itself educative: "Participation develops and fosters the very qualities necessary for it; the more individuals participate the better able they become to do so" (Pateman 1970: 42–43).

Pateman's key contribution to democratic theory, developing the observations of Mill and Cole, was to emphasize the linkage between the workplace and politics. She observed that most people spend a large part of their daily lives in the workplace, usually in authoritarian organizations where they exercise little influence over their work. The hierarchical, bureaucratic organizations typical of capitalist liberal democracies give people little opportunity to hone their democratic skills. Yet the workplace is in many respects a political system very similar to government, notably because "the business of the workplace provides an education in the management of collective affairs that is difficult to parallel elsewhere" (Ibid: 43).[2] Pateman argued that by democratizing the workplace – transferring ownership and control to the workers – individuals will be able to participate in routine decision-making affecting their immediate work environment, an arena in which they have first-hand knowledge. As Macpherson (1977: 104) later put it, individuals involved in workplace democracy "are getting experience of participation in decision-making in that side of their lives – their lives at work – where their concern is greater, or at least more immediately and directly felt, than in any other."

The next, crucial, step in Pateman's argument is that because "people learn to participate by participating, and that feelings of political efficacy are more likely to be developed in a participatory environment," (Ibid: 105) the effect of democratizing the workplace will also escalate beyond the factory gate. As workers find that they can exercise greater control over their working lives, they will seek to shape other aspects of their lives by participating in civic and political institutions. Moreover, having learnt to participate at work they will have acquired the confidence, skills and desire to participate in civic society. In short, workplace democracy will turn workers into citizens.

Pateman (1976) believed that workplace democracy should be encouraged primarily for instrumental reasons:

> The aim of organizational democracy is democracy. It is not primarily increased productivity, efficiency, or industrial relations (even though these things may even result from democracy); rather it is to further justice, equality, freedom, the rights of citizens, and the protection of the interests of citizens, all familiar democratic aims.
>
> (Pateman 1976: 22f.)

Other benefits may follow, notably by encouraging greater economic equality, which, in turn, enhances democracy by equipping individuals with the "independence and security necessary for (equal) participation" (Pateman 1970: 43). But the key claim, reiterated by democratic theorists such as Macpherson (1977) and Mason (1982), is that the educative experiences of participation in the workplace will spill over into the wider polity.

The spillover thesis is underpinned by some big claims about the relationship between workplace experience and political efficacy. It is important, therefore, to clarify what Pateman meant by political efficacy. She defined it by directly linking the general sense of personal effectiveness and self-confidence nurtured by the act of participation with political efficacy or competence, and she drew approvingly on Almond and Verba's observation that "the belief in one's competence is a key political attitude" (Pateman 1970: 46). Pateman discussed political efficacy primarily in terms of the "psychological benefits" (p. 46) accruing from participation; or, as Mason (1982: ch. 4) put it, participation at work nurtures the attitudes and skills, or psychological traits, associated with a "participatory persuasion." This language exposed Pateman to the criticism that she was applying a narrow behaviorist use of the term, but she subsequently made clear that she had a "multi-dimensional" understanding of political efficacy, which encompassed psychological as well as normative (the extent to which norms of political efficacy have been absorbed) and cognitive (knowledge and belief about the operation of the political system) dimensions (Pateman 1971: 298). Indeed, a central part of her explanation for low public participation was that if the experiences and perceptions of the operation of the political system leave citizens with a sense of frustration and powerlessness, then "apathy is a realistic response, it does not seem worthwhile to participate" (Pateman 1971: 298) – which, she argued, is a cognitive rather than a psychological response.

The key questions posed by the spillover thesis concern the relationship between the workplace experience and political efficacy. Pateman distinguishes two separate, but related, processes: first, between workplace participation and the development of an individual's personal effectiveness and political efficacy; and, second, between this political efficacy and wider political participation. However, the precise nature of these two processes needs to be demonstrated rather than just asserted. In particular, the linkage between workplace participation and the transformation of individual attitudes and behavior generates many questions. Will all forms of workplace participation produce a similar effect, or will the mode, intensity and quality of participation generate different outcomes? Will subjective perceptions of participation affect the development of political efficacy; if individuals do not enjoy the process of participation or doubt its value, can it still exert a positive impact? What internal and external factors will shape the individual's experience of workplace participation? The answers to these questions will help us to explain why, as is revealed in the next section, there is limited empirical evidence supporting the simple spillover thesis.

Evidence for the spillover thesis?

One major weakness of Pateman's work, as she conceded (1970: 106–107), was that when she wrote there was very little evidence supporting her core claims. She was unable to draw on the experience of fully worker-owned enterprises, apart from Scott Bader, where a benevolent entrepreneur transferred ownership to his workforce. Consequently, she drew heavily on studies of participation in conventional businesses to argue that workplace participation enhances personal and political efficacy. She also examined the Yugoslav system of self-management and worker councils, although her tentative optimism was not supported by later studies that raised serious doubts about the extent of participation in these enterprises[3] (notwithstanding the difficulty in making meaningful comparisons between public participation in Yugoslavia and contemporary Western liberal democracies).

Remarkably, over 35 years later, there are still very few studies that investigate empirically the link between workplace and public participation, and these offer only limited support for the spillover thesis.[4] Wajcman (1983: 182) found that the experience of working in a small British women's co-operative had little impact on individual political consciousness, and even for the women who participated actively and assumed new responsibilities, "the increased confidence and knowledge they gained through these activities never found expression beyond the confines of the factory." A few studies, notably Elden (1981) and Mason (1982), have followed Pateman in seeking to show that workplace participation in conventionally owned companies enhances personal and political efficacy, but the link to political participation is still usually presumed rather than proven (Greenberg *et al.* 1996: 307). Several studies have indicated some weak statistical links between various forms of workplace participation and political participation (Lafferty 1985; Smith 1985; Peterson 1992; Sobel 1993).

The major exception is Greenberg's (1986) work on the plywood co-operatives of the American Pacific North West. Greenberg's findings were mixed (pp. 119–131). He detected no evidence of greater political efficacy amongst co-operative workers. Whilst he found *lower* levels of involvement in community organizations (such as trade unions, parties, churches) amongst co-operative members compared with conventional organizations, over time worker-owners reached parity with workers in conventional firms, which is consistent with the educative assumption of the spillover thesis. He found a weak association between workplace participation and political participation, although it was only statistically significant for community involvement and attendance at government meetings, but not for voting and party campaign activity. Significantly, it was those workers participating actively in co-operative governance who were most likely to be involved in wider democratic politics and that the longer workers had been involved in workplace decision-making, the higher their rates of political participation. However, in a follow-up investigation of three co-operatives, an ESOP and a range of conventional firms ten years later (which identified important weaknesses in the earlier study), Greenberg *et al.* (1996: 306) found that "members of the most democratic enterprises were the least likely to participate in outside politics." In short, the most important and thorough test of the spillover thesis is inconclusive.

Thus there is only limited empirical evidence supporting the spillover thesis, and what there is suggests that the relationship between workplace participation and public participation may be more complex than Pateman acknowledged. Indeed, drawing on their findings, Greenberg *et al.* (1996: 305) offer a respecification of the *simple spillover thesis* to take account of: (a) the possible differential effects on political participation of direct and representative forms of workplace participation; (b) the possibility that the pathway between workplace and political participation may be indirect, and mediated by psychological factors such as self-confidence and a sense of mastery; and (c) the possibility that participation in an economically troubled enterprise might diminish political participation. Each clarification explicitly questions the direct relationship between workplace participation and the development in individuals of a "participatory persuasion." This focus on the first step in the spillover thesis is important: after all, if the educative effect of workplace participation is more context specific than proponents of the spillover thesis acknowledge, then its wider impact on public participation will be limited. Fortunately, although few political scientists have tested the spillover thesis, there is extensive evidence about worker co-operatives in the sub-disciplines of industrial relations and organizational studies thesis that helps answer the questions identified in the previous section about the way that workplace participation affects individual attitudes and behavior. Consequently, I argue below that the revisions identified by Greenberg *et al.* (1996) represent only the starting point for a further respecification of the spillover thesis, but first it is important to be clear about what is meant by participation.

Defining workplace participation

Pateman (1970: 68–72) distinguishes between pseudo, partial and full workplace participation. *Pseudo* participation refers to the plethora of management-initiated schemes designed to persuade workers to accept decisions that have already been made; she rightly rules these out of consideration. *Partial* participation involves a process whereby two or more parties influence each other, but final power to decide rests with one party (management) alone. *Full* participation gives each individual member equal power to determine the outcome of decisions. Pateman further distinguishes between *lower* and *higher* levels of management: lower level decisions affect the day-to-day control of shop floor activity, whereas higher level decisions relate to the operation of the entire enterprise, such as investment and marketing. She notes that partial participation typically involves only lower level decisions, but full participation could take place at either level. Finally, Pateman distinguishes between *democracy* and *participation*. Partial participation could occur without any democratization of the authority structures in an organization, as could full participation at the lower levels of management; but a system of industrial democracy would involve full higher level participation by employees.

Pateman's original statement of her participatory theory of democracy assumed that democratization of the entire firm was required in order to produce the required psychological effect on political efficacy. She amended this assumption in the light of her survey of the (albeit limited) evidence, which suggested that full participation at lower levels might have some positive impact on political efficacy. However, she remained convinced that higher level participation would be more effective in nurturing political efficacy and providing workers with the skills required for wider public participation (Pateman 1970: 74). Consequently, it seems reasonable to judge the spillover thesis on the "best case scenario" of organizations that are genuinely democratized, with ownership and control residing in the hands of the workers. Therefore the following analysis focuses on the experience of worker co-operatives, where the workers own and control their workplace.

Developing a participatory persuasion

This section draws on empirical studies of worker co-operatives to identify seven variables that mediate the impact of participation on individual workers. The first two variables relate to participatory structures and the remaining five variables concern the subjective experience of participation.

Co-operatives have adopted a wide range of democratic structures, ranging from direct, participatory democracy to indirect, representative democracy. Co-operatives organized on participatory lines were the norm amongst the mass of grassroots collectives that sprang up in the 1960s and 1970s across North America and Europe, as well as in many other small co-operative businesses (Case and Taylor 1979; Mansbridge 1980; Rothschild and Whitt 1986; Cornforth *et al.* 1988). Some were organized on pure collectivist principles, with all decisions requiring consensus; others had active member participation in higher and lower level decisions, alongside some indirect participation via an elected management committee. However, representative structures have been more common, predominating in the large co-operative sectors in France (Batstone 1983) and Italy (Earle 1986), most larger British co-operatives (Cornforth *et al.* 1988; Mellor *et al.* 1988), the US plywood co-operatives studied by Greenberg (1986) and in the thriving Mondragon federation of over one hundred co-operatives in the Basque country (Whyte and Whyte 1988; Cheney 2002).

Greenberg *et al.*'s respecified model states that the simple spillover thesis should be revised to take account of the possible differential effects on political participation of direct and representational forms of participation. Their findings suggest that direct forms of participation, where workers engage more frequently in decision-making, are more likely to have the kind of educative impact suggested by Pateman. The co-operative literature suggests an even more complex relationship, because the choice of participatory structure and the degree of active participation by workers is strongly influenced by two variables: the origins of a co-operative and organizational size.

The *origins* of a co-operative may shape both the choice of structure (between indirect and direct participation) and the intensity of member participation. There are several typologies of co-operatives based on their origins (e.g. Paton 1978; Cornforth *et al.* 1988: pp. 8–10), but the four main types are endowed, defensive, alternative and job creation co-operatives. *Endowed* co-operatives involve the transfer of the ownership of an existing company to its employees, as at British co-operatives Scott Bader (Pateman 1970: 80–83), Fairblow Dynamics (Paton and Lockett 1978) and Topline Typewriters (Carter 1987). The benevolent former owner, true to the paternalism that prompted the handover, typically imposes strict conditions for the control of the enterprise that involve a representative structure and limited opportunities for higher and lower level worker participation. *Defensive* co-operatives, such as the three "Benn co-operatives," are formed by employees in the hope of preserving their jobs after the closure of a business.[5] They are often an act of desperation. The workers seize on the co-operative idea not because they have always wanted to run their own business, but because it offers the best chance of salvaging some jobs after a factory closure. Initially, the members (usually shopfloor workers used to undemocratic management structures) have no strong wish to participate actively in decision-making, preferring to appoint or elect managers to make decisions (Wajcman 1983; Carter 1987), or allow union representatives to act on their behalf (Eccles 1981). *Alternative* co-operatives, such as the wave of grass-roots collectives that flourished in the 1960s and 1970s, are set up primarily for social or political (rather than economic) reasons. The members join these co-operatives precisely because they reject the conventional bureaucratic organization structures of the capitalist firm in favor of democratic, collectivist, structures, and because of the product or service provided, such as wholefoods or bicycle repairs. Studies of American collectives (Rothschild and Whitt 1986) and Scottish alternative co-ops (Oliver 1984) found member profiles to be typical of new social movements: young, well-educated, transient individuals keen to exercise control over their lives. Finally, the *job creation* co-operative is a catch-all category for several kinds of co-operative. As these range from a co-operative set up by unemployed workers with support from a local development agency to groups of professional lawyers or architects, it is hard to make any firm claims about their participatory characteristics.

The origins of a co-operative may influence the attitudes and behavior of the workforce towards participation. For example, in an endowed co-operative the workers are "conscripts" in the sense that participation has been imposed on them from the top; typically the workforce will be divided between those who relish the opportunity to get involved, and others who are uninterested (Paton and Lockett 1978; Carter 1987). In an alternative co-operative, however, it is more likely that most members will regard democratic structures as intrinsically desirable and will wish to utilize them. By contrast, in defensive co-operatives most members are initially uninterested in, or at least uncertain about, participation. Eccles (1981), for example, observed very little workforce participation over five years in one radiator manufacturing co-operative of 750 members. Yet Carter's (1987) study of the first three years of a small shoe co-operative charted the gradual development of participatory activity and its associated skills as members acquired a taste for workplace participation that supported Pateman's claim that people can learn to participate. Thus the origins of a co-operative can influence both the choice of participatory structure and the extent to which workers utilize those formal participatory structures.

One difference between the co-operatives studied by Eccles and Carter was organizational *size*. An analysis of several American grassroots collectives led Mansbridge (1980) to conclude that democracy can work effectively only in a relatively small group, although Rothschild and Whitt (1986: 92–95) found no precise cut-off point beyond which democratic control yields to oligarchy. Nevertheless some delegation of responsibilities usually occurs in co-operatives larger than 15–20 members, when collective processes become less practical; the critical question then is how far co-operatives with representative structures allow (or encourage) active participation by the workforce. In a study of Israeli kibbutzim, Rosner (1983) found that participation in both the factory and community diminishes as the assembly grows in size. Yet larger co-operatives still usually boast greater participation than conventional firms of a similar size. A study of six San Francisco (partially worker-owned) scavenger firms found that worker-owners were widely perceived as exercising a greater amount of influence within the organization than comparable groups of workers in other types of firm (Russell *et al.* 1979). But are positive perceptions of participation sufficient to nurture political efficacy? One study of Mondragon reported that around one-third of members regarded themselves as participating either directly or indirectly in making important decisions, compared with just 7 percent in equivalent capitalist firms (Bradley and Gelb 1983: 54), even though the General Assembly of members usually met just once a year, only a handful of workers were involved in the elected management council and there was little evidence of an active participatory culture. Significantly, after a strike at the largest Mondragon co-operative in 1974, the size of co-operatives was restricted to a maximum of 500 workers and social councils were introduced in each co-operative – in effect a network of work-based shop stewards – where members can discuss job and workplace issues with management. It seems that organizational size is therefore important in mediating both the mode of a participatory structure and the way it operates, but what of the experience of participation for individual co-operative members?[6]

The spillover thesis presumes that workers will have a positive response to participation – that people will like it, value it, even develop a thirst for it. Indeed, many workers clearly do prize the co-operative experience. Mondragon workers display high levels of vertical trust between managers and workers, and high commitment, involvement and motivation (Bradley and Gelb 1983), while workers in American plywood co-ops (Greenberg 1986) and Israeli kibbutzim (Rosner 1983) value participation. Similarly in grassroots co-operatives in the USA and the UK, members were strongly committed, involved and satisfied in their work (Oliver 1984; Rothschild and Whitt 1986: ch. 6).

However, what if participation does not have this positive impact? Participation comes in many shapes and forms; not surprisingly, therefore, other studies report that many people are either apathetic or negative about it. But if individuals have a negative experience of workplace participation, will they develop the political efficacy predicted by the spillover thesis? In a significant finding, Greenberg *et al.* (1996) report that the representative form of participation actually *diminishes* political participation, and that it undermines their sense of mastery, which they tentatively explain in terms of "whether the experience of participating in decision making at work is a positive or negative experience" (p. 320). In the remainder of this section five variables are identified that may shape the attitudes and behavior of workers towards participation: forms of informal control; member expectations, the external economic environment, job autonomy and conflict.

First, to what extent do the formal structures of control reflect what really happens? Put differently, do the processes of *informal* control reflect the formal structure? There is certainly no guarantee that the existence of direct participatory structures will result in active participation by all workers. Numerous case studies have shown that many members prefer to let others get on with decision-making (Wajcman 1983; Carter 1987; inter alia). A constant refrain from active co-operative members, notably managers and committee members, is that the wider workforce does not participate actively in meetings or take responsibility for decisions. Indeed, many co-operatives experience a process of *organizational degeneration* (Webb and Webb 1914; Cornforth *et al.* 1988: ch. 6) whereby control becomes increasingly concentrated in the hands of a few and a range of capitalistic organizational practices, such as a management hierarchy and division of labor, are adopted. Degeneration can result from both internal and external pressures. The most powerful internal pressures are associated with the "iron law of oligarchy," which states that direct democracy is inefficient and that elected leaders in democratic organizations will seek to become a ruling elite (Michels 1959). External pressures arise from the critical tension facing a democratic organization operating within a market economy, which make it difficult for co-operatives to avoid falling back on capitalist organizational practices (Nichols 1980: 25). Whilst there is extensive debate about the inevitability of degeneration (see Cornforth *et al.* 1988: ch. 6; Estrin and Jones 1992), no one doubts that it happens, and where degeneration does occur it may obstruct the development of political efficacy, as few members will be participating actively.

The *expectations* of members can also profoundly affect the impact of workplace participation. Unrealistically optimistic expectations may have a negative long-term impact on member attitudes and behavior. This problem seems particularly acute in endowed co-operatives. Long (1982) found that after the conversion of one firm to worker-ownership, a period of stable job attitudes was followed by a reduction in commitment, involvement and motivation, which he explained as the result of workforce expectations of greater influence being raised, but then dashed. Similarly, at Fairblow Dynamics (Paton and Lockett 1978) conversion to a co-operative increased formal participation, but it had little impact on satisfaction because raised expectations were soon dissipated by the members' perception that managerial prerogatives remained unchanged. Expectations can also lead to disillusionment in alternative collectives where "high expectations and the sense of mission in collectives may lead to more intense, engaging work, but engagement exacts a price: stress" (Rothschild and Whitt 1986: 156). The combination of emotional intensity, interpersonal conflict and tendency to overwork frequently results in the burn-out of some of the most active members of small co-operatives, characterized by growing disillusionment that the organization is not living up to their high expectations. The experience of defensive co-operatives is quite different. Where the co-operative option is simply a pragmatic strategy to secure employment, the opportunities offered by participation engender lower expectations, so that members may regard even a small amount of influence positively. If members do actively engage in direct participatory structures, they are regarded in a very positive light (Carter 1987). However, once participatory structures are introduced, all the problems and frustrations faced by a struggling defensive co-operative are likely to be expressed through them, thereby turning the democratic forum into a harbinger of bad news – an arena characterized by gloom and doom. At KME Kirkby, Eccles (1981: 377) observed how the initial expectations and mood of "trust, some excitement and hope" gradually declined through "puzzlement, disappointment and recrimination" to "apathy, fatalism and suspicion."

The *external economic environment* is another mediating factor because "participation in decision making in economically troubled enterprises might undermine the positive link between workplace and political participation" (Greenberg *et al.* 1996: 323). Both the historic (Webb and Webb 1914; Shirom 1972) and contemporary (Cornforth *et al.* 1988) records of co-operatives show that many have struggled on the margins of economic survival or failure. Defensive co-operatives, formed by rescuing a failing enterprise, usually struggle from the start and many survive for only a few years (Eccles 1981; Wajcman 1983). New-start co-operatives, like so many other small businesses, either quickly collapse or struggle under the permanent shadow of bankruptcy. In such dire economic circumstances, co-operative workers are effectively engaged in self-exploitation: working long hours for low pay in poor "sweatshop" conditions (Wajcman 1983; Mellor *et al.* 1988). But no longer do they work a "nine to five" day and forget work when they pass through the factory gate; instead they participate in decision-making, and may become stressed by the business worries they take home with them. In such circumstances it is hardly surprising that the experience of participation may be negative. As Greenberg *et al.* (1996: 320) observe, participating in the running of a failing enterprise must be a "deeply demoralizing experience." How far can workers get a sense of mastery if all they do is struggle against apparently irresistible forces?

Nor are individuals likely to develop a sense of mastery without possessing some control over their immediate work environment. The absence of *job autonomy* is a key factor contributing to the alienation that characterizes the work experience in many capitalist enterprises. Alienation has several dimensions, notably powerlessness, meaninglessness, isolation and self-estrangement (Blauner 1964). If the day-to-day work of co-operative members remains unchanged – if they still feel powerless, if their job is boring – then the introduction of formal democratic decision-making structures may have little impact on their working lives. Many of the causes of alienation appear to lie elsewhere. For Blauner, technology is the critical factor, as it makes some work intrinsically repetitive, monotonous or unpleasant. As Eccles wryly commented about the shopfloor at the newly formed KME Kirkby co-operative, "It is difficult to tell a man with a welding torch still in front of him that he's part of a new system" (1981: 382). Whether working in a democratic or an authoritarian workplace, boring work is boring work.

It could be countered that no work is intrinsically alienating; from a subjectivist viewpoint it depends on what meaning people ascribe to it. In a co-operative members may feel a sense of ownership and involvement that is absent from the capitalist workplace such that even the most mundane of tasks is invested with purpose and meaning. Yet, whilst this argument might hold in the heady early days after a new participatory system is introduced, it is hard to believe that such positive attitudes could be sustained over the longer term. So a key question is whether a worker-owned enterprise could make different decisions about the use of technology.

However, the scope for members to exercise choice over the organization of work may be constrained by external factors. In his seminal study of the labor process, which was critical of both technological and subjectivist explanations of alienation, Braverman (1974) relocated the study of workplace alienation within the broader capitalist system. Although his approach has attracted much criticism, his basic message remains important: what goes on inside the workplace will be profoundly influenced by events beyond the factory gate. As noted above, every co-operative in a capitalist market will be under pressure to adopt existing work processes characterized by hierarchical control and division of labor. At Mondragon, the conventional hierarchical work organization, despite an openness to methods of job enrichment, allows workers limited control over their daily work experience (Bradley and Gelb 1983). Greenberg (1986: 98) found little evidence that worker ownership in the plywood co-operatives brought control over the technical division of labor or prevented self-exploitation in terms of health and safety at work. As small businesses, many co-operatives are also locked into dependent sub-contracting relationships with powerful corporations that allow co-operatives little autonomy over the organization of the work process (Bate and Carter 1986; Mellor *et al.* 1988). If external constraints prevent workplace democracy from giving members increased control over the work process (including technology) and reforming their day-to-day work experience, then members are likely to feel a sense of powerlessness that is a poor basis for the development of a "participatory persuasion." In short, worker participation without job autonomy is unlikely to increase political efficacy.

Worker ownership, by removing the structural (capital/labor) conflict of interests of the conventional capitalist enterprise, does not magically remove *conflict* in the workplace. On the contrary, a plethora of case studies show that conflict seems endemic to the co-operative experience. Ironically, democratic structures, by encouraging more people to get involved in decision-making, create ample opportunities for dispute, both in the formal setting of meetings and through informal clashes over the roles and responsibilities of members (Cornforth *et al.* 1988). Where a dual structure of control persists, with (elected or appointed) managers controlling day-to-day activities, there is also plenty of scope for structural conflict (Eccles 1981; Wajcman 1983). Even Mondragon, the great co-operative success story, experienced a strike in one factory. Where structural conflict can be dissipated, interpersonal conflict may still flourish. Mansbridge (1980) argued that conflict in small democratic settings can be more difficult to handle than in larger bureaucratic, rule-bound organizations. In the co-operative there is less social distance between manager and worker and personality clashes – often between (former) friends – can quickly spiral out of control. The greater commitment of co-operative members may exacerbate the emotional intensity of conflict, as people feel strongly about work issues, take their worries home with them and are less willing to compromise. This is not to say that serious conflict is inevitable or necessarily damaging, but, as Gamson and Levin (1984) observed, co-operatives need to manage it constructively. Yet the evidence shows that many do not (Mansbridge 1982; Rothschild and Whitt 1986: 65–66; Cornforth *et al.* 1988: ch. 8; Mellor *et al.* 1988: 116–117).

The five variables discussed in this section demonstrate that participation may not always provide a positive experience for workers, which suggests the conclusion that participation may only result in heightened political efficacy in specific contexts.

Discussion

There is very little empirical support for the simple spillover thesis. The lack of evidence partly reflects the absence of rigorous research, which itself is a function of the paucity of worker co-operatives. What research there is offers only limited support for spillover in specific contexts. In this chapter I have drawn on the extensive empirical literature on co-operatives to show how the processes underpinning the spillover thesis are much more complex and uncertain than its proponents suggest. Building on the revisions suggested by Greenberg *et al.* (1996), a further respecification of the simple spillover thesis has been outlined which incorporates several other variables that shape the relationship between workplace participation and political efficacy.

First, the mode and intensity of participation will mediate the educative impact of participation. It cannot just be assumed that democratic structures will be educative. Direct participation, by empowering workers on the job, is likely to provide the confidence, skills and sense of mastery needed to become active citizens, but indirect participation via representative structures provides little opportunity for face-to-face participation and therefore seems less likely to contribute to personal and political efficacy. Two further variables – organizational origins and size – by influencing the mode and intensity of participation will shape the participatory experience of individual co-operative members. The origins of a co-operative may shape the impact of particular forms of participatory decision-making. For example, the representative forms of participation characteristic of endowed and defensive co-operatives can be expected to generate different responses from their members. A direct participatory structure may have a different impact in a small defensive co-operative of manual factory workers compared with a grassroots co-operative of young, university-educated individuals. There may also be an organizational size beyond which full participation at higher levels of management cannot take place. Thus the Greenberg *et al.* (1996) respecification of the simple spillover thesis, which states that direct and representative forms of participatory decision-making at work may have different effects on political participation, needs to be amended to note the possible differential impact of (a) organizational origins and (b) organizational size.

Second, the potential for participation to nurture a "participatory persuasion" is context specific. Whilst there is evidence that participation can produce positive attitudes and behavior amongst the workforce, it may also have a negative effect. Five variables have been identified that can influence the subjective response of workers to participation: forms of informal control, individual expectations, the external economic environment, the degree of job autonomy and the level of interpersonal conflict. Any of these variables can turn participation into a negative experience for individual members. Where someone finds participation disappointing, frustrating, demoralizing or stressful, then it is far less likely (although not impossible) to increase political efficacy. Thus the simple spillover thesis should be respecified to state that the relationship between workplace participation and political efficacy may be undermined where: (a) a small elite exercises informal control and the majority of workers do not engage actively in decision-making; (b) positive expectations of the process of participation are unfulfilled; (c) the external environment constrains organizational autonomy, particularly (following Greenberg *et al.* 1996) where the enterprise is economically troubled; (d) members exercise little control over their individual job; and (e) there are high levels of interpersonal conflict. In short, the personal and political efficacy that is the prerequisite for "spillover" is likely to be a rare beast.

This chapter has focused on the first part of the spillover equation, but it is important to note that the processes underlying the second part of the equation – the relationship between political efficacy and public participation – are also complex and uncertain. For example, one study shows that indirect participation via representative structures in the plywood co-operatives actually diminishes wider political participation, which may be explained by the members' negative response to the poor economic performance of the enterprise (Greenberg *et al.* 1996: 320–322). Even if direct workplace participation does nurture personal and political efficacy, it is not certain that individuals will have the inclination to engage in wider politics. Direct participation is very resource intensive; it takes time and energy, and can be very stressful, as illustrated by the high degree of burn-out that Rothschild and Whitt (1986) discovered in alternative collectives. In short, will politicized workers have any energy left to participate beyond the factory gate?

There are two more fundamental theoretical objections to the second stage of the spillover thesis. Schweizer (1995) argues that workplace democracy is unlikely to encourage political participation because it is conceptually wrong to expect humans to become more civic-minded and politically efficacious in contemporary representative (or, as he calls it, republican) liberal democracies. Indeed, if direct participation within the workplace were to generate participatory, co-operative and egalitarian attitudes, Schweizer (1995: 377) suggests that the workers would be more likely to regard the impersonal, remote institutions of the liberal democratic polity as meaningless and therefore be even *less* likely to participate in them. A second problem with the spillover thesis is that other factors may exert a more profound impact on political efficacy than the workplace experience. The socio-economic background of workers, notably education, may be a critical variable, as will the attitudes to work that members bring with them into the workplace (Carter 1987). External factors, notably the market, will also play a vital mediating role. Greenberg (1986) found that plywood members were actually less public spirited and community-oriented than the norm; they were characterized by self-interested, individualistic attitudes and these values seemed to increase according to the length of time spent in the co-operative!

In conclusion, the simple spillover thesis has fundamental problems, particularly with regard to its claims about the relationship between workplace participation and political efficacy. Building on the work of Greenberg *et al.* (1986), this chapter has offered a further respecification of the thesis that identifies seven variables that mediate (and constrain) the educative impact of participation.

Unfortunately, while co-operatives and other forms of full participation remain scarce, it will be very difficult to test this respecified model. Meanwhile, there is little empirical support for the promotion of workplace democracy as a practical institutional solution to the problem of declining public participation.

Notes

1 This chapter is a revised version of an earlier paper published in the *British Journal of Politics and International Relations* 8, 2006: 410–426.

2 Robert Dahl (1985) develops this analogy in an alternative normative justification for workplace democracy based on its beneficial impact on the wider polity. He regards economic democracy, or self-governing enterprises, as a positive counter-weight to the might of corporate capital, which, by accruing disproportionate political power and generating extreme economic inequalities, represents a pernicious threat to the well-being of liberal democracy. Drawing a parallel between the relationships between the state and its citizens and between a business and its employees, he argued that "If democracy is justified in governing the state, then it must also be justified in governing economic enterprises; and to say that it is not justified in governing economic enterprises is to imply that it is not justified in governing the state" (Dahl 1985: 111).

3 See various contributions in Dunn and Obradović (1978, parts 3, 4 and 6).

4 There are several possible explanations for the dearth of research. Interest in workplace democracy has waned over the last two decades, partly because worker-owned enterprises remain rare. Worker participation schemes that involve full participation (see next section) are also uncommon and often short-lived. There are also significant methodological complexities involved in comparing worker responses to participation both longitudinally and between participatory and non-participatory enterprises.

5 Tony Benn, as UK Secretary of State for Industry in 1974–1975, provided financial and political support for three defensive co-operatives: *Scottish Daily News*, Triumph Meriden, and KME Kirkby (Coates 1976; Eccles 1981).

6 Of course, co-operative origins and organizational size will also indirectly influence the attitudes and behavior of workers towards participation.

References

Bate, P. and Carter, N. (1986) "The Future for Producer Co-operatives," *Industrial Relations Journal*, 17: 57–70.

Batstone, E. (1983) "Organisation and Orientation: A Life-Cycle Model of French Co-operatives," *Economic and Industrial Democracy*, 4: 139–161.

Blauner, R. (1964) *Alienation and Freedom*, Chicago, IL: University of Chicago Press.

Bradley, K. and Gelb, A. (1983) *Co-operation at Work: The Mondragon Experience*, London: Heinemann.

Braverman, H. (1974) *Labor and Monopoly Capital*, New York: Monthly Review Press.

Carter, N. (1987) "Control, Consciousness and Change: A Study of the Development Processes of a Worker Co-operative," PhD Thesis: University of Bath.

Case, J. and Taylor, R. (eds) (1979) *Co-ops, Communes and Collectives*, New York: Pantheon.

Cheney, G. (2002) *Values at Work*, Ithaca, NY: Cornell University Press.

Coates, K. (1976) *The New Worker Co-operatives*, Nottingham: Spokesman.

Cornforth, C., Thomas, A., Lewis, J. and Spear, R. (1988) *Worker Co-operatives*, London: Sage.

Dahl, R. (1985) *A Preface to Economic Democracy*, Cambridge: Polity.
Dunn, W. and Obradović, J. (eds) (1978) *Workers' Self-Management and Organisational Power in Yugoslavia*, Pittsburgh, PA: University of Pittsburgh Press.
Earle, J. (1986) *The Italian Co-operative Movement*, London: Allen & Unwin.
Eccles, T. (1981) *Under New Management*, London: Pan.
Elden, J. (1981) "Political Efficacy at Work: The Correlation between More Autonomous Forms of Workplace Organisation and a More Participatory Politics," *American Political Science Review*, 75: 43–58.
Estrin, S. and Jones, D. (1992) "The Viability of Employee-Owned Firms: Evidence from France," *Industrial Relations and Labor Reviews*, 45: 323–338.
Gamson, Z. and Levin, H. (1984) "Obstacles to the Survival of Democratic Workplaces," in R. Jackall and H. Levin (eds) Worker Co-operatives in America, Berkeley, CA: University of California Press, pp. 219–244.
Greenberg, E. (1986) *Workplace Democracy*, Ithaca, NY: Cornell University Press.
Greenberg, E., Grunberg, L. and Daniel, K. (1996) "Industrial Work and Political Participation: Beyond Simple Spillover," *Political Research Quarterly*, 49: 287–304.
Lafferty, W. (1985) "Decision Making Involvement and Socioeconomic Resources in Norway: A Normative-Empirical Analysis," *Scandinavian Political Studies*, 8: 1–32.
Long, R. (1982) "Worker Ownership and Job Attitudes: A Field Study," *Industrial Relations* 21: 196–215.
Macpherson, C. (1977) *The Life and Times of Liberal Democracy*, Oxford: Oxford University Press.
Mansbridge, J. (1982) "Fears of Conflict in Face-to-Face Democracies," in F. Lindenfeld and J. Rothschild-Whitt (eds) *Workplace Democracy and Social Change*, Boston, MA: Porter Sargent, pp. 125–137.
—— (1980) *Beyond Adversary Politics*, New York, NY: Basic.
Mason, R. (1982) *Participatory and Workplace Democracy*, Carbondale, IL: Southern Illinois University Press.
Mellor, M., Hannah, J. and Stirling, J. (1988) *Worker Co-operatives in Theory and Practice*, Milton Keynes: Open University Press.
Michels, R. (1959) [1915] *Political Parties*, New York: Dover.
Nichols, T. (ed.) (1980) *Capital and Labour*, London: Fontana.
Oliver, N. (1984) "An Examination of Organisational Commitment in Six Workers Co-operatives in Scotland," *Human Relations* 37: 29–46.
Pateman, C. (1976) "A Contribution to the Political Theory of Organisational Democracy," in G.D. Garson and M. Smith (eds) *Organisational Democracy*, London: Sage, pp. 9–30.
—— (1971) "Political Culture, Political Structure and Political Change," *British Journal of Political Science*, 1: 291–305.
—— (1970) *Participation and Democratic Theory*, Cambridge: Cambridge University Press.
Paton, R. (1978) *Some Problems in Co-operative Organisation*, Milton Keynes: Open University.
Paton, R. and Lockett, M. (1978) *Fairblow Dynamics Ltd.*, Milton Keynes: Open University.
Peterson, S. (1992) "Workplace Politicisation and its Political Spillovers: A Research Note," *Economic and Industrial Democracy*, 13: 511–524.
Rosner, M. (1983) "Participatory Political and Organisational Democracy and the Experience of the Israeli Kibbutz," in C. Crouch and F. Heller (eds) *Organisational Democracy and Political Processes*, Chichester: Wiley, pp. 455–484.

Rothschild, J. and Whitt, A. (1986) *The Co-operative Workplace*, Cambridge: Cambridge University Press.

Russell, R., Hochner, A. and Perry, S. (1979) "Participation, Influence and Worker-Ownership," *Industrial Relations*, 18: 330–341.

Sartori, G. (1962) *Democratic Theory*, Detroit, MI: Wayne State University Press.

Schweizer, S. (1995) "Participation, Workplace Democracy and the Problem of Representative Government," *Polity*, 27: 359–377.

Shirom, A. (1972) "The Industrial Relations Systems of Industrial Co-operatives in the United States, 1880–1935," *Labour History*, 13 (fall): 533–551.

Smith, S. (1985) "Political Behaviour as an Economic Externality," in D. Jones and J. Svejnar (eds) *Advances in the Economic Analysis of Participatory and Labor Managed Firms*, Greenwich: JAI Press.

Sobel, R. (1993) "From Occupational Involvement to Political Participation: An Exploratory Analysis," *Political Behaviour*, 15: 339–353.

Wajcman, J. (1983) *Women in Control*, Milton Keynes: Open University Press.

Webb, S. and B. (1914) "Co-operative Production and Profit Sharing," *New Statesman*, Special Supplement, 14 February.

Whyte, W. and K. (1988) *Making Mondragon*, Ithaca, NY: Cornell University Press.

Part V

Democratic reform and local government

10 Mobilizing for participatory democracy?

The case of democracy policy in Sweden

Stig Montin

Introduction

Sweden is often considered a forerunner regarding welfare and democracy. For example, according to the 2002 UN Human Development Index, Sweden is among the five most developed countries in the world, together with Norway, Iceland, Austria and The Netherlands (UNDP 2002). Regarding measures of democracy – such as participation in elections – Sweden also is at the top of the list. According to empirical studies on social capital, trust in welfare institutions and general trust in other people, Sweden again emerges in a leading position among all the established democracies (Putnam 2002; Rothstein 2002).

Despite the fact that Sweden fares well compared with other democracies, Swedes are not optimistic regarding the state of their democracy. They are concerned by several developments that they perceive as problems which need to be addressed. Voter turnout has declined continuously during the past 20 years in Sweden. At the federal level, it reached a peak in the 1976 Parliamentary Elections with a 91.8 percent turnout. In 1991, voter turnout was 86.7 percent and in the most recent election (2002), it went down to 80.1 percent. At the local level, voter turnout was 84.3 percent in 1991 and went down to 77.7 percent in the 2002 election. Sweden is also one of the countries where trust in politicians has declined most dramatically since the late 1960s. According to annual surveys, the proportion of voters expressing distrust in politicians and political parties increased from 46 percent in 1968 to 75 percent in 1998 (Holmberg 1999).

A cornerstone in the early stages of Swedish democracy was the popular mass movements (*folkrörelser*) such as the labor movement, the farmers' movement, the temperance movement and the free churches. The women's movement, the peace movement and the environmental movement are considered to be contemporary versions of these traditional means of organizing collective action (Micheletti 1995). Empirical research shows that membership in traditional popular mass movements decreased during the 1990s. Between 1992 and 2000 the number of those who did not participate at all in associational life increased by roughly 20 percent (Vogel *et al.* 2003). The importance of contemporary new social movements has declined in Sweden as well. Finally, the budgetary crisis at the beginning of the 1990s is an important issue of concern in the Swedish context. The resulting downscaling of the welfare state via cutbacks in social policies tends to heighten political distrust, especially if people feel that they have experienced distributive and procedural injustice (Kumlin 2002).

These problems provided the background to the decision of the Social Democratic Government in 1997 to scrutinize the problems of democracy and to formulate a policy on democracy. A parliamentary commission (Government Commission on Swedish Democracy) appointed in October 1997 provided a first stimulus for this new policy field. Shortly after the parliamentary election in 1998, which brought heavy losses for the Social Democratic Party but which nevertheless allowed the party to stay in government, Prime Minister Göran Persson appointed a Minister of Democracy. Three years later, in 2002, the government proposed an official democracy policy to the Riksdag.

On the surface, this appears to be the standard way of enacting political reforms in Sweden, but it is not. First and foremost, the topic was unusual. For the first time, the government aimed at an overall evaluation of Swedish democracy with all its problems and solutions. The appointment of a Minister of Democracy, formally placed in the Ministry of Justice, represents a new policy instrument to tackle problems of democracy. From a procedural point of view, the attempt to overhaul the Swedish democratic system produced an unusually high level of open conflict in consensus-oriented Sweden. Those who were in favor of radical change were soon confronted with more cautious voices who suggested shunning the risk of reform and adhering to the old institutions.

The chapter comprises four sections: the first section provides a brief presentation of the process and the rhetoric surrounding the debate on democratic reform in Sweden; the second section discusses four proposals that were rejected by the Commission on Democracy; the third section presents the objectives of the democracy policy as well as a follow up of these objectives; finally, the fourth section suggests some explanations as to why the Social Democratic Government hesitated in moving towards a more radical renewal of Swedish democracy.

A new policy field: democracy policy

Political reforms and institutional change in Sweden normally presumes decisions that ought to be made in the Riksdag. The process leading to these decisions usually starts with a government initiative. Before the government can draw up a legislative proposal (government bill), there is a broad-based inquiry into the issue including social and political elites. In the case of the development of a democracy policy, a parliamentary commission (Government Commission on Democracy) was appointed by the government in September 1997. In accordance with the tradition of Swedish public committees, its members were appointed by the government from a group of candidates who were nominated by the political parties within the Riksdag. The members were assisted by experts from the fields of culture, the labor market and industry, as well as by ministerial officers. The chairman of the commission was a former minister of the earlier Social Democratic Government with strong roots within the party. A principal secretary was recruited by the chairman to take the overall executive responsibility for the inquiry. The commission, following standard procedures, operated independently of the government for about two years from October 1997 to 15 February 2000. Then it presented the report *A Sustainable Democracy* (Government Commission Report 2000: 1) to the government.[1] The report was referred for consideration to local governments, interest group organizations and other relevant bodies of Swedish society.

In addition to the final report, the output of the commission consisted of 15 research volumes with contributions from approximately 100 scholars from 12 disciplines. This material was distributed free of charge to all Swedish municipal libraries, high school libraries, study circle associations and adult education centers (*folkhögskolan*). The idea was – and this was explicitly supported by the Prime Minister, Göran Persson – that the material should be discussed all around the country in study circles (Amnå 2006).

After the 1998 parliamentary election, the Swedish Prime Minister appointed a Minister of Democracy. However, government decisions in Sweden are made collectively, not by single ministers. A minister cannot instruct any public authority how to deal with a particular issue. All ideas about how to revitalize democracy had, thus, to be anchored among all other ministers, especially the Prime Minister. The appointed Minister of Democracy (Britta Lejon) was not in a strong political position either. She worked hard to establish *demokratipolitik* (politicy on democracy) as a new policy field and she was able to score some victories in pursuit of this goal. She initiated, for example, the appointment of a Parliamentary Commission on Local Government Democracy which presented a report in 2001 (Government Commission Report 2001: 48). Many of the proposed measures in the ensuing democracy policy in 2002 were based on the work of this specific commission as well as on work of the Commission on Democracy. However, she did not manage to convince the Prime Minister or other leading politicians of the Social Democratic Party to adopt a bottom-up, participatory perspective on democracy as it was also suggested by the Commission on Democracy. Britta Lejon was dismissed as Minister of Democracy in October 2002.

There is no tension at the rhetorical level in the Swedish debate on democracy between the traditional political party-controlled representative model on the one hand and the participatory and deliberative model on the other. The formula used by the Commission on Democracy suggested "more of participatory democracy with strong deliberative qualities" (GCSD 2000). This phrase is rooted in a tradition where self-organization and direct democracy is considered to be no less important than the predominating political party-controlled and output-oriented discourse on democracy (Amnå 2006). It was accepted by the government and the prime minister at the level of rhetoric. However, the measures proposed finally in the 2002 Government Bill on Democracy Policy deviated in quite substantial ways from the proposal that was made by the commission. Ultimately, the Social Democratic Government did not approve the quite radical participatory-oriented suggestions made by the commission. The aftermath of the Commission on Democracy exposed traditional tensions of interest within the traditional Labor Movement and other social democratic-affiliated organizations and the Social Democratic Party.

The politics of democracy: four rejected proposals

As indicated above, the Commission on Democracy and the government shared, rhetorically, the same abstract vision with regard to the development of a participatory and deliberative democracy within the frame of the representative system. However, when it came to implementing specific measures in order to realize this vision, conflicting ideas and institutional interests emerged from behind the veil of rhetorical consensus.

Only a few of the commission's proposals were actually intended to challenge the institutions of representative democracy. In fact, many ideas of institutional renewal were focused on how to revitalize representative government. However, those few farther-reaching proposals coming from the commission immediately became the subject of critical comment. The general argument of critics was that the representative system might be put at risk through too far-reaching reform efforts. A more specific concern was that too much participation outside representative institutions would give already influential social interests an even stronger say in politics, which was seen as a threat to political equality (Amnå 2006).

In order to specify and explain the tension between the view of the commission on the one hand and the view of the government and other defenders of the current institutional arrangements on the other, four commission proposals will be presented and discussed in the following. We will deal in this section with the proposals to have separate election days, to allow for direct elections of district boards, to strengthen the system of local referendums and to provide the opportunity for Internet voting in ordinary elections.

Separate election days?

The question of separating the elections days used to be put on the Swedish political agenda from time to time. Since 1965, all elections (to municipal assemblies, county assemblies and the Riksdag) are held on the same day. In this respect, the Swedish system is quite unique. In most other European democracies, national and local elections are held on separate election days. The Social Democratic Party has been in clear opposition to this proposal since the mid-1960s, while most of the right-wing parties argued in favor of separate election days. The Left Party has been ambivalent, as have been the Christian Democrats. Occasionally during the 1990s, there was a majority in favor of a constitutional change separating local elections from the national election. However, due to the fact that this reform demands a change in the constitution, the Riksdag has to make two subsequent majority decisions with an election in-between. This means that any coalition of parties in favor of this proposal has to make sure that a majority would still be available after the next election.

The Commission on Democracy argued that separate elections would facilitate the election campaigns, thus having a mobilizing effect on voters, not least within the party organizations. The commission has been aware of the arguments against separate elections such as the threats of declining voter turnout in municipal elections and of people being incapable of distinguishing between the different elections. However, "in the situation of imminent collapse in which the Swedish party system now finds itself, there is reason to carefully consider several ways to stimulate party work and local political discussions" (GCSD 2000: 11). Furthermore, according to the Commission on Democracy, local authorities have become increasingly important for citizens and separate elections would further strengthen their accountability.

In the ensuing Government Bill on Democracy Policy, the question of separating the election days was not even mentioned. The issue was handled by another parliamentary commission on constitutional matters which had been assembled earlier to handle other issues related to constitutional change. A majority on that commission (the Social Democratic Party, the Left Party and the Christian Democratic Party) clearly stated that they preferred the existing system of one election day for all types of elections (Government Commission Report 2001: 42). Their argument was that separate elections would cause the voter turnout to decrease, which was unacceptable from a democratic point of view, and that the joint elections had until then been no threat to the accountability of local governments. Thus, the commission declared that the revitalization of local democracy could certainly be achieved without such adventurous experiments. The only empirical support for this statement is that in countries where election days are separate, election turnout is lower than in Sweden. The uncertainty of what separate election days might lead to was interpreted as a risk rather than a possibility.

Direct elections of district boards?

Several municipalities established municipal district boards during the 1980s. A district board is a standing committee with responsibility for several policy areas (social, cultural, leisure policies and primary education) within a municipal district. Most of them were abolished in the aftermath due to the perception that the expected increase in citizen participation and revitalization of the political parties did not materialize. During the 1990s, the attention was focused on other types of reforms such as market-oriented management, user participation and overall budget control. In the view of leading local politicians and managers, the district boards were then regarded as more or less unfashionable. However, in the largest cities (Stockholm, Gothenburg and Malmö), a political majority still considers district boards an important tool to ensure democracy as well as efficiency. The members of the city district boards are elected by the municipal assembly, which means that they are indirectly elected. One of the proposals from the GCSD (Government Commission on Swedish Democracy) was to introduce direct elections to the city district boards, "in order to increase transparency and the opportunities for citizens to decide who will represent them" (GCSD 2000: 12). Such reform would open up representative democracy at the sub-municipal level.

The proposal was rejected by another parliamentary commission (Government Commission Report 2001: 48), which argued that the democratic advantages of direct elections would not outweigh the disadvantages. Consequently, the question of direct election to district boards was taken off the democracy policy agenda. The most important reason for the rejection was that direct elections might lead to unequal distribution of services, as well as conflicts between municipal and sub-municipal political majorities. Equal distribution and central political control is considered to be more important than direct local citizen political influence. As in the case of the notion of separate election days, centralized political coordination and control is put before uncertain experiments in order to enhance citizen participation within the representative system.

Local referendums?

Direct democracy, such as advisory referendums at the national or local level, has not been of any great importance in Swedish political culture. The idea of municipal referendums has been subject to political debate several times but was consistently rejected until the mid-1990s. In 1994, rules concerning advisory local referendums were adopted (Municipal Referenda Act) and incorporated into the Local Government Act. A majority in the assembly can initiate and decide on a local referendum, but it can also be put on the agenda of the assembly by at least 5 percent of the electorate. In practice, this means that if at least 5 percent of the voters (by list of names) suggest a local referendum concerning a particular issue, the assembly must take it into consideration. Despite the advisory nature of citizen-initiated local referendums, local politicians adopted a reserved attitude towards this measure. Between the years 1994 and 2003, local assemblies debated 76 citizen initiatives, but only in four cases did the assemblies decide on a local referendum.

The lack of enthusiasm among local politicians for citizen-initiated referendums became an issue of concern for the Commission on Democracy. The commission generally stated that it should be more difficult for assemblies to refuse to arrange these kinds of referendums. This was later followed up by another commission which suggested that if 10 percent of the voters in a municipality demand a local referendum, the assembly should be obliged to arrange the referendum (Government Commission Report 2001: 48). The proposal was discussed in the government proposal on democracy policy in 2002, but the Social Democratic government decided to withdraw the issue from the agenda with the argument that it should be subject to further consideration (Government Bill 2001/02: 80, p. 49). Since 2002, a majority in the Riksdag has asked the government on two occasions to clarify its position, but the government has hesitated to make any final statement concerning the change of rules for local referendums. The current position from the Ministry of Justice is that municipal assemblies should be bound to arrange "broad citizen consultations" at the request of 10 percent of the electorate (Ministry of Justice 2004b). The reactions from both the Social Democratic Government and among local politicians strongly indicate that the question of citizen-initiated local referendums is perceived as a serious challenge to the dominating model of citizen participation. According to the model of party-based representative democracy, citizen initiatives should be made through ordinary channels, or at least be controlled by specific restrictions.

Internet voting?

The proposal regarding the use of modern information and communication technologies (ICTs) to facilitate local democracy, has reached a prominent position on the Swedish political agenda. At the municipal level ICTs can be used in many ways, such as to publish policy records online, to publish documents online before committee meetings, to conduct policy debates via discussion forums, to conduct online polls or online referendums, and to implement Internet voting. The technical prerequisites for using ICTs in the political process are available in terms of the expanding infrastructure (broadband) and the increasing number of Internet users. In 2001, 80 percent of the Swedish population between 16 and 64 years of age had access to a computer at home, and 70 percent had access to the Internet at home. Around three-quarters of the population use the Internet at home or somewhere else (Statistiska Centralbyrån 2002). In light of the government's vision of a high level of citizen participation, it should be expected that ICTs are considered an important part of any reform policy. A particular issue being discussed is Internet voting (Olsson and Åström 2002). More than half of the population would prefer to vote via the Internet in national, regional and local elections and referendums, if there were a choice (Statistiska Centralbyrån 2002).

The Commission on Democracy suggested that Internet voting should be tested in the context of experiments, for example, in local communities or in conjunction with school elections. The argument was that such experiments could provide initial evidence regarding the capacity of Internet voting to stimulate interest and participation in politics (GCSD 2000). The commission also pointed to technical problems that have to be solved in the context of electronic voting, especially the need to secure the secrecy of the ballot.

The government turned down the commission proposal on the use of ICTs. It adopted a more cautious approach than the commission and other actors, and the bill on democracy was more focused on the problems of electronic democracy rather than on the opportunities. Apart from the security concerns, the government emphasized the dignity and symbolic importance of voting in public on election day (Government Bill 2001/02: 80, p. 44). E-democracy is considered important, but more in terms of gathering opinions and conducting debates rather than in terms of voting. This hesitation towards Internet voting indicates in an odd way a conservatism which does not sit well with the general support for any kind of technical development in Sweden. When it comes to traditional institutions such as elections, the Social Democratic Government focuses on the threats rather than the opportunities (Olsson and Åström 2002).

So far, we can conclude that many of the commission proposals as well as proposals from other parliamentary commissions were considered to be too challenging from the perspective of the government and local political leaders. The critics' main argument was that these reform measures would weaken the basis of the political parties and that they therefore should not be implemented. The depiction of the four cases supports the case of historical institutionalism which claims that change usually takes place within the established overall institutional framework and is informed by previous choices (March and Olsen 1989; Hall and Taylor 1996). In other words, the power of the traditional institutions is maintained by incumbent political engineers who argue that new forms of participation might jeopardize the role of these institutions.

In short, the previous analysis indicates that, *rhetorically*, there were quite similar statements from the Commission on Democracy, the Minister of Democracy and the Prime Minister by the end of 1997. Despite this rhetoric, a few years later, several proposals from the commission were rejected and the Minister of Democracy was dismissed. This, however, is not the end of the story. Politics on democracy did become a new policy field and the government did formulate a proposal on how to enhance citizen participation.

Democracy for the new century

In spring 2002, the Social Democratic Government put forward a government proposal (government bill) in the Riksdag, entitled *Democracy for the New Century*. The policy was defined as a "cornerstone of the overall democracy policy the government has actively pursued since 1998" (Ministry of Justice 2002).

The title *Democracy for the New Century* indicates that the democracy policy should address fundamental issues and contain innovative and long-term initiatives. According to the proposal, it is important to preserve the traditional channels of representative democracy. Within this framework, the aim is to enhance citizen participation between elections and to increase the importance of dialogue and deliberation in the democratic process (Government Bill 2001/02: 80, p. 30).

The long-term and short-term objectives are stated as follows:

- Participation in elections should increase considerably at the national, the local, and the EU level. A short-term objective is that the voter turnout should increase in the 2002 election.

- An increasing share of the population shall hold some kind of political position of trust. A short-term objective is that the number of representatives in municipalities and county councils shall increase by 10,000 by the year 2010. The number of people who have had a political position of trust at least once in their life, shall also increase.
- Citizens shall have better opportunities to participate and exert influence on the political process. The share of people who participate shall also increase.
- The opportunities for citizens to exert influence in the political process shall be more equal than today. The proportion of young people, unemployed people, and people with a foreign background who participate in the political process shall increase.

(Government Bill 2001/02: 80, p. 31)

In order to attain these goals, several more or less concrete measures were suggested, referring to all levels of political life, ranging from neighborhoods to the European level of government. However, most of the concrete means for reaching the goals of increased citizen participation were focused on the local government level:

- Improving the working conditions for political representatives,
- Making special efforts in order to facilitate the integration of disabled representatives in decision-making,
- Giving the right to all members (not just the electorate) in the municipality to suggest items for the Municipal Assembly Agenda,
- Giving the possibility for those other than representatives to be appointed onto drafting committees in the assembly,
- Introducing different kinds of citizen panels or other types of citizen advisory organizations,
- Introducing youth advisory boards,
- Giving sub-local, self-administrative bodies a wider competence (these bodies consist of user representatives and personnel representatives),
- Improving the use of ICTs for administrative and democracy-oriented purposes, and
- Improving the possibility for the public to control private entrepreneurs who produce public financed service.

(Government Bill 2001/02: 80)

There are only a few municipalities (approximately ten of 290) which have implemented a larger number of these proposals in the context of an overall comprehensive strategy to increase citizen involvement. However, single measures have been introduced in many municipalities such as citizen advisory organizations (97 percent), the right for all inhabitants of a community (not just the electorate) to suggest items for the Municipal Assembly agenda (approximately 50 percent), different kinds of citizen panels (20 percent) or different types of youth advisory boards (50 percent), and improving the use of ICTs for democracy-oriented purposes (approximately 30 percent) (Gilljam, Jodal and Cliffordson 2003). It should be noted that many of these arrangements are not new. For example, user boards in schools were introduced in many municipalities during the 1990s.

In 2004, the Ministry of Justice ran an evaluation of the new democracy policy based mainly on research reports (The Government Offices 2004). The first objective was to increase election turnout. The 2002 election was held only a few months after the democracy policy was passed in the Riksdag. The turnout dropped by about 6 percent in the national election and by about 7 percent in the local election. It was, however, less than the decrease in electoral participation between 1994 and 1998. Of most concern was the continuing decrease in election turnout among first-time voters. The election turnout among foreigners did not decrease, partially due to various state-financed projects such as *Time for Democracy*. Swedish research on voting behavior indicates that the act of voting is still held in high esteem by Swedes, but the continuing decrease in party identification makes them less anxious to vote.

The second goal was to increase the share of the population holding some kind of political position of trust. Up to now, it could not be reached because the number of local representatives continues to decrease. It seems that there is a strong tendency towards smaller and more centralized political organizations rather than towards more inclusive and participatory ones. The political organization in most municipalities changed during the 1990s in order to increase efficiency, and one way of doing this was to reduce the number of committees. It was done within the context of a broader New Public Management reform initiative (Montin 2000). Another reason is the growing problem of recruiting new members to the political parties which is conditional on being nominated for a political commission. In addition, it is not unusual that representatives, for different reasons, leave their elected position between two elections (Government Commission Report 2001: 48). In addition, although women are highly represented in municipal assemblies and committees, many other groups are under-represented and this under-representation is even more pronounced at higher levels in the political hierarchy.

The third and fourth goals aimed to increase citizen participation between elections and to achieve political equality. According to research on this topic, it is hard to conclude whether the general level of political participation has increased or decreased over the last 20 years in Sweden. However, it is clear that the forms of citizen participation have changed. There is less participation in political parties and more participation in political activities initiated by citizens themselves. What worries the government and municipal leaders is the growing gap between traditional and non-traditional participation, especially among young people, and the fact that a lot of people, especially foreigners, are more or less politically passive. According to a recent national scientific survey, the democracy-oriented projects and other efforts at the local government level have so far failed to make local democracy more vital or to increase political trust among citizens in general (Gilljam and Jodal 2005).

All in all, research on the implementation of the Swedish democracy policy indicates that the new policy has not yet had any significant impact, apart from triggering specific local projects designed to increase election turnout among immigrants. It would be premature to come to a conclusion at this early point in time, but it is safe to say that Swedish political elites, especially in the party realm, have not put much effort into making any significant changes to support citizen participation via the reform of democracy.

The democracy policy in Sweden is mainly focused on the local level of government (see for example Ministry of Justice 2004a). One important reason as to why most of the concrete measures were oriented towards the local government level is that local governments in Sweden have a prominent position as they are responsible for the major part of carrying out national welfare policies. Local governments (including county councils) employ about one-quarter of all gainfully employed people in the country, and their expenditure counts for 20 percent of GNP (2003). Another reason is that the local government level is historically considered to be one of the cradles of democracy in Sweden. However, the government has been criticized for not taking a broader view of the problems of democracy and for watering down the proposals coming from the Minister of Democracy in drafting its government bill. In the final democracy policy there are no specific measures to strengthen the individual citizen's possibilities to participate, to be involved, and to make a difference (Amnå 2006). The more comprehensive perspective taken by the Commission on Democracy and the government rhetoric by the end of the 1990s was turned into a paper tiger that consisted of rhetoric and somewhat limited changes in the Local Government Act.

Why the hesitation?

There are several reasons why the Swedish democracy policy lags behind the political rhetoric surrounding it. We do find indications of some willingness to debate more innovative and critical ideas. However, the more critical voices in the political debate on democratic reform proved to be stronger, and prevailed. In the final section I will deal with the question of why the incumbent discourse has been dominant.

One explanation draws attention to how the welfare state is organized. Compared with many other welfare states, local governments in Sweden are responsible for most welfare functions, from the cradle to the grave. Output legitimation (government for the people) is, in general, considered to be more important than input legitimation (government by the people). Needs and wants among citizens are supposed to be aggregated and balanced by the political parties and civil servants within professionalized municipal organization. Increasing citizen participation might actually mean the mobilization of strong interest groups which can put too much stress on the local political system and make it less politically equal. On the other hand, controlled forms of citizen participation can be fruitful in order to legitimate difficult political priorities. This is, in short, a reasonable explanation as to why the Social Democratic Government rhetorically prefers increased citizen participation but actually rejects those reforms which are considered as dangerous for the system. When different kinds of participatory models are discussed in commission reports and government bills, a warning finger is often raised. There should not be too much participation beyond the representative scheme because it could jeopardize political equality (Government Bill 2001/02: 80).

The way in which local and national politicians argue for or against participatory democracy has also to be put in a wider historical and ideological context. This context acts as a frame for the process of implementing the reform proposals and determines what should, and can, be done. There is an ideological resistance to participatory democracy which can be traced back in history. Although this is not the place to elaborate upon the general historical political debate concerning different models of democracy in Sweden, one particular historical path of ideas should be emphasized. It is strongly linked to the labor movement and the Social Democratic Party. Social Democratic domination has been the trademark of the twentieth century. The party has been in government for more than 70 years in total. This means that the ideas developed within the labor movement and the Social Democratic Party have been of great importance for contemporary ideas on how to develop democratic institutions, not least concerning local self-government and local government democracy.

At the beginning of the twentieth century there was (and still is) a tension between two poles in socialist political thought: movement socialism and state socialism (Dahlkvist 1999). The tension has been obvious in the Social Democratic Party as well as in the Left Party (the former Left Party Communists). The different strategies are more about means than ends. Crucial values of democracy, such as popular sovereignty, political equality and the self-realization of individuals, are of similar importance in each of the strategies.

Movement socialism takes as its point of departure the organization of the working class. It is the self-organization of workers and their own experiences which, according to this view, should form the basic substance of a new society. In terms of the institutional dimension, this means that democratic movements should constitute the basis for self-administration, that forms of direct democracy should be adopted and that representative democracy should be most responsive to the demands of the citizens. Democratization or democratic renewal of society is, from this point of view, something that should develop from the bottom to the top.

State socialism, on the other hand, puts an emphasis on the state and the central government. Society should be democratized from above, by a centralized democratic constitutional state. The party (the Social Democratic Party and the Left Party, respectively) constitutes the most important basis and the most important instrument for the cohesion of society. In terms of the institutional dimension this means that it is the party-controlled representative democracy that should be renewed when democracy is to be renewed. Legislation and other forms of regulation from above are important to define the boundaries between legitimate and illegitimate citizen participation.

Historically, from the end of the nineteenth century to the 1950s, when the relation between movement socialism and state socialism was debated in the context of party congresses, the term *local democracy* had nothing to do with the actual municipalities, according to movement socialistic thinking. The municipalities were considered to be part of the state power. Local democracy was something that should be developed through workers' economic, social, cultural and political self-organization (Dahlkvist 1999: 23). There were some movement socialistic contributions on the view of the role of municipalities at the beginning of the twentieth century (Östberg 1996: 111) but, in general, the role of municipalities in the creation of the welfare state and local democracy became defined within the frame of state socialistic thinking after the Second World War. State integrationism has been the dominating idea regarding the role of local self-government and local democracy ever since (Strandberg 1998).

Subsequently, strong party control and strong state control are important features in the creation of the decentralized welfare state and in the renewal of local democracy. The proposed democracy policy contains traces of the old statist socialist view. According to this view, democratic renewal should be a top-down project or bottom-up initiatives should, at least, be assessed and legitimated by traditional democratic institutions. With this historical link in mind, the resistance towards several renewal proposals can be understood.

Movement socialism had without doubt some effect on the process of formulating a Swedish Democracy Policy. Other Swedish political parties (the Green Party, the Liberal Party and the Centre Party) fueled this process by actively advocating a more participatory-oriented local democracy and a stronger local self-government. However, the notion that the party dominates, and that the representative process should be organized in a top-down fashion, has not been questioned. It is clear that citizens, in general, are considered to be political citizens, who with the right support can be active and responsible in the process of handling common matters. Thus, the old tension surrounding the different ways of how to organize a democratic society is certainly still alive.

Note

1 An English summary is found in GCSD 2000.

References

Amnå, E. (2006) "Playing with Fire. Or: Why the Swedish Mobilization for Participatory Democracy Had to Fail," *Journal of European Public Policy*, 13 (forthcoming).

Dahlkvist, M. (1999) "Den instängda demokratin. Rörelsesocialism och statssocialism i svensk arbetarrörelse," in *Civilsamhället som demokratins arena*. Demokratiutredningens skrift, no 29, SOU 1999: 112, Stockholm: fakta info direkt, pp. 7–68.

GCSD (2000) *Sustainable Democracy. Policy for Government by the People in the 2000s*. Report of the Government Commission on Swedish Democracy. Official

Government Reports, SOU 2000: 1. English translation 12 September 2000 of the recommendations made by the Commission, Stockholm: Regeringskansliet, Ministry of Justice.

Gilljam, M., Jodal, O. and Cliffordson, O. (2003) *Demokratiutveckling i svenska kommuner. Del I. En kartläggning av vad som gjorts*, Göteborgs universitet: CEFOS.

Gilljam, M. and Jodal, O. (2005) Demokratiutveckling i svenska kommuner. Del III. Kommunala demokratiseringar – vägen till en mer vital demokrati? Göteborgs universitet: CEFOS.

Government Bill 2001/02: 80, Demokrati för det nya seklet.

Government Commission Report (SOU 2000: 1) *En uthållig demokrati. Politik för folkstyrelse på 2000-talet. Demokratiutredningens betänkande*, Stockholm: Fritzes.

Government Commission Report (SOU 2001: 42) *Den gemensamma valdagen och andra valfrågor. Slutbetänkande av 1999 års författningsutredning*, Stockholm: Fritzes.

Government Commission Report (SOU 2001: 48) *Att vara med på riktigt – demokratiutveckling i kommuner och landsting. Bilagor till betänkande av kommundemokratikommittén*, Stockholm: Fritzes.

Hall, P.A. and Taylor, R.C.R. (1996) "Political Science and the Three New Institutionalisms," *Political Studies*, 44: 936–957.

Holmberg, S. (1999) "Down and Down We Go: Political Trust in Sweden," in P. Norris (ed.) *Critical Citizens: Global Support for Democratic Governance*, Oxford: Oxford University Press, pp. 103–122.

Kumlin, S. (2002) *The Personal & The Political. How Personal Welfare State Experiences Affect Political Trust and Ideology*, Göteborg: Department of Political Science, Göteborg University.

March, J.G. and Olsen, J.P. (1989) *Rediscovering Institutions: The Organizational Basis of Politics*, New York: Free Press.

Micheletti, M. (1995) *Civil Society and State Relations in Sweden*, Aldershot: Avebury.

Ministry of Justice (2004a) Democracy policy. Fact Sheet. December 2004 www.regeringen.se/content/1/c6/03/58/26/ba6b920f.pdf (accessed 1 August 2005).

—— (2004b) *Samråd efter folkinitiativ*, Ds 2004: 4, Stockholm: The Government Offices.

—— (2002), *Democracy for the New Century*. www.sweden.gov.se/content/1/c6/01/62/74/8923a8b7.pdf (accessed 1 August 2005).

Montin, S. (2000) "Between fragmentation and co-ordination. The changing role of local government in Sweden," *Public Management*, 2: 1–23.

Olsson, J. and Åström, J. (2002) "eSweden: Hare or Tortoise?," Paper presented at IPSA Research Committee 05, Comparative Studies of Local Government and Politics, Marburg, June 14–15.

Östberg, K. (1996) *Kommunerna och den svenska modellen. Socialdemokratin och kommunalpolitiken fram till andra världskriget*, Stockholm: Symposion.

Putnam, R.D. (2002) "Conclusion," in R.D. Putnam (ed.) *Democracies in Flux. The Evaluation of Social Capital in Contemporary Society*, Oxford: Oxford University Press, pp. 393–416.

Rothstein, B. (2002) "Social Capital in the Social Democratic State," in R.D. Putnam (ed.) *Democracies in Flux. The Evaluation of Social Capital in Contemporary Society*, Oxford: Oxford University Press, pp. 289–331.

Statistiska Centralbyrån (2002) *Privatpersoners användning av datorer och Internet 2001*, Stockholm: Statistiska centralbyrån (scb.se).

Strandberg, U. (1998) *Debatten om den kommunala självstyrelsen 1962–1994*, Hedemora: Gidlund.

The Government Offices (2004) *Demokratipolitik.* Regeringens skrivelse 2003/04: 110. www.regeringen.se/content/1/c6/01/20/65/2f226da0.pdf (accessed 1 August 2005).

UNDP (2002), Human Development Report 2002 hdr.undp.org/reports/global/2002/en/pdf/HDR%20PR_HDI.pdf (accessed 1 August 2005).

Vogel, J., Amnå, E., Munck, I. and Häll, L. (2003) *Associational life in Sweden. General Welfare, Social Capital, Training in Democracy*, Stockholm: Statistics Sweden, Report no 101.

11 Democratic renewal in local government?

Top-down strategies for bottom-up involvement

Jacob Aars

Introduction

Much has been said and written in recent years about the claim that local democracy in Norway is in crisis. The most striking symptoms of crisis are the decline in electoral turnout and diminishing membership of the political parties. Public authorities in Norway, on both the central and local levels, have initiated various strategies to counteract what is generally seen as an undesirable development. What we are witnessing is a somewhat paradoxical development where political rights and popular political participation are being furthered by political elites. Historically, participatory rights have been established through a long popular struggle. These days it seems as if public authorities are running after the masses to make them participate. The elites struggle to bring the citizens back in. On a positive note these programs may be capable of laying down the foundations of participation from below. However, one sometimes suspects that government-sponsored democracy programs aim at involving the public as accomplices to elite policies.

A vital, but infrequently posed question is whether top-down initiatives can possibly succeed in creating bottom-up engagement. Furthermore, when initiatives for public involvement come from the political elites themselves, they might have some important implications for the kind of involvement that is being generated. Hence, another related questions concerns the forms of participation created through government-initiated democracy programs.

This chapter addresses these two questions through analysis of a specific program initiative in Norway. I will focus on a Norwegian local democracy program initiated by the Norwegian Association of Local and Regional Authorities (KS). Twenty local authorities took part in this program with various projects aimed at strengthening political involvement and activity among local residents. The KS sent out an invitation to all Norwegian local authorities to submit, if interested, project proposals. The participating municipalities were granted NOK50,000 (about €6,200) each. The grants were raised to NOK70,000 (€8,700) after two years. Another possible incentive to take part in the program was the prospect of taking part in a network of municipalities working on similar projects. The democracy program ran from 1996 to 2000. I shall review the more important results and conclusions from this program for democratic renewal. The democratic experiments in the various authorities are considered in a comparative context in which the experience from the Norwegian work is evaluated in relation to experience with equivalent projects in the other Scandinavian countries and in Great Britain.

On the basis of this review, the paper will then present a critical discussion of what has been called *democratization policy* (Olsson and Montin 1999: 31; Petersson 2001). Olof Petersson (2001) defines democratization policy as follows:

> The term democratization policy refers to the assessments and decisions that affect the realization of the idea of popular government. The aim of democratization policy is to create political institutions that satisfy the demand for citizens' participation in government, a constitutional state and political effectiveness. Responsibility for democratization policy lies primarily with the state, but also with the EU, with local and regional authorities, as well as with voluntary organizations and other sectors of civil society.
>
> (Olof Petersson 2001: 4)

Democratization policy specifies an object to be influenced (turnout and/or political participation in general), it specifies an objective (increase participation and achieve better equality [in participation]), it aims to specify a set of effective strategies for accomplishing the desired increase in participation. Thus, democratization policy meets several of Ranney's classic criteria for a public policy (Ranney 1968: 7). However, the strategies for attaining the specified goals are by no means clear. An important part of the policy is therefore to collect systematic information as to what strategies may be effective.

Both Olsson and Montin, and Petersson maintain that democratization policy can be initiated by parties and other organizations as well as by public authorities. However, the impression is that, to a considerable extent, it is central and local authorities that take the initiative for democracy projects at the local level. In this chapter we will therefore concentrate on the kind of public policy that aims to influence conditions for local democracy. We will discuss the question of whether it is possible to promote bottom-up involvement by means of top-down strategies. Is democratization policy a program for strengthening popular political participation or for controlling it? Following on from the preceding question, we will discuss whether the top-down approach strengthens certain kinds of involvement: when initiated by elites, does democratization policy tend to encourage involvement of a kind that supports these very elites?

The link between democracy and political participation: how strong is it?

We cannot conceive of democracy without some form of popular participation, yet theories of democracy assess the importance of this involvement differently. Some believe that democracy is best served when the greatest possible number of people assumes an active role. The substance of political decisions should be the result of varied and unlimited participation. Others believe that it is of paramount importance for a well-functioning democracy to channel and regulate popular involvement.[1]

Government-initiated democracy programs may leave the impression that popular participation is an unquestionable good, but theories of democracy, however, do not agree on how much participation is healthy for democracy. On closer inspection we may also suspect that top-down democracy initiatives aim to control participation rather than to enhance it. Robert Salisbury (1975) has pointed out that one tradition within democratic theory is preoccupied with participation primarily as a source of legitimacy for governing elites:

> Insofar as the citizens participate in governmental affairs, through voting and whatever other means exist, they give their consent to decisions and so legitimize those decisions and the regime that makes them.
>
> (Robert Salisbury 1975: 326)

Accordingly, top-down efforts to enhance participation should be interpreted as a strategy in the struggle to secure popular support for the political system. The same strand of theory that Salisbury refers to argues that democracy entails strict regulation of the opportunities for popular involvement. The elitist democratic tradition is based on the idea that the populace does not participate directly in the political process. Instead, the political elite makes decisions on behalf of the people (Schumpeter 1961: 269; Sartori 1965). The role of the people is to elect their own leadership. In this case, democracy is a matter of regulating involvement rather than of opening it up. The influence of a community's citizens is limited to the choice of who will govern them. However, democratization policy appears to be based on the insight that political systems in the longer term cannot function properly without the energy of popular participation. Political power is characteristically vulnerable and, thus, cannot in the long run be upheld without the confirmation given from popular support.

Popular involvement is a necessary source of energy for a democratic system. Without it, the system would ultimately be unable to function. On the other hand, there is a danger of this energy increasing to a point where it disables the political system. Theories of political participation are therefore characterized by a certain ambivalence towards popular participation. The defining idea of democracy is that it is the people who govern their own affairs. Participation thereby reflects a population's self-government. Most people would however agree that spontaneous self-organization has to be contained within a framework of institutions that regulate relations among a community's citizens and which give direction to the energies represented by that involvement. Democracy therefore entails both spontaneity and rules. For a political system to be regarded as democratic, its institutions must be flexible enough to be changed in response to shifts in fundamental values among the citizens they serve.

Government-initiated democracy programs are efforts to manipulate the institutional context within which civic involvement is taking place. Democratization policy is an effort to influence democracy's forms, not only substantial policy issues. Some projects aim to strengthen traditional representative channels of participation, whereas others promote more direct participatory forms. On the other hand, the various democracy projects are directed at different participatory roles. A rough distinction can be drawn between the projects that define the residents primarily as citizens and the projects that define residents as users or consumers of local services.

Manipulating the institutional context: direct or indirect participation?

In Norway, democracy at the municipal level combines elements of indirect and direct forms of democracy. In local elections, local elites compete for the support of the electorate. Voters show their confidence in candidates by voting for them, or they express their dissatisfaction by withholding their votes. Having won a local government mandate, a candidate is relatively free to use his/her discretion to influence decisions in ways that best serve his/her conception of what is good for the local community. On the other hand, Norwegian local democracy has clear features of participatory democracy. First, a relatively large portion of the population is mobilized as local councillors or as members of municipal boards and committees. According to the 2003 Local Election Survey, 6 percent of the respondents reported that they had served as local councillors at some point. An even greater figure is involved in local politics as candidates for election or as members of municipal committees. This broad political involvement via public offices becomes particularly clear when we look at recruitment to such positions over time (Aars and Offerdal 1998: 218; Offerdal and Ringkjøb 2002: 128). In addition, people participate in many other ways than merely through the electoral channel. They participate through organizations, events or open hearings. Another important form of participation is direct contacts with local politicians or local administration.

The primary objective of the Norwegian democracy program was to encourage engagement within the existing institutional framework, although several local authorities also experimented with new forms of participation. Where attempts to increase engagement through new forms of participation are successful, there is also the potential to promote the construction of new institutions. New forms of involvement can develop into challenges to established institutions. In this sense, the initiative taken by the KS has the potential to give rise to new local political institutions.

The willingness of many local authorities to experiment with new forms of participation seems to reflect the idea that more arenas for participation imply better democracy. But the foundations for this assumption are somewhat vague. It is not self-evident that more possibilities for participation automatically result in an improved local democracy. More channels of involvement certainly do imply a greater choice of means by which citizens can express themselves politically. A greater diversity of social groups can be drawn into the political process, since the opportunities for the individual to find a personally suitable form of political expression are more numerous. However, if democratic arenas are being dispersed to a greater diversity of forms one must assume that the individual has the resources to orient him or herself in a complex landscape. In this sense, more channels of influence do not necessarily lead to more people becoming involved in political work, but simply that those who were already active acquire more ways to make their influence felt.

If new arenas for participation primarily represent new channels of influence for those who are already active, then it might be argued that such modifications undermine democracy rather than strengthen it. In this case, the best way to defend democracy would probably be to limit means of participation rather than to increase them. If opportunities for involvement were confined to just a few arenas, it would be easier to regulate who becomes involved by means of formal arrangements.

Manipulating participatory roles: citizen or user/consumer?

Involvement in local politics implies more than just taking part in elections and protests. Local authorities consult with local residents ever more frequently, since the latter are the consumers of the services provided by the former. Direct user influence or user representation is a form of participation of growing importance for many people. *New Public Management* has turned user influence into an important management tool (Øgård 2000). According to this view, it is of crucial importance to develop indicators for the quality of public management activities. Regular feedback from the users of local authority services is considered an important indicator for the quality of the services offered. User surveys that measure levels of satisfaction with offered services are being conducted with increasing frequency to gather information about the quality of services.

By means of user surveys and other forms of user influence, residents can play a part in determining the content of the services offered by their local authorities. User influence therefore represents an important channel of participation. In addition, this form of participation presupposes specific views of participation and of local authority institutions.

Local residents participate by making use of certain services, or as potential users of those services. As users they are for one thing affected by how the service is designed. It is therefore considered reasonable that the user is accorded some influence over what is offered in the service. Such considerations are based on *assessments of affectedness*. A second consideration is that the users of public services are assumed to be better placed to influence those services than non-users. Those with the greatest experience of a certain field of service will also have the best knowledge of how policy is framed within that field. This is a *knowledge assessment*.

In Norway, local residents regard their local authorities primarily as providers of services to the people who live in the respective area. It would appear that residents define themselves more as users of local authority services rather than as citizens of the community (Pettersen and Rose 1997). Several analysts have claimed that popular involvement in local politics ought therefore to take the role of the service user as its basic premise rather than the role of the citizen (Rattsø and Sørensen 1997; Ståhlberg 1996). This would enable the inhabitants of a community to influence politics more directly, and not just via political parties and elected representatives. Moreover, their influence would then be exerted in areas where the conditions for their involvement are particularly good.

Various kinds of criticism have been leveled at the view that local democracy should be based to a greater extent on user influence. One criticism is that people's engagement would thereby become *individualistic* and that this would amount to a "privatization" of their relations with the local authorities (Hansen 1995). Users' engagement is stimulated only when their immediate interests are affected, and their interest in the political commonality remains slight. Social rights have undermined the significance of political rights. Another related critique is that user influence results in a *fragmentation* of politics. Users become engaged in single issues and devote little attention to the contexts in which those issues occur. An important argument for local democracy is precisely that people's proximity to matters that affect them should make it easier for them to weigh up different fields of concern in relation to one another. Thus, they will be better placed to set reasonable priorities. The user will be less interested in seeking solutions that serve the community as a whole (Eriksen and Weigård 1993).

But a person's role as user is complementary to his or her role as citizen. Anyone who gets involved in politics will always be more concerned with some issues than with others. Many people get engaged in politics through their interest in a single issue. But in becoming involved in local political processes, the resident's sense of engagement is almost invariably stimulated by the similar involvement of others and by aspects of politics as a whole. In this way links are forged between the particular and the general, or between the individual and the collective (Sørensen 1998: 138f.). Moreover, someone who is concerned about, for example, the issue of local schools, will be obliged to argue how the conservation of this particular structure can be beneficial for the community as a whole. In this sense, there is an implicit relationship between the roles of the user and the citizen. The conflict between these two participatory roles might arise because local authorities often wish to consult residents exclusively as users of one particular service. This precludes the possibility of evaluating this one field of concern in relation to the many others. Local authorities seek to draw upon the views of residents as if they constituted a kind of expert commission.

An entirety always consists of parts. Any political engagement will necessarily entail linkage between the specific and the general. Just as politics cannot function properly without certain higher-level judgments, it cannot function well without engagement in concrete issues. With this in mind we can say that the roles of service user and citizen are situated on different levels. Since the two roles are complementary rather than competing, it is no easy matter to compare empirically the degrees to which the two roles are played out.

A classification of participatory forms

In Table 11.1 I have placed a number of forms of participation along two dimensions that emerge from the discussion thus far as especially important. On the one hand, a distinction is drawn between direct and indirect forms of participation. On the other, we distinguish between forms of participation based on the individual's role as either citizen or service user. This gives four combinations. We find the traditional *representative democracy* in the combination of indirect participation and the role as citizen. The form of participation in this case is the electoral channel and political parties. The status of being eligible for political positions is also an aspect of indirect democracy. Where the role of the citizen is combined with direct participation we might well talk of *participatory democracy*. In principle, local residents can participate in all kinds of issues relevant to the community as a political entity, whereby typical forms of engagement would include public debates and hearings. Direct protests will also belong in this category, insofar as they constitute an expression of the way the public is directly affected by political processes. The combination of the service-user role and indirect participation is called *interest group democracy*. Here, participation

Table 11.1 Classification of participatory forms

	Direct	*Indirect*
Citizen	Participatory democracy • Public debates • Popular meetings • Protests • Referendums	Representative democracy • Elections • Parties • Elected positions
Service user/client	Needs democracy • User management • User surveys – as input for the administration • Exit – choosing some services in preference to others	Interest group democracy • Participation through voluntary associations • User representation • User surveys – as indicators for elected representatives

occurs via those elected to represent certain organized interests or service-user interests. Examples of this type of participation will include participation in terms of voluntary institutions, but also user representation in various organs affiliated to community institutions such as schools or health institutions will fall into this category. The characteristic of the final category, *needs democracy*, is that user interests are channeled directly into the political decision-making process. In this respect we have already mentioned user surveys. In a system where public services are offered to competitive tender, one can imagine that the user exerts influence over the substance of policy by choosing between different service providers.

The participatory projects that comprise the program *Democracy, Participation and Government* were grouped into seven main categories by the initiators, the KS:[2]

1 Political parties
2 Initiatives aimed at specific groups
3 Community processes
4 Participation for sustainable development
5 User surveys as tools of democracy
6 Information and communication technology (ICT) in local democracy
7 Deliberative hearings

The various projects combine features from several of the types presented in Table 11.1. One of their overriding aims has been to strengthen election turnout. Several local authorities have implemented measures to strengthen participation via political parties. These forms of participation fall under the category of traditional representative democracy. Projects aimed at specific groups can also be placed in this category. Most notable in this respect are projects intended to strengthen the role of women, young people and immigrants in the electoral channel and in publicly elected bodies. Within the category that we have called participatory democracy we find local authorities that have focused their efforts on various forms of hearing, including deliberative hearings. But here we also find those that have worked to establish structures for broader public debate, especially projects that emphasize the use of information technology as a tool of local democracy. It is also reasonable to place in this group those local authorities that have worked with local community processes. Among the communities that aim to promote involvement for sustainable development we find examples of both direct and indirect forms of participation. Others can be placed in the category of interest group democracy, insofar as the involvement often takes place via voluntary organizations. User surveys represent the most important form of user-based participation within the program. Several local authorities have worked with user surveys as a kind of participatory tool. In Table 11.1 this is characterized as a form of direct participation, although we can also imagine how user surveys could be employed in a more advisory capacity, as a source of information that may well be of significance and interest to elected representatives.

Experiences from the Norwegian democracy program

In the following we will use the various thematic headings presented above to take a closer look at what was learnt from the KS democracy program.

Political parties in local authorities

The problems that political parties have experienced in relation to recruitment and member participation were considered a focal issue for the democracy program. A paradox faced by the political parties is that their position has become both weaker and stronger in the field of local politics. Where the internal processes of town halls are concerned, their importance has increased (Bäck 2000), while at the same time, their connections with the electorate have grown weaker. As far as the KS and the various local authorities were concerned, it was considered important to strengthen popular participation by rehabilitating the political parties among the communities' residents. The parties were thus defined as a vital means of reinforcing popular engagement. At the same time there was a normative motive behind this emphasis on the parties. The KS and the local authorities *wished* to channel participation through the parties.

Several of the local authorities involved in the democracy program conducted projects that aimed to strengthen the position of the parties in local politics. The most important project was carried out in the municipality of Jevnaker ahead of the 1999 local election. On the basis of a survey of local party board members and of core groups within the population, two developmental experiments were carried out. The first was intended to change the ways the parties developed their manifestos. Residents were invited to make suggestions for the parties' election programs, and the parties collaborated in the distribution of the resulting publications. The goal of the second experiment was to provide training for potential list candidates, preferably candidates under 30. A research institution (The Eastern Norway Research Institute) was put in charge of the training program, offering information on topics such as the role of local councillors and the workings of political parties. The program experiment was successful in the sense that it aroused considerable interest among residents. The training experiment was far less successful owing to poor attendance; only a handful of the target group turned up.

In connection with the party project, a large survey of party members in the county of Telemark was undertaken. Both this survey and the survey conducted in the municipality of Jevnaker showed that activity in regional party offices was low, and perhaps equally important, not all party activity was focused on the agenda of the local government. In other words, it appears that party activity at the municipal level is largely governed by the local political issues of the day. If, however, one considers the activity of party members over time, it turns out that many are inclined to accept official posts during their time as members. Yet at any one time only relatively few are active. Even those who regard themselves as passive members show some engagement if we study activity over time.

Projects involving particular groups

The principle aim of the KS democracy program was to increase overall participation, but some concern was also expressed regarding the established pattern of participation. The aim was to address the imbalance between those groups within society that were over-represented, and others that were under-represented in the political channels of involvement. The idea was to stimulate greater interest and participation among groups that are usually among the least active in local politics. The projects focused on three social groups: (a) children and young people, (b) immigrants and (c) women. Apart from seeking to stimulate increased participation, the projects built on the (tacit) idea that political involvement would lead to better integration within the local community of groups that have in varying degrees been socially marginalized.

The municipality of Orkdal carried out a successful project with direct elections to a Youth Council.[3] Most parties succeeded in running lists for the election, and turnout was high, namely 79 percent. The election was held using its own lists and following its own election campaign. The actual voting took place under the auspices of the local schools. The legitimacy of such a youth council is no doubt greater when its representatives are directly elected than when they are appointed by, for example, smaller student councils.

In the municipality of Skjervøy an important part of the project work was aimed at strengthening the participation of women in local politics. The procedure involved a combination of work conducted through political parties and efforts to set up a women's network within the community. The political parties conducted a campaign to increase the proportion of women on their electoral lists. In addition, various meeting places for women were established and courses were offered to female list candidates. The project work in Skjervøy was successful in the sense that female representation in local government increased from 28 to 40 percent after the election in 1999.

Local community processes

As we have already seen, local self-government is based partly on the idea that people should organize their own interests. For this value to be put into practice, it is necessary that the residents within a certain geographic area have some sense of community and belonging to that area. But local communities are not always neatly reflected by administrative divisions. In many cases, a municipality will encompass several local communities. Some of the municipalities that took part in the KS democracy program wanted to strengthen local democracy by enhancing local community identities. In this case, the respective projects were aimed at involving residents in local planning procedures, such as the redevelopment of a local area or the construction of port facilities for leisure boats. Various methods were employed to achieve this objective.

Two local authorities were especially active in working with local community procedures, Sauherad and Karmøy, albeit through different approaches. In both municipalities it was considered that the division of the municipality into smaller sub-municipal units served to integrate rather than fragment the area as a whole, despite the fact that the methods used by the respective local authorities differed in other respects. Offerdal and Espeland (2000) described the work in Sauherad as first and foremost a *project*, whereas the work in Karmøy was for them primarily a *process*. Characteristic of the projects in Sauherad was that the local administration defined clear objectives for the work to be done in the five smaller zones that participated. Various local associations in the built-up areas took part in the implementation of specific projects. In Karmøy the populations of the nine sub-municipalities were invited to participate in discussions about strengths and weaknesses of the respective local community. Subsequently measures were proposed to improve those aspects of the local communities that the residents had identified as problematic. Whereas Sauherad conducted a carefully managed project, Karmøy pursued an open process. A key difference between the two projects was the manner in which they handled conflict. In the former, conflicts were resolved, or at least put to rest, through the local authorities' use of power. In Karmøy, conflicts were either left unresolved or they were resolved by referring them to the municipality's central political structures.

In both Sauherad and Karmøy it was considered important that local councilors remained outside the local community processes during their early stages. Later they were gradually drawn into the work, but the delay was sufficient to allow a new stratum of active residents to form. During the first phase of the work, these people seemed to identify little with the municipality as a whole, but when it came to the nomination process for the elections of 1999, several of those most active in the local community processes were nominated for the party lists, and subsequently elected into local government. Thus from having been opponents of local political institutions, some community activists assumed key functions within those institutions.

Involvement for sustainable development

Several of the participating municipalities focused on promoting involvement in single issues. One such field of concern was environmental protection and sustainable development. The most active municipalities in this field chose different strategies by which to arouse interest and strengthen participation. Surveys were carried out to assess people's environmental behavior, local meetings were organized, and various neighborhood consultations were arranged whereby the politicians were fetched out to the areas where residents actually live. A number of deliberative hearings on environmental policy were also held, but these will be discussed when we turn to the general subject of hearings below.

In the municipality of Os, Hedmark, a series of community meetings were held on the subject of "Community Values for the Future." All in all 5 percent of the population attended one of the meetings. However, as was the case in many projects, the participants did not represent a cross-section of local society. For instance, 63 percent were male, and the general impression was that most attendants were well above 40.

Although the local authorities sought to promote participation, they did so in terms of only one issue. It could be said that the problem with the field of environmental policy is that it is rarely a scene of major conflict. For the municipalities involved in the experiments, one aim of the projects was to promote understanding and active support for broadly defined local environmental policies. There was therefore little scope for disagreement. However, political involvement presupposes disagreement. Participation is expected to be supportive; otherwise it is deemed undesirable. Democracy is unnecessary where solutions are obvious. The participation that the projects sought to harness in the field of environmental policy involved asking people to support and implement a few political goals that they had had no chance of influencing. This is problematic because it is conflict that rouses engagement. Participation is employed for the purpose of confirming elite policies.

User surveys as tools of democracy

It might appear somewhat odd that user surveys should be included as an instrument in a program on democracy. But this reflects the fact that many local authorities consider user or resident surveys an important source of information on people's attitudes to various issues. Although the filling out of a user survey might seem fairly trivial as a political act, for some respondents it will nevertheless require greater effort than voting in an election. Compared with other more demanding forms of political involvement, user surveys have the advantage of allowing all sections of the population to have their say (Verba 1996). Such surveys allow one to study the attitudes of a representative sample of the population. Most other forms of participation are based on self-selection, but where people decide for themselves whether or not to get involved, such participation tends to be socially imbalanced. And from the point of view of democracy, user surveys have a further advantage: each participant is allowed only one vote. At public meetings, some participants will always be more active than others. In a user survey, each person's participation counts only once. Each participant is accorded equal significance.

But this method also has its problems when viewed from a democratic perspective. First, user surveys give people few chances to discuss and form opinions on the issues in question. There is therefore a certain danger that user surveys register attitudes, and that the respondents have not had the opportunity to arrive at these attitudes after giving the matter thoughtful consideration. Perhaps they only provide us with superficial opinions (Converse 1970). Second, there is the danger that the extensive use of user surveys can transform political questions into merely administrative concerns. The democracy program provided several examples of this. For one thing, the administration normally decides on the questions and in many cases how they were formulated. This gave the administration control of a significant aspect of the political agenda.

Another thing was that politicians often seemed to shy away from their role as politicians when interpreting the results of such surveys. Politicians were preoccupied with the question of whether their own municipality had achieved better or worse results in the relevant field of concern than other municipalities, or whether the results represented an improvement or a decline compared with earlier surveys. They were less interested in evaluating the results relative to their own views on what constituted the important issues for their area. User surveys represent a tool for tapping into opinion whenever it is needed or convenient, and in some cases it would appear that this technology causes important political judgments to be deferred or sidelined.

ICTs in local democracy

Great hopes have been attached to the possible implications of information and communication technology (ICT) for political engagement. In the KS democracy program, several municipalities chose to focus on new technology in order to communicate with their residents. The level of ambition varied. Some wished to employ the new technology to provide residents with information about political issues and things that were happening in the area. Others wanted to establish channels for two-way communication, for example, by publicizing the e-mail addresses of elected representatives. Yet others wanted to set up Internet discussion sites that would allow residents not only to communicate directly with the local authorities but also to discuss issues among themselves.

The relevant technology is in a process of rapid development, and many changes took place in the four years of the project period. Still, major developments have taken place after the program was concluded. Certain limited results were achieved, although in some municipalities the projects were hampered by a failure to implement the necessary technical solutions. In other municipalities the problems had more to do with organizational capacities. The implementation and maintenance of systems to provide information and opportunities for discussion via the Internet called for a considerable work investment, and many municipalities simply lacked the necessary resources.

One lesson learnt from this exercise concerned the difficulty of establishing lively Internet debates. Despite a major effort by the municipality of Kongsberg to initiate such a discussion, few people got involved. One municipality did succeed in stimulating an Internet debate with many contributions. This concerned the closure of a music school in Skjervøy. In this case the debate was intense, but short lived.

Deliberative hearings

What motivated the so-called deliberative hearings was a wish to create forms of participation that would be both broad based and deep in commitment. In other words, they should involve a numerous and preferably representative cross-section of the population, while also providing opportunities for discussion and deliberation prior to decision-making. Deliberative hearings were held in three municipalities: Nordland (county), Stord and Kongsberg.[4] In addition, a hearing was planned in Os in Østerdalen, but this had to be cancelled due to insufficient response.

The hearings were preceded by surveys, in which a representative sample of the population was asked to respond to questions concerning the theme of the projected hearing.[5] The subjects were asked whether they would be willing to take part in the hearing. Those who declined were asked to respond to a similar survey at a later date. These respondents would constitute a control group, whose responses could be compared with those who participated in the hearing.

Concerning the scale of participation, it turned out that many who initially declared themselves willing to participate in the hearing eventually failed to turn up. In Nordland, 114 persons were enrolled as participants, but 83 eventually turned up. Defection was approximately the same at the other hearings. Although the participants were selected to represent a cross-section of the population, the make-up of the group that actually took part was lop-sided. The aspect of self-selection meant that the resultant group perpetuated many of the biases found in traditional forms of political participation. Most significantly, there was a disproportion of men and middle-aged participants.[6]

With regard to the content of the contributions, we registered that relatively few participants changed their opinions as a result of the hearings. In fact, the proportion of those who changed their opinions was about the same in the control group as among those who took part. Moreover, it would appear that the control group exhibited an observational effect. The fact that those in the control group knew that they would be interviewed later meant that they reflected on the responses they would give the second time. This apparently influenced opinion formation just as much as participation in the actual hearings.

The Norwegian experiments from a comparative perspective

The Norwegian experiments in democracy are far from unique. Many of the problems that have been sketched for Norway are also encountered elsewhere in the Scandinavian countries. Similarly, the other Scandinavian countries have also resorted to various measures to strengthen local democracy. But in Britain as well, efforts have been made to achieve democratic renewal.

Using the classification worked out in Table 11.1, we would have to define many of the British measures as *needs democracy*. In other words, residents become involved in political processes primarily in virtue of their being customers or users of municipal services. Privatization and competitive tendering are regarded as means not just of improving the efficiency of public services, but also of strengthening residents' influence over the services provided. The prevalence of these strategies is far greater in Great Britain than in Norway. The democratic element of competitive tendering consists in giving local residents, in their capacity as customers, influence over public services by allowing them to choose certain service providers while rejecting others.

Complaints procedures and user surveys are very widely used by local authorities in Britain. In 1997, both instruments were regularly employed by some 90 percent of British municipalities, whereas just over 20 percent introduced direct user control for certain types of service. Moreover, more than 60 percent of British local authorities reported that they had established so-called user forums, in which users are consulted about the services on offer (Leach and Wingfield 2000: 49).

In addition to the market-oriented strategy, many local authorities in Britain have implemented what we classified in Table 11.1 as participatory democratic measures. These tend to be relatively traditional forms of involvement, such as public meetings or open question sessions with local authority officials. But on top of this, there have been several experiments with so-called focus groups, and a few municipalities have made use of citizen juries. The idea behind the latter is that a relatively small but representative sample of the population (10–25 people) comes together for a certain duration in order to develop a position on a particular political issue (Smith and Wales 2000). On a larger scale, a number of deliberative polls have also been conducted in Britain, along the lines described earlier in this paper (Fishkin 1995), but the polls have not dealt with local matters and did not target participation at the local level specifically.

These democratic initiatives in Britain must be seen in connection with changes that have been made in relation to municipal self-determination. The British Labour Party has put forward a program to revive local government in Great Britain, which was subjected to a process of fragmentation under Margaret Thatcher's government, but which has continued under New Labour leadership. Popular influence over local politics is difficult to achieve when local authorities have been deprived of their traditional responsibilities and these in many cases are transferred to non-elected bodies.

In Sweden the question of local democracy has received considerable attention for many years, as is reflected in the large number of democratic audits that have been conducted. Sweden has adopted many of its ideas from Great Britain. First and foremost, Sweden has gone much farther than Norway in offering its public services to competitive tender, a process that Stig Montin has dubbed *free choice democracy*. In his review of local democracy initiatives in Sweden, Montin concludes that the threat that people might swap from one institution to another (exit) is seen as having a far greater effect than involvement in a user organ (voice) (Montin 1998: 40). Elsewhere it has been reported that many Swedes are critical of the privatization of municipal services.[7] It would appear that the Swedish population has grown more critical towards the idea of privatization after an initial period in which it was very positive. One probable reason for the increased skepticism is the exposure of serious failings in the provision of care at a number of homes for the elderly.

The Swedish municipalities have also conducted a number of other experiments aimed at strengthening popular participation. Olof Petersson mentions examples such as sub-municipal committees, purchaser–provider arrangements, referendums and the use of ICT. In addition, some municipalities have conducted trials with citizen juries or citizen panels (Montin 1998: 36). There have also been examples of projects similar to those in Sauherad and Karmøy in Norway, which take the local community as their starting point (Montin 1998: 55ff.).

In many ways, Finland has followed a path similar to that of Sweden, towards greater privatization and increased competitive tendering. Tavastehus has become known for its cultivation of market solutions. In 1997, the Finnish Ministry of Home Affairs initiated a program to strengthen participation in the country's local politics. Eighteen municipalities took part in the program. In contrast to the program of the KS in Norway, the one in Finland was initiated by the ministries. In other respects the two programs had many points of resemblance. One group of municipalities was primarily concerned with organization at the sub-municipal level. Another group focused on involving young people in local political decision-making processes. A third group concentrated on improving local authority contacts with residents in their capacity as service users (Kettunen 2001).

In Denmark there have been no major programs to improve participation in local politics. Part of the explanation for this might be that the need for such programs has been assessed as less considerable. Disregarding the local elections of 1974, when voter turnout was dramatically down on other years, electoral participation in Denmark has for a long time been relatively stable at around 70 percent (Bjørklund and Kjær 2002: 90).

Whereas Great Britain, Sweden and Finland have developed arrangements whereby their residents influence policy in terms of their consumer choices, Denmark has placed greater emphasis on direct user influence (Goul Andersen 2000: 49). Denmark has developed opportunities for participation by means of *voice* rather than *exit*. Political influence is channeled via so-called institution boards directly at the activities of the separate municipalities rather than towards structures on the central political level.

Local community-based commissions or sub-municipal committees are less common in Denmark than in Sweden and Norway. For four years, Copenhagen conducted an experiment with neighborhood councils that were eventually discontinued following a plebiscite (Bäck 2002). Other experiments with sub-municipal organization have been conducted in Herlev, Ejby and Grantoften in Ballerup (Hansen 1997: 273). Danish research in this field has however also identified a less formal type of neighborhood organization, whereby residents in a neighborhood or local community organize themselves on their own initiative in order to find solutions to concrete, everyday problems. A particular local activist role has developed in Danish society, the *everyday maker*. Since this role is essentially non-ideological, those who take it on have a certain power to influence established local political institutions and political parties (Bang and Sørensen 2000). In some respects, this form of local community activity comes close to the classic ideal of popular self-organization.

Norway has not gone as far as Sweden, and certainly not as far as Great Britain, in privatization and competitive tendering. Neither has the Danish model, with its direct user involvement, been copied to any notable extent by local authorities in Norway. Something of the same ideal of self-organization can be seen in Norwegian local community processes, but the latter have not been made independent of local political institutions in the way that the *every-day maker* has become in Nørrebro in Copenhagen. Instead, local community processes in Norway are initiated at the municipal level and in time the activists tend to become integrated with traditional local politics.

One feature that all the Scandinavian countries and Great Britain have in common is that their respective local authorities are all striving to develop some form of democratization policy. In Great Britain and Sweden the premises for such policy are heavily influenced from the central level by means of various committees. Centrally initiated programs for democratic renewal also exist in Norway, but they are not as extensive as in the former countries. The democracy program of the Norwegian Association of Local and Regional Authorities (KS) must be regarded as one such initiative, but other moves to stimulate local democracy through municipal development schemes have also come from the Ministry of Local Government and Regional Development (KRD). In addition, many local authorities enact/implement their own initiative to carry out experiments in the field of democratic renewal. In some cases the KS and the KRD are able to finance such locally initiated projects. In the next part of this chapter we shall discuss some of the fundamental questions relating to public democratization policy.

Conclusion and discussion

What kinds of participation do public democracy initiatives create? I shall attempt to throw some light on this question by referring to some examples from the KS democracy program. One lesson learnt from the KS program was that when participation was managed by political elites, the forms it assumed tended to support these elites. Popular involvement was highlighted as crucial for the survival of local democracy, but not all forms of involvement were equally desirable. For example, the program had the clear aim of promoting participation through the political parties. As we have seen, some of the work was devoted to this objective. Other, more direct forms of participation were used with utmost caution, but the political parties were still regarded as a precondition for the strengthening of local democracy. For the party-governed KS system it was problematic to work on forms of participation that might threaten the established party structures within the municipality.

In some cases it was clear that the project municipalities wanted to control the agenda of the various experiments. In making them accessible to broad involvement, one also ran the risk of questions being asked about earlier measures taken by the local government. For example, the local authorities in Kongsberg wanted to conduct a hearing about the extension of a major trunk road beyond the point where it had passed the town, but no debate was encouraged concerning the route of the road up to that point. It is understandable that local politicians should want to uphold the resolutions that had already been passed.

Nevertheless, it became clear that the route of the road *to* the town was far more controversial than its continuation *beyond* the town. On the one hand, the local government was interested in having an open and spontaneous debate, but on the other, it wanted to keep the debate strictly under its own control.

The Kongsberg authorities found it difficult, if not impossible, to determine the course of the free debate. Participants at the hearing discussed alternative routes for the trunk road, both for the section before the town and the section after it. There was no way to restrain people's engagement. This example illustrates that the democracy experiments entailed a potential loss of control for the local authorities that initiated them. Even top-down initiated democracy is risky for the political elites. Although the authorities wished to guide participation in certain directions, this proved difficult in practice – especially in the case of experiments that were successful in the sense of attracting wide support.

We see that public democratization policy often leads to attempts to regulate popular participation. Equally important to efforts to ensure the broadest possible participation is the provision of a framework in which that participation should occur. But participation is by its very nature difficult to regulate, especially when broad and inclusive. The side effects of democratization policy therefore become an important argument for the public to become involved in the issue of democratic measures: when many people become engaged, the resultant activity can be beneficial to the community. The aforementioned experience of the local authorities in Karmøy serves as a good example in this respect.

Another argument for why local and other public authorities ought to assume responsibility for promoting democratic development is that such democracy experiments imply a non-static conception of democracy: the form of these experiments amounts to an acknowledgment that democracy requires continual renewal. In effect, democracy itself is regarded as a continuous experiment in which one is constantly looking for new institutions.

In support of the public democracy program it might also be said that such programs can have positive effects on the pattern of participation, in other words on how participation is distributed among different social groups. Studies have shown that political involvement via new and untraditional channels is often more uneven than it is when it occurs via traditional mechanisms, such as elections and political parties (Fiorina 1999; Parry *et al.* 1992: 73). Where new forms of participation develop from private or small-group initiatives, we might justifiably speak of a participation market. In this market, the strongest stand out most and these are the ones with the most resources. In the past the political parties played an important role by giving political training to people who had not received such skills during their upbringing (Rokkan and Campbell 1960). But with the parties failing to activate broad sections of the population via the membership channel, it is perhaps important that the public authorities create arenas of participation that are inclusive and which provide political training to the groups that have traditionally been least active. At least we should ask the question: If parties and associations fail to even out differences in resources among the citizens, could public authorities play their part?

One of the lessons learnt from this work is that popular participation is to be regarded as a resource for a political system. Accordingly, elites take part in a struggle to get ordinary citizens to confirm their elite positions and actively support the work that they do. This struggle appears to have generated a new policy area, called "democratization policy." A possible consequence of elite-sponsored democracy is that democracy and public participation is not treated as an integrated part of the political process. Instead democracy is conceived as a sector of its own. Thus, to local political elites public participation is only desirable as long as it does not influence actual political outcomes.

It was just as important for those local authorities that initiated democracy experiments to steer and delimit popular participation, as it was to stimulate that participation. Despite the diverse projects contained in the democracy program, it is hard to escape the conclusion that efforts to enhance public involvement have been strictly directed from political and administrative elites. The constant lament of the political elite about the lack of popular involvement can often be interpreted as a wish that more people would show interest in the important work performed by that elite. Hence, many of the municipalities involved explicitly attempted to strengthen representative forms of participation. In other projects we witnessed efforts from the local authorities to direct popular involvement and public debate, instead of enhancing it. Presumably, spontaneous debates were in reality conducted under firm guidance. Agendas were mainly decided by local authorities, and the projects left little room for the public to influence what issues would be brought up. The democracy projects promoted by local authorities had a strong element of supportive participation. However, some of the projects may contain prospects for institutional renewal. And when local authorities conduct experiments to strengthen local political engagement and participation, activity is also stimulated that the elite cannot easily control. In other words, the unintended consequences of democratization policy are often just as important as the intended.

Notes

1 For an overview on different models of democracy regarding the role of political participation see Chapters 1 and 2 in this volume.
2 For each of the project categories mentioned here a handbook of ideas has been published: Jensen (2000), Offerdal and Espeland (2000), Aars (2000a, 2000b), Guldvik (2000), Andersen and Rugset (2000), Lesjø and Offerdal (2000). The descriptions of the various areas of activity that follow draw on these sources among others.
3 The youth council was handed advisory authority over a set of issues considered to be particularly relevant to young people. Furthermore, the youth council was granted a sum of money to spend according to the youth councillors' own preferences.
4 A thorough report on the hearing in Nordland has been given in Aars and Offerdal 2000.
5 The design of the hearings was partly modeled after James Fishkin's Deliberative Polls (Fishkin 1995).
6 The male proportion was somewhat above 70 percent in all three hearings. Furthermore, those above 45 were strongly over-represented among the participants, whereas those under 30 were just as strongly under-represented.
7 *Kommunaktuellt* 6 June 1999.

References

Aars, J. (2000a) *Brukerundersøkelser som demokrativerktøy*, Oslo: Kommuneforlaget.

—— (2000b) *Få folket i tale! Utvidede folkehøringer som hjelpemiddel til å styrke demokratiet i kommunene*. Oslo: Kommuneforlaget.

Aars, J. and Offerdal, A. (2000) "Representation and Deliberative Politics," in N. Rao (ed.) *Representation and Community in Western Democracies*, Houndmills, Basingstoke: Macmillan, pp. 68–93.

—— (1998) "Local Political Recruitment in Crisis? A Comparison of Finland and Norway," *Scandinavian Political Studies*, 21: 207–231.

Andersen, T. and Rugset, S.A. (2000) *Hvordan kan medvirkning organiseres? Eksempler på medvirkning til bærekraftig utvikling*, Oslo: Kommuneforlaget.

Bang, H. and Sørensen, E. (2000) "The Everyday Maker: Building Political Rather Than Social Capital," in P. Dekker and E. Uslaner (eds) *Social Capital and Participation in Every Day Life*, London: Routledge, pp. 148–161.

Bjørklund, T. and Kjær, U. (2002) "Valgdeltakelsen ved lokalvalg i Norge og Danmark – forskjeller og likheter," in B. Aardal (ed.) *Valgdeltakelse og demokrati*, Oslo Kommuneforlaget, pp. 89–111.

Bäck, H. (2002) *Fragmentation and Consolidation in the Big City: Neighbourhood Decentralisation in Six Scandinavian Cities*, Paper presented at the 2002 ECPR Joint Session of Workshops, Torino, 22–27 March.

—— (2000) *Kommunpolitiker i den stora nyordningens tid*, Malmö: Liber.

Converse, P.E. (1970) "Attitudes and Non-attitudes: Continuation of a Dialogue," in E.R. Tufte (ed.) *The Quantitative Analysis of Social Problems*, Reading, MA: Addison-Wesley, pp. 168–189.

Eriksen, E.O. and Weigård, J. (1993) "Fra statsborger til kunde. Kan relasjonen mellom innbyggerne og det offentlige reformuleres på grunnlag av nye roller?," in *Norsk Statsvitenskapelig Tidsskrift*, 9: 111–131.

Fiorina, M.P. (1999) "Extreme Voices. A Dark Side of Civic Engagement," in T. Skocpol and M.P. Fiorina (eds) *Civic Engagement in America*, Washington, DC: Brookings/Russell Sage Foundation, pp. 395–427.

Fishkin, J. (1995) *The Voice of the People: Public Opinion and Democracy*, New Haven, CT: Yale University Press.

Goul Andersen, J. (2000) "Det lille demokrati. Nærdemokratiet i den offentlige sektor," in J. Goul Andersen, L. Torpe and J. Andersen (eds) *Hvad folket magter. Demokrati, magt og afmagt*, København: Jurist- og Økonomforbundets Forlag, pp. 47–79.

Guldvik, I. (2000) *Blant de få utvalgte? Økt deltakelse i lokalpolitikk fra barn, unge, innvandrere og kvinner*, Oslo: Kommuneforlaget.

Hansen, A.D. (1997) "Lokaludvalg: nogle teoretiske perspektiver," in P. Gundelach, H. Jørgensen and K.K. Klausen (eds) *Det lokale. Decentral politik og forvaltning*, Aalborg: Aalborg universitetsforlag, pp. 265–289.

Hansen, T. (1995) "Lokalt demokrati ved et vendepunkt?," in T. Hansen and A. Offerdal (eds) *Borgere, tjenesteytere og beslutningstakere. Festskrift til Francesco Kjellberg*, Oslo: TANO AS, pp. 75–93.

Jensen, T.Ø. (I samarbeid med flere) (2000) *Internett i lokaldemokratiet*, Oslo: Kommuneforlaget.

Kettunen, P. (2001) *Developing Local Democracy in Finland*, Paper presented at the X. Nordic Local Government Research Conference, Åbo.

Leach, S. and Wingfield, M. (2000) "Public Participation and the Democratic Renewal

Agenda: Prioritisation or Marginalisation?," in L. Pratchett (ed.) *Renewing Local Democracy. The Modernisation Agenda in British Local Government*, London: Frank Cass, pp. 46–59.

Lesjø, J.H. and Offerdal, A. (2000) *Partiene – lokalsamfunnets støtte?*, Oslo: Kommuneforlaget.

Montin, S. (1998) *Lokala demokratiexperiment, Demokratiutredningens Skrift Nr. 9*, SOU 1998: 155.

Offerdal, A. and Espeland, H. (2000) *Prosess eller prosjekt? Lokalsamfunnsutvikling, nærmiljø og lokal planlegging*, Oslo: Kommuneforlaget.

Offerdal, A. and Ringkjøb, H.-E. (2002) "Medlemsgrunnlag og medlemsaktivitet i lokale partilag," in O. Bukve and A. Offerdal, A. (eds) *Den nye kommunen. Kommunal organisering i endring*, Oslo: Samlaget, pp. 112–133.

Olsson, J. and Montin, S. (eds) (1999) *Demokrati som experiment, Försöksverksamhet och förnyelse i svenska kommuner*, Ôrebro: Novemus.

Øgård, M. (2000) "New Public Management – markedet som redningsplanke?," in H. Baldersheim and L.E. Rose (eds) *Det kommunale laboratorium. Teoretiske perspektiver på lokal politikk og organisering*, Oslo: Fagbokforlaget, pp. 27–55.

Parry, G., Moyser, G. and Day, N. (1992) *Political Participation and Democracy in Britain*, Cambridge: Cambridge University Press.

Petersson, O. (2001) *Demokratipolitik*, Stockholm: Studieförbundet Näringsliv och Samhälle.

Pettersen, P.A. and Rose, L.E. (1997) "Den norske kommunen: Hva har politikerne ønsket, og hva ønsker folket?," in H. Baldersheim, J.F. Bernt, T. Kleven and J. Rattsø (eds) *Kommunalt selvstyre i velferdsstaten*, Oslo: Tano Aschehoug, pp. 91–127.

Ranney, A. (1968) "The Study of Policy Content: A Framework for Choice," in A. Ranney (ed.) *Political Science and Public Policy*, Chicago, IL: Markham, pp. 3–21.

Rattsø, J. and Sørensen, R.J. (1997) "Kommunen som serviceprodusent/tjenesteyter: Hva forteller norsk kommuneforskning om kommunesektorens effektivitet?," in H. Baldersheim, J.F. Bernt, T. Kleven and J. Rattsø (eds) *Kommunalt selvstyre i velferdsstaten*, Oslo: Tano Aschehoug, pp. 127–158.

Rokkan, S. and Campbell, A. (1960) "Citizen Participation in Political Life: Norway and the United States of America," *International Social Science Journal*, 12: 69–99.

Salisbury, R.H. (1975) "Research on Political Participation," *American Journal of Political Science*, 29: 323–341.

Sartori, G. (1965) *Democratic Theory*, New York: Praeger.

Schumpeter, J.A. (1961) *Capitalism, Socialism and Democracy*, London: Allen & Unwin.

Smith, G. and Wales, C. (2000) "Citizens, Juries and Deliberative Democracy," *Political Studies*, 48: 51–65.

Ståhlberg, K. (1996) *Herre i eget hus: 12 debattinlägg om nordiska kommuner i förandring*, LOS-senteret rapport 9605, Bergen: LOS-senteret.

Sørensen, E. (1998) "New Forms of Democratic Empowerment. Introducing User Influence in the Primary School System in Denmark," in *Statsvetenskaplig Tidskrift*, 101: 129–144.

Verba, S. (1996) "The Citizen as Respondent: Sample Surveys and American Democracy, Presidential Address, American Political Science Association, 1995," *American Political Science Review*, 90: 1–7.

Conclusion

Can participatory engineering bring citizens back in?

Thomas Zittel

The chapters of this volume suggest participatory engineering to be a universal rather than a secular phenomenon. Their authors detect efforts to affect political participation positively through democratic reform across a number of established democracies. McLaverty and Morris report on policies in Scotland which open up the new Scottish Parliament to citizens in order to render it more responsive. Montin points to the Swedish Government's large-scale program to strengthen local democracy and Aars describes similar efforts in Norway. Baglioni and Moeckli both direct our attention to direct decision-making in Switzerland and elsewhere across the globe as an option for democratic reform. Rahat and Hazan take us to Israel, where political parties experiment with party primaries to increase party membership. Carter's chapter travels across the Atlantic reporting on experiments with worker co-operatives in the US. This selective survey is by no means exhaustive and a more comprehensive and systematic inventory should be the focus of future research efforts. However, the evidence presented in this volume stresses the need to undertake such an endeavor.

I started out in my chapter with the hypothesis that political actors who aim to engineer political participation via institutional means might face a *reform dilemma*: Those policies least effective could be most feasible and vice versa. The notion of effectiveness means that reform policies are able to link the institutional and the behavioral levels of analysis in theoretically plausible ways and that they are suited to increase the level of participation without compromising other values of modern government. The notion of feasibility implies that reform policies are likely to be implemented in the course of political decision-making.

The initial hypothesis in my opening chapter fares well in light of the evidence presented in this volume. Many of the policies analyzed in the chapters of this volume aim to stimulate engagement within the existing institutional framework of liberal democracy. They focus on marginal institutional changes that alter details of liberal democracy without changing its core elements and that stress strategies of *cost-efficient democratization* at best. This includes concrete reform measures such as: strengthening the role of citizens as consumers of community services at the local level; increasing the appeal of political parties by allowing for more intra-party democracy (i.e. via party primaries or by opening up the process of formulating party manifestos); increasing the transparency of the parliamentary process; and decreasing the cost of participation, for example via the introduction of online voting.

Reforms that stay within the framework of established liberal democracy are not without meaning from the perspective of participatory engineering. This is for two reasons. First, they might imply side effects or non-intentional results that point beyond the established framework of liberal democracy. As Jacob Aars put it, democracy experiments entail a potential loss of control for those authorities that initiated them. This observation raises questions regarding the specific conditions for loss of control and vice versa prerequisites for control that have to be addressed in future research. Second, a temporal series of marginal changes or a combination of several small-scale reforms might alter the nature of representative government in the long run, changing the role of representatives from being trustees to being delegates. From a functional point of view, reformed representative structures would then serve as a basis for "quasi-direct decision-making" and would thus be elements of a strategy of expansive democratization. The analysis of the Scottish case by McLaverty and Morris points in the direction of such a "cumulative reform process." A number of changes in the details of the representative system might add up here to "something bigger." However, the effectiveness of both types of reform process is left to chance and is thus clearly second to a more holistic process that stresses the theoretically plausible strategies of integrative and expansive democratization in the first place.

Those authors who focus on direct democracy in this volume did not detect a massive push towards *expansive democratization*. As Moeckli suggests, the referendum device has been used to an increasing degree across the globe. But he stresses in his comparative analysis that it serves in many countries as a plebiscite used by the political majority rather than as an instrument of participatory democracy and thus expansive democratization. If we gauge direct democracy from this perspective, Switzerland is the beacon of participatory democracy with California in close proximity. Montin's analysis on the use of the referendum device at the local level supports Moeckli's point. He demonstrates the wariness of Swedish officials to relax requirements for advisory citizen initiatives in Swedish communities. The local assembly by majority decision remains to be the prime initiator of local referendums that thus serve as plebiscites rather than instruments of participatory democracy.

Strategies of integrative democratization that I envisaged in my chapter as the most effective instruments of participatory engineering are pursued on a very cautious and hesitant note in light of the analyses presented here. Carter's analysis on workplace democracy portrays this means of participatory engineering implicitly as an old-fashioned instrument that has been pushed to the back of the engineer's tool kit. Experiments with worker co-operatives that are at the center of his survey of the literature date back to the 1970s and 1980s. Programs to revitalize local democracy flourish in a number of countries as Montin and Aars stress in their chapters. However their analyses also suggest that these efforts proceed without providing viable incentives to communities to implement specific policies and without raising questions regarding the scope of local jurisdictions and constitutional reforms. Given this void, efforts to revitalize local democracy remain to be "project-driven" and thus a rather insignificant means of participatory engineering.

The analyses of Aars and Montin point to important additional means of *integrative democratization* at the local level. This includes programs to educate traditionally marginalized groups of citizens, as well as efforts to organize deliberative processes in community politics. However, their analyses stress that these efforts are again "project-driven" and lack a solid institutional basis. This does not render them irrelevant for research on participatory engineering. Experiments and pilots can of course become the breeding ground for more comprehensive change. They can diffuse across communities and thus can be the cornerstone of bottom-up institution building. They thus have to be closely watched from this angle by means of cumulative and comparative research.

What are the politics of the reform dilemma outlined above? This question is answered in different ways by different authors in this volume. Montin stresses in his chapter the gap between a far-reaching rhetoric of democratization on the one hand and actual policy-making that restricts itself to piecemeal change on the other. His explanation points to state socialism as a dominant ideological paradigm in Sweden that frames the behavior of political actors as well as the actual meaning of their reform rhetoric. Thus, according to Montin, *ideas* matter most, when it comes to the politics of participatory engineering. Aars, as well as Rahat and Hazan, suggest that the politics of democratic reform is primarily driven by a conflict of *interests* in the minds of political elites. While they aim to secure popular support and thus the legitimacy of their own positions, they are also eager to minimize the loss of political autonomy and control. While decreasing support in terms of turnout and organizational membership triggers their activities towards participatory engineering, the particular means of participatory engineering are initialized by their interests in control and autonomy. McLaverty and Morris's analysis of the Scottish case suggests that *historical junctures* defined by the absence or the disruption of an established institutional frame, as well as the absence or the disruption of historical legacies, provide a unique opportunity for democratic reform.

Each of these three perspectives on the politics of participatory engineering stimulates important follow-up questions and speculations for further research. (a) Do political elites share similar interests in the course of participatory engineering and do we really observe the predominance of a mass-elite cleavage in this policy area, as suggested above? One might reason that the degree and type of political pluralism in a given system patterns the type of reform policy that is chosen. I would assume that a higher level of political pluralism triggers a more complex pattern of conflict within competing elites, higher levels of conflict and eventually more far-reaching reform policies. (b) How and why do which ideas of democracy affect actual decision-making in the course of participatory engineering? One might consider that with social change and with the growing heterogeneity of the societies of established democracies, prevalent ideas and paradigms of democracy will gradually loose their grip on the political discourse and the aggregation of social interests. (c) How does the external environment come into play and how does it affect the behavior of political actors? Contextual changes such as the crisis of the fiscal state and the economic need for efficiency should put pressure on political elites to consider new opportunities for citizen involvement to balance the loss of "output legitimacy" with an increase in "input legitimacy."

Does participatory engineering makes a difference at the individual level of politics? The chapters in this volume lead to a cautious conclusion regarding this question that forms the core of this volume. This can be partly explained by the more recent origins of many reform initiatives. In many cases it is simply too early to come to a conclusion yet. However, this can also be explained by the observation that incremental, marginal strategies of democratic reform, which are considered least effective above, dominate the current practice of participatory engineering. Let me conclude with a systematic summary of the main findings regarding the impact of the three strategies of democratization outlined earlier. The main message of this summary is that the politically all-too-obvious path of incremental engineering within the established frame of liberal democracy is the least effective to pursue.

Strategies that aim at marginal or cost-efficient democratization produced as expected no or negative effects in light of the analyses in this volume. McLaverty and Morris refer in their assessment to data from the Scottish Social Attitudes Surveys in 1999 and 2001 that report a sharp decrease in political efficacy. While in 1999, 64 percent of the respondents claimed that ordinary people have a say in how Scotland was governed, in 2001 only 38 percent thought so. Along with a drop in turnout from 58.4 percent in 1999 to 50 percent in 2003 these data suggest that the reform of parliamentary representation in Scotland had little impact at the individual level. Montin concludes that the Swedish initiatives developed and implemented at the local level between 1997 and 2002 did not prevent turnout dropping again in the 2002 elections by about 6 percent (parliamentary elections) and 7 percent (local). He also points to research concluding that the Swedish democracy policy has so far failed to involve more citizens in local politics and increase political trust (pp. 357–359).

Rahat and Hazan relate predominantly negative effects with marginal forms of democratization. They find a short term increase of party membership as an effect of the introduction of party primaries. But according to the authors, this increase was not sustainable and it was also paralleled by a decrease in the quality of participation. They observe party membership becoming more superficial in terms of emotional attachment and identification with the party one was member of.

Strategies that aim at expansive democratization produced positive effects according to the chapters in this volume. Baglioni finds in the Swiss Canton of Berne, where there is a comprehensive system of direct democracy, a higher use of direct democracy, higher political interest and higher engagement in political parties compared with the Swiss Canton of Vaud, which has a more restricted system of direct democracy. He stresses in his multivariate analysis other factors such as personal resources and the size of the community, but concludes that institutions do matter. Moeckli finds in a cross-national comparison that the level of participation (in the election of officeholders and referendums) is lowest where the opportunities for participation are greatest – particularly in Switzerland. However, he makes the theoretical argument that direct democracy nevertheless has a positive impact on the electorate's involvement in political decisions and on the system's responsiveness to the electorate. He claims in contrast to the initial expectations regarding measures of expansive democratization that comprehensive forms of direct democracy serve to educate and socialize the electorate and that it increases its overall satisfaction with the system. He furthermore argues that it affects the political process by allowing oppositional groups to break down corporative structures and to gain a voice in the negotiation phase of the process. According to Moeckli, high levels of participation in the decision stage are no longer necessary because of this effect. Both claims are theoretically plausible but have to be supported by empirical data. Baglioni's positive evaluation of direct democracy also raises the question whether this holds true for cases other than Switzerland where the institutions of direct democracy are embedded in a particular cultural and historical context.

Strategies that aim at integrative democratization produced positive effects in light of the findings of the chapters in this volume, but with a big "but." The "but" stresses that these effects are very context dependent, that strategies of integrative democratization work in most indirect ways, and that they will work in the long run, at best. Maloney and Jordan argue in their chapter that non-participation is partly explained by the group structure itself rather than by an Olsonian rational calculus and the motivation to free ride. According to the authors, proactive marketing and recruitment strategies, as well as the conviction that a group is effective, have positive effects on the decision of individuals to join these groups. This finding suggests that any reform policy stimulating the group structure of modern democracies or that visibly aims to increase the impact of social groups on decision making would have pay-offs in terms of political participation. The particular type of reform activity needed to stimulate and revitalize group structures remains to be subject to further research.

Uslaner's analysis in this volume questions the meaning of engagement in civic associations for the attitudinal level and suggests economic and non-corruption policies as an integral element of any strategy of participatory engineering. He studies in his chapter the foundations of trust that many students of social capital and civil society have held to be a result of political and civic engagement. He strongly argues against this view and perceives trust as something that we learn early in life from our parents and that is very stable. However, Uslaner's empirical analysis points to two effects of the state on trust. States can enact public policies that foster the level of economic quality such as universal welfare policies. Uslaner finds that states with high equality are high on trust. Democratic governments with fair and non-corrupt administrations are also higher on trust than authoritarian and corrupt states. Uslaner's interpretation here is that the state does not produce trust but that it sustains trust. With this argument he makes the important point that social policies as well as anti-corruption policies might be an important integral part of any strategy of integrative democratization.

Carter's survey of the literature finds little evidence supporting a simple relationship between workplace democracy and political efficacy. His conclusion is that specific participatory structures might have a limited impact on political efficacy and participation when operating in specific contexts. Direct forms of participation in decision-making compared with representative forms via a management board along with moderate expectations of workers, a positive economic situation of the company and high job autonomy are most likely to produce a positive relationship between workplace democracy and political efficacy. In line with Uslaner, the latter two variables highlight the role of the economy as an important variable that intervenes in the relationship between forms of expansive democratization and individual behavior.

Does the context of modern democracy prevent us from implementing any form of participatory democracy as Fuchs argues in his chapter? The answer is certainly yes if we equate participatory democracy with a comprehensive structural model of democracy distilled from the practice of ancient Athenian democracy. The answer is no if we break down participatory democracy to a set of strategies for democratic reform that are rooted in theories of political behavior. Implementing any of these strategies might eventually lead to hybrid models of democracy that go beyond the simple dichotomy between liberal and participatory democracy. As many of the chapters of this volume suggest, this process is already underway in many established democracies and thus poses important questions that we aimed to raise with this volume. Obviously the considerations and answers presented here regarding the policies, politics and behavioral effects of participatory engineering are tentative rather than conclusive and written in stone. However, they provide a systematic basis for further research on the subject of participatory engineering that will hopefully develop, for it is of utmost importance for the development of modern democracy in a changing world.

Index